PRAISE FOR *Andy Andrews*

"*The Traveler's Gift* effectively combines self-help with fiction . . . sustaining momentum while simultaneously passing on instructions for positive thinking . . . an exemplary job at providing positive suggestions for overcoming life's obstacles . . . this is an author to watch."
—Publishers Weekly

"Andrews' book will engage your mind and inspire your heart."
—Hyrum W. Smith, Co-Chairman of the Board, Franklin Covey

"Andy Andrews will challenge you to reach your fullest potential."
—John C. Maxwell, Founder, The INJOY Group™

"This is the best inspirational book written since Og Mandino wrote *The Greatest Miracle in the World*."
—Charlie T. Jones, Author of *Life is Tremendous*

"*The Traveler's Gift* touched me in a way no other book ever has."
—Barbara Johnson, Humorist and Best-selling Author

"Andy Andrews has done it again. This book will inspire you, touch your heart and soul, and change you in every way you desire!"
—Don Hobbs, Chairman and Cofounder, Hobbs & Herder Advertising

"Andy Andrews' words—both written and spoken—are a significant and enduring presence in the lives of our Squadron Commanders around the world."
—Michael W. Wooley, Lieutenant General, USAF Commander, Air Force Special Operations Command

The Traveler's Gift

Mastering the

SEVEN DECISIONS

That Determine Personal Success

THE TRAVELER'S GIFT

Seven Decisions That
Determine Personal Success

Mastering the
SEVEN
DECISIONS

That Determine Personal Success

An Owner's Manual to the New York Times Bestseller
The Traveler's Gift

Andy Andrews

THOMAS NELSON
Since 1798

NASHVILLE DALLAS MEXICO CITY RIO DE JANEIRO BEIJING

CONTACT ANDY

To book Andy for corporate events, call

(800) 726-ANDY (2639)

For more information, go to

WWW.ANDYANDREWS.COM

The Traveler's Gift © 2002 by Andy Andrews
Mastering the Seven Decisions © 2008 by Andy Andrews

Published in Nashville, Tennessee, by Thomas Nelson. Thomas Nelson is a registered trademark of Thomas Nelson, Inc.

Thomas Nelson, Inc., titles may be purchased in bulk for educational, business, fund-raising, or sales promotional use. For information, please e-mail SpecialMarkets@ThomasNelson.com.

Scripture quotations noted KJV are from The Holy Bible, KING JAMES VERSION.

Scripture quotations are taken from the HOLY BIBLE: NEW INTERNATIONAL VERSION®. © 1973, 1978, 1984 by International Bible Society. Used by permission of Zondervan Publishing House. All rights reserved.

The "NIV" and "New International Version" trademarks are registered in the United States Patent and Trademark Office by International Bible Society. Use of either trademark requires the permission of International Bible Society.

ISBN 978-0-8499-4679-0
ISBN 978-0-7852-6428-6 (Traveler's Gift hc)
ISBN 978-0-7852-7322-6 (Traveler's Gift sc)
ISBN 978-0-8499-4679-0 (Traveler's Gift special edition)
ISBN 978-0-7852-6141-4 (Mastering the Seven Decisons hc)

CIP information on file with publisher. Available upon request.

Printed in the United States of America

09 10 11 12 13 LBM 5 4 3 2 1

THE TRAVELER'S GIFT

*Dedicated to
Robert D. Smith,
a champion—
and the inspiration
for this book*

In great deed, something abides. On great fields, something stays. Forms change and pass, bodies disappear but spirits linger to consecrate ground for the vision place of the soul. And reverent men and women from afar and generations that know us not and that we know not of, shall come here to ponder and to dream and the power of the vision shall pass into their souls.

—JOSHUA LAWRENCE CHAMBERLAIN, 1828–1914

ONE

HEADLIGHTS SWEPT THE HOUSE AS THE TAXI TURNED out of the driveway. David Ponder stood alone on his front lawn looking at the home where he and his wife, Ellen, had lived for more than twenty years. David lowered himself onto the grass. Nausea poured over him as he felt panic enter his very soul. Like a serpent easing up his spine and wrapping itself around his throat, it wasn't a quick, devastating attack, but a slow, gripping realization that life, as he knew it, was over. He was forty-six years old. He had no job. He had no money. He had no purpose.

A short time later, David stood in the doorway of his daughter's room. It had literally been a month since he'd seen her awake. Lately, his work schedule had been frantic. As a last-ditch effort to save his employer from takeover, he often left home before daylight and rarely returned until well after his family had gone to bed. Several times during the past few weeks, he had not come home at all.

David gently placed his briefcase next to the dresser and moved toward the bed. His only child's breathing seemed loud in the quiet room. Sinking to his knees, David reached out to stroke her hair. It was so soft. The Cinderella night-light she'd cherished since her fourth Christmas cast an angelic glow on her perfect face. Jennifer Christine Ponder. "My little Jenny," he murmured. David remembered the very moment she had been born . . . twelve years ago today. He glanced at the clock on the nightstand: 2:18 A.M. *Okay,* he thought disgustedly, *so it was twelve years ago yesterday.* A tear slipped down his cheek.

"David?" It was Ellen. Moving into the room, she touched his shoulder. "I thought I heard you come in. Is everything all right?"

David looked up into his wife's face. Her hair was a mess from sleeping, and of course, she had on no makeup. She wore a long white T-shirt that contrasted with her medium-length dark hair. Her brown eyes were sleepy, but she was as beautiful to him as the day they had met twenty-five years ago.

Ellen knelt beside her husband. With her fingers, she brushed the hair from his forehead.

"David," she said again, "are you all right?"

He took her hand in both of his, brought it to his lips, and said simply, "No."

At 5:00 A.M., Ellen lay asleep on her side with her head on David's chest. David was on his back, wondering how she could possibly sleep. He wasn't sure if he'd ever sleep again. For almost two hours, he'd told Ellen everything that had happened that evening.

Late that afternoon, David and a team of management personnel had gathered in the executive conference room. By five, they had begun working the phones, feverishly soliciting stockholder support. It was a desperate, last-ditch attempt to prevent a hostile buyout by a predatory conglomerate. Final notice reached the conference room shortly before midnight. Despite their best efforts—tears, pleas, prayers, and curses—the takeover had been completed. All executive and supervisory positions at the plant were terminated effective immediately.

A security guard had entered David's office less than fifteen minutes after the phone call and offered to help clean out his desk. Within the hour, David was at the guard house near the plant entrance, waiting for a taxi. After twenty-three years of service, David had been asked to relinquish the key to his office, the key to the gym, and the key to his company car.

As he lay awake, David thought about his life. He and Ellen had met the day after both graduated from Iowa State University. David had a degree in business and was determined to make his mark with a Fortune 500 company, while Ellen, with her degree in education, wanted to teach. For two years they dated. People often asked if they were brother and sister. David's height was their only difference. He, at six-foot-two, was taller than she, but the dark hair, brown eyes, and thin body type gave them a similar look.

They would have been married sooner had it not been for David's insistence on finding a career job before settling down. He worked in his father's shoe store as a stopgap measure while sending out résumés all over the country. Ellen had already been teaching fifth grade for almost a year when David was accepted as a management trainee for a chemical company in Dallas. They were married almost immediately.

David became immersed in his work. He felt that he had found a position that would allow him to be in control of his family's future. Ellen enjoyed teaching and taught right up until Jenny was born and then never went back. Financially, the family struggled a bit on one income, but it was a sacrifice they were willing to make to have one parent at home full time for their daughter.

"Ellen," David said as he squeezed her arm.

"What, honey?" she mumbled.

"Is Jenny mad at me?"

"What?" Ellen asked.

"Is Jenny mad because I missed her birthday?"

Ellen put her arms around David. "No, honey. Jenny is fine."

"*I'm* pretty mad about it, you know . . . honey . . . Ellen?"

David sighed. Ellen had already drifted back to sleep. The world could be coming to an end, and Ellen would have no problem sleeping. He never understood how she did that. She usually laughed and said she knew he'd always take care of her. *If that is true,* David thought, *how is she sleeping now? Isn't it obvious that I am failing miserably in that department?*

Staring into the darkness, David remembered walking the moonlit beach on the island of St. John. Their honeymoon to the Caribbean had been a gift from her parents. Ellen's dad owned a lawn care business and had insisted on dipping into his savings for the honor of beginning his daughter's marriage in a special way. And it was special. They walked on the beach and talked for hours. At one point, David remembered, he had taken Ellen's face in his hands and said, "I promise you everything," and she had not laughed. He had been serious, and she knew it.

For more than ten years they prayed for a child, and when Jenny came along, their lives seemed complete.

5

David put his energy and focus into providing a home and lifestyle in which his family would prosper. But his work at the plant, while it did provide a living, never seemed to provide a life. As David told a friend one day, "I'm working so hard to live where we want to live that I don't actually get to live there."

As the years passed, their savings were slowly depleted. A computer business David put together with an old fraternity brother was gone in two years, and rising interest rates had soured their real estate investments. Subsequently, the college fund that had been started for Jenny when she was born was used to put braces on her teeth only six months ago. David tried vainly to recall if the price he had paid the orthodontist covered everything. *Funny, the things one thinks about at a time like this,* David mused. *If I haven't already paid for having them removed, Jenny just might be wearing braces when she's thirty.*

David's mind drifted back to the beach on St. John. "I promise you everything," he had said. He felt the bile rising in his throat. David looked at Ellen, still sleeping peacefully beside him. *I promised you everything,* he thought, *and now I've provided nothing.* Quickly, David got out of bed, stumbled into the bathroom, and threw up.

Around seven, Ellen woke up alone. Putting on her housecoat and slippers, she went into the kitchen where she found her husband sitting at the breakfast table. It seemed strange to her to see him in jeans and a T-shirt. For years David had been the first one awake in their family, and by this time, he had always been ready to walk out the door in a coat and tie. It was obvious to Ellen that he had not slept at all. "Good morning, dear," she said.

"Jenny's not up yet," David said. "Coffee's made."

She looked at him for a moment. "David," she said, "everything will be fine." He turned and stared out the window into the backyard. "David," she said again, "everything is going to be okay. We've been through tough times before."

"I'm forty-six, Ellen," David said. "Forty-six-year-old executives are not being hired anywhere except McDonald's. We have a second mortgage on this house, you know. Your car is not paid for, and I don't have one anymore. I get no severance from the plant because I didn't opt out in the package deal they offered last year. We don't have any money, and I don't know where to borrow any more. This is more than a tough time, and we have *not* been through this before."

"So what are we going to do?" Ellen asked.

"I don't know," David answered. "I have no clue."

TWO

SEVEN MONTHS LATER, DAVID FELT LIKE A BEATEN man. The health insurance coverage from his former employer had run its course, and the part-time job David took at a hardware store provided little more than minimum wage. Ellen was making more money than he was. She had placed hand-printed advertisements on bulletin boards all over town and was cleaning houses five days a week. Every day for months, David continued to search for a job. The seemingly endless stream of rejections confused him. *At least I'm on my way up*, he kept telling himself. *It can't get any worse.* But it did.

That morning had dawned cold and hard. It was everything David had always hated about winter. The sky was the color of dirty water, and the below-freezing temperature, carried by a nasty wind, cut David like the thrusts of a thousand knives. Struggling into the used car he had bought with a loan from his father, David cursed at nothing and no one in particular.

The car seemed to David a constant reminder of his failure. He had answered an ad in the newspaper and paid a high school kid nine hundred dollars for what he had hoped would be temporary transportation. It was a two-door Dodge Colt, mostly faded silver except for the right fender, which was black. The brake lights quit about ten minutes after David completed the sale, and the heater had never worked in the first place.

Shivering as he drove to work, David's mind was as numb as his body. Ellen had been up most of the night with Jenny. The child had suffered with a fever and sore throat now for three days, and with the lack of sleep, none of them were feeling well. Jenny, however, was truly sick. It was the fifth or sixth time she had been ill this winter. David had lost count.

When he had gotten out of the shower that morning, he heard Ellen hanging up the phone. "Who was that?" David asked.

"It was Dr. Reed's office, David," she said. "I've got to take her in to see what's wrong. Tylenol isn't handling this."

"What kind of parent am I?" David said aloud, interrupting his reverie as he pulled the Colt into a parking place behind Marshall's Hardware. "What kind of *person* am I? What has happened to me?"

When Ellen mentioned the doctor, he blew up. Where did she think the money was coming from, he yelled, and of course, she yelled right back that she'd steal it if she had to. This was their daughter, she shouted. Didn't he care about that anymore? As David left the house, he went by Jenny's room to kiss her good-bye. She had big tears rolling down her face. Jenny had heard everything.

About ten that morning, David was loading shingles on a flatbed truck in front of the store. He was grateful for the activity. The shingles were heavy, and they gave him somewhere to focus his anger. "Ponder!" someone yelled. David looked up. It was Mr. Marshall, the owner of the store. A tall, lanky old man with curly white hair and a red nose, he was leaning out the back door, motioning to David. "Phone call," he barked as David strode past him into the warm store. "It's your wife. Make it quick. I've told you about personal calls."

"Ellen," David said as he picked up the phone. "Where are you?"

"I'm at home," she said. "We just got back from the doctor."

"What did he say?"

"David, it's her tonsils."

"Okay?"

Ellen paused. "Honey, Dr. Reed said her tonsils have to come out. He said we need to have it done right away."

"Ponder!"

David looked around. It was Mr. Marshall. "Let's go, son," he said. "I got a driver waiting on you."

"David? Are you there?" he heard Ellen ask through the phone.

"Yes. Yes, I'm here," he said. "Ellen, we have no insurance."

"I've already checked," she answered. "The operation, including the hospital, will only cost eleven hundred dollars."

David was stunned. "We don't have eleven hundred dollars," he said.

"We can put it on a credit card."

"Hey, Ponder. This is the last time I'm going to tell you. Get off the phone," the store owner warned.

David put his hand over his ear, trying to concentrate on the conversation with his wife. "We don't have any room on a credit card, Ellen. Every card is maxed out."

Ellen started to cry. "Then we'll just have to borrow the money, David. Jenny is sick."

"I know Jenny's sick, honey, but we can't borrow anything. We're a month behind on the house, two months on your car. No bank will touch us. My parents don't have any more money to loan, and God knows, yours don't. With your dad's lawn business, they struggle through the winter just to make it themselves."

Ellen could hardly talk through her tears. "Oh, David. What are we going to do?"

"Don't worry," he said. "I'll get the money somehow. Maybe I can work overtime here. Or maybe I can get an advance. I'll get the money." As Ellen continued to cry, David pleaded with her: "Honey, please calm down. I have to go. I'll take care of this, I promise. I love you." He hung up the phone.

Turning to move from behind the counter, David met Mr. Marshall face-to-face. "I'm sorry . . . ," he started to say, but the old man cut him off.

"Your next job, you need to pay attention to the rules," Marshall said.

David was confused. "Excuse me?" he asked.

"You can come back on Friday, and your check will be waiting. I'm letting you go."

"I'm . . . I'm fired?" David stammered. "I'm fired because I used the telephone?" Marshall stood there with his arms crossed. "My daughter is sick." The old man didn't say a word. David was incredulous. He pointed at the phone. "That was my wife calling because my daughter is sick." David paused, then said once more, this time in almost a whisper, "My daughter is sick." Raising and lowering his hands in a helpless gesture and shaking his head, David turned and walked slowly out the door.

Reaching the car, David fumbled for the keys and laughed. He had experienced a brief mental flash of the car not starting. "Mr. Marshall," he saw himself saying, "my car won't start. May I use your phone?" Twisting the key in the ignition, David laughed again as the car roared to life.

Obviously, he thought, *I am laughing because I am cracking up.* As David wheeled out of the hardware store parking lot, he wondered, *If I'm sane enough to recognize insanity, does that mean I'm okay after all?* He laughed again. This time he actually laughed until he cried.

Out on the interstate, David drove past the exit for home. Traffic was light, and it was only 11:15. No reason to go home and share the big news with Ellen just yet. *Ellen doesn't deserve this*, David thought. *And Jenny certainly did not choose me for a father. A year ago, I was on top of the world, and now, I can't even provide for my family.*

David pulled onto the shoulder. Bowing his head, he clasped his hands together. "Oh, God," he said aloud. "Oh, God . . ." He stopped and was silent for almost a minute. "Oh, God . . . ," he began again. After another minute, he put the Colt into gear and moved back onto the highway. *I can't even pray*, he thought.

On an impulse, David took the Grayton exit. Almost forty miles from home, he was driving to nowhere in particular. *Just like my life*, he thought, *going nowhere in particular, nowhere special. Didn't I used to think I had a purpose?* David wondered. *Wasn't I accomplishing something?*

David looked at the speedometer. It read seventy. There were no other vehicles anywhere in sight. He pressed a little harder on the accelerator. Eighty . . . eighty-five. As he flew over hills and around curves, David became oblivious to the speed. Ninety miles per hour. His thoughts were also racing at a furious pace. Ellen was still young. She was beautiful. If he weren't around, she could find someone else to take better care of her and Jenny. *I still have life insurance*, he thought. *Would they be better off without me? Would everyone be better off without me?*

Without any further conscious thought, David jammed his foot on the accelerator, pressing it down to the floorboard. The little car screamed as David gripped the steering wheel, trying to drive away from his life. With tears streaming down his face, he rolled the window down and steered into a straightaway. The freezing wind seemed to clarify his thoughts. "Why am I here?" David said aloud. "Why is this . . . why is everything happening to me?" He pounded his hand on the steering wheel, let his foot off the accelerator for a second, and then stomped it to the floor again. "Why . . . me?" he screamed. "Why me?"

At that instant, David's moment of despair intersected with an icy bridge. Covering a small stream, the bridge was no more than fifty feet long, but its sheet of black ice sent the speeding car careening into a spin. Tires screeching, David's car bounced off the guardrail as he crossed the short bridge and found himself still on the highway. He fought desperately for control as the car fishtailed from side to side and finally swerved off the road.

Many people, when faced with a life-or-death crisis, talk of seeing their past scroll before their eyes. They experience childhood, adolescence, and many years of living all in one split second. In that moment, one person might feel remorse while another gains an acceptance of the inevitable and receives a peaceful calm. David Ponder, on the other hand, had only questions in his heart as his car careened helplessly toward a giant oak tree. With his remaining conscious thought, David removed his hands from the steering wheel and raised them as fists to the sky. "Please, God!" he cried. "Why me?"

And then . . . nothing.

THREE

"PLEASE GET OFF THE FLOOR AND SIT IN THIS CHAIR."

Slowly, David opened his eyes and looked directly into the face of a man who seemed vaguely familiar. A small, older gentleman, his short almost-white hair was neatly combed, contrasting with the slightly disheveled appearance of his clothes. The sleeves of his dress shirt were rolled up at the elbows, and his red-and-black-striped tie was loosened at the collar. Atop his sharp nose sat a pair of round spectacles that were thick enough to make his clear blue eyes seem huge.

"This is a very inconvenient time for me," the man said. "Just sit right there and be very quiet." Turning quickly, he walked toward a huge hand-carved desk. Settling himself behind it and picking up a stack of papers, he grumbled, "As if I don't have enough happening right now."

Confused, David glanced around. He was sitting on a large Persian rug, his back against the wall of an ornate, high-ceilinged room. Directly to his left was the hard-backed mahogany chair that had been indicated by the man who was now intently sorting papers across the room. To his right, a globe stood on a pedestal in front of an unlit fireplace.

Easing up and into the chair, David said, "I'm thirsty."

Without looking up, the man replied, "I'll get you something in a bit. For now, please be quiet."

"Where am I?" David asked.

"Look here now." The man cursed as he slammed the stack of papers down on the desk and pointed a finger at David. "I politely asked you to be quiet, and I'm expecting you to do it. You are in Potsdam, Germany, a suburb of Berlin in a free zone presently controlled by the Red army. It is Tuesday, July 24, 1945." Taking a deep breath and appearing to calm down, he reached for his work again. Separating the papers, he said, "There now, sit and chew on that for a while."

David wrinkled his brow. *I must be in a hospital,* he thought. *This is a creepy old place. And if this guy is my doctor, he has a horrible bedside manner.* Sitting absolutely still, trying to collect himself, David watched the man at the desk. *Why would he tell me I'm in Germany?* he wondered. *And the Red army thing? I must have a head injury. Is this some kind of psychiatric exam?*

He tugged at the collar of his dark blue sweatshirt.

Uncomfortably warm, David noticed a water pitcher and some glasses on a small table near a window directly across the room. He stood up and walked slowly to the water. From the corner of his eye, David saw the man behind the desk briefly glance up, frown, and go back to his work.

David quietly poured a glass of water and, drinking it, looked out the window. He was obviously in a second-floor room of this building or house or whatever it was. Below him, no more than fifty feet away, was the bank of a slow-moving river. There were no people boating, no children playing—in fact, he didn't see anyone at all. "Something isn't right here," David muttered as a breeze crossed his face and rustled the drapes beside him.

Reaching his arm through the open window, David was almost startled to find that the air was warm and humid. Then he realized what had been bothering him. It was the air itself. The air was *warm*. Every tree within sight was full of leaves, and the grass in the yard below him was green. In the dead of winter?

Putting his glass down on the table, David placed his hands on the windowsill and pushed his whole upper body through the opening. Yes, it was hot, he decided, and pulled himself back inside. *What kind of place is this?* David wondered. *Why are the windows open in the first place? As hot as it is, the air conditioning should be running full blast.*

As he moved back toward his seat, David looked around

for a thermostat. There wasn't one that he could see. The only temperature-controlling device was an old heater that someone had put in the fireplace. *Not that* that *heater would do anyone any good*, he thought. *It's so old, it looks like it could have been made in . . .* , David stopped in midstride. In a soft voice, he said aloud, ". . . 1945."

Wheeling suddenly, David faced the man behind the desk. The white-haired gentleman looked up and slowly pushed his work to the side. A slight smile on his thin lips, he leaned back into his chair, crossed his arms, and peered curiously at David.

David's mind raced furiously. *Potsdam . . . Potsdam . . .* , he thought. *Why is that name so familiar?* Then, like a thunderbolt, it came to him. Potsdam, Germany, he remembered from a television documentary, was the site of the famous war conference after which the decision had been made to drop the atomic bomb on Japan during World War II.

A shudder passed through his body as David put his hands to his head. *Think, think*, he commanded himself. *Who attended the war conference in Potsdam? It was Churchill, Stalin, and . . .* All the breath seemed to go out of David at once as he groped for the chair behind him. Sitting down heavily, he stared at the man in front of him. "You're Harry Truman," he said in a shocked tone.

"Yes," the man said, "I am. Though at the moment I would give anything to be almost anyone else."

Swallowing audibly, David said, "They call you 'Give 'Em Hell Harry.'"

Truman grimaced. "I never give anybody hell," he snorted. "I just tell the truth, and they think it's hell."

Removing his glasses, he rubbed his eyes and said, "Obviously, I'll not be getting any peace from this point on, so we might as well go ahead and talk." Putting his glasses back on, he rose and came out from behind the desk. "By the way," he said, "why *not* you?"

"Excuse me?" David asked.

"Why . . . not . . . you?" Looking directly into David's eyes, he enunciated the words carefully, separating them as if he were speaking to a child. "I believe that is the answer to the last question you asked before you arrived."

David frowned. Trying to remember, he said, "I was in an accident, I think."

"Yes," Truman said, "that's sometimes how this happens. And the last question a person asks is often, 'Why me?' Of course, 'Why me?' is a question great men and women have been asking themselves since time began. I know the thought has occurred to me more than once during the past few days. It's hard for me to believe that twenty-five years ago, I was a clerk in a clothing store!" Truman extended his hand and pulled David to his feet. "What's your name, son?"

"David Ponder. Am I okay?"

"Well, David Ponder, if you mean 'Am I dead?' the answer is no. If you simply mean 'Am I okay?'" Truman shrugged, "I'm not sure. I've never been given any information on how these things turn out."

Suddenly, David relaxed. Smiling, he said, "I understand. I'm dreaming, right?"

"Maybe you are," the president said, "but, David, I'm not. And even if you are dreaming, that's not a problem. For centuries, dreams have been used to communicate instruction and direction to people of purpose—great men and women. God used dreams to prepare Joseph for his future as a leader of nations. He gave battle plans to Gideon in a dream. Joan of Arc, Jacob, George Washington, Marie Curie, and the apostle Paul were all guided by their dreams."

"But I'm an ordinary guy," David said. "I'm nothing like any of the people you've mentioned—great, I mean—and I'm certainly no apostle Paul. I'm not even sure I believe in God anymore."

Truman smiled as he put a hand on David's shoulder. "That's all right, son," he said. "He believes in you."

"How can you be certain of that?" David asked.

"Because," Truman responded, "you wouldn't be here if He didn't. Occasionally, someone is chosen to travel the ages, gathering wisdom for future generations. It's as if the Almighty literally reaches down and places His hand on a shoulder, and in this particular case," the president peered over his glasses, "it was *your* shoulder."

A sharp knock at the door drew their attention. Without waiting for a response, a large, stocky man strode into the room. It was Fred Canfil, Truman's special bodyguard. Formerly the U.S. marshal from Kansas City, Fred was temporarily attached to the Secret Service and had become a favorite of the president and his family. "I'm sorry to barge in like this, sir," he said as his eyes surveyed the room. "I thought I heard you talking to someone."

"No, Fred," Truman said as he looked directly at David, "no one here." Then motioning toward the door with his hand, he said, "If you'll see that I'm not disturbed?"

"Of course, Mr. President," Canfil said as he slowly backed out, a concerned look on his face. Still glancing about, he added, "I'll be escorting you to the conference room within the hour, but if you need me before then . . ."

"You'll be right outside," Truman said as he ushered his bewildered friend from the room, "and I won't hesitate to call for you. Thank you, Fred."

As the president closed the door, David asked, "He can't see me?"

"Apparently no one can," Truman replied. "No one, that is, except the person you came to visit. Of course, that makes me look a little crazy," he said with a grin, "in here, all alone, talking to myself." Quickly, he wiped the grin off his face and continued, "But I shouldn't think anyone would find it strange. I have ample reason to be talking to myself, what with everything that's going on here." Truman cocked his head and looked at David from the corner of his eye. "It is curious how you people always seem to show up during critical points in *my* life."

"So this has happened to you before?" David asked.

"Yes," Truman said, "three times now since I became president, you being the third. The first time was the night Roosevelt died. I was all alone in the Oval Office, and this kid just appeared out of nowhere. Fred came busting through the door—almost gave me a heart attack. It was strange that no one could see him but me."

"The kid?"

"Yeah, the kid." Truman paused. "I say 'kid.' He was a teenager actually. He was having trouble deciding whether or not to finish college."

David was incredulous. "That doesn't seem to be a problem big enough for the president."

"What are you here for?" Truman asked.

"I don't know."

"Well," the president said as he moved across the room, "at least the kid had a question." Leaning against the desk, he motioned for David to sit in a chair near the globe. "Anyway, there was a lot of pressure for him to stay in school."

"What did you tell him to do?" David asked.

"I didn't tell him to do anything," Truman replied. "That's not my part in all this. I offer perspective. The ultimate outcome of anyone's life is a matter of personal choice." The president continued, "I was evidently his second visit. He had just spent an hour or so with Albert Einstein."

David shifted uncomfortably in his seat. "Will I be going somewhere after this?"

"Yes, you will," Truman said. "Several different places actually, but don't worry. They will be expecting you."

"So you knew I was coming?"

"I was informed as you might expect—in a dream—the other evening," Truman said. Walking around behind his desk, Truman opened the right top drawer. Removing a folded piece of paper, he handed it to David and said, "I was instructed to prepare this for you. This is the essence of why you are here. It is one of the Decisions for Success. This is the first of seven you will receive. You are to keep it with you, reading it twice daily until it is committed to your heart. For only by committing this principle to your heart will you be able to share its value with others."

David started to unfold the page. "No, no," the president said as he put his hands over David's. "Don't read it now. You must wait until our meeting is finished. As soon as you read these words, you will immediately travel to your next destination. Amazing, actually. You read the last word and—bang!—you're gone!"

David reached over and touched the globe, unconsciously turning it to the United States. "Do you know my future?" he asked.

"Nope," Truman said. "Can't help you there. And wouldn't if I could. Your future is what you decide it will be. Now you, on the other hand, could probably tell me mine." As David opened his mouth to speak, the president held out his hands as if to ward off the words. "Thanks, but no thanks. God knows, there are enough influences coming to bear without you telling me what I already did!"

"You say my future is what I decide it to be," David ventured. "I'm not sure I agree with that. My present is certainly not of my making. I worked for years to finally end up with no job, no money, and no prospects."

"David, we are all in situations of our own choosing. Our thinking creates a pathway to success or failure. By disclaiming responsibility for our present, we crush the prospect of an incredible future that might have been ours."

"I don't understand," David said.

"I am saying that outside influences are not responsible for where you are mentally, physically, spiritually, emotionally, or financially. You have chosen the pathway to your present destination. The responsibility for your situation is yours."

David stood up. "That's not true," he cried angrily. "I did a good job at the plant. I could've taken early retirement, but I stayed. I stayed to help the company remain afloat, and I was fired. It was not . . . my . . . fault!"

"Sit down," Truman said softly. Drawing a chair around to face David, who was trembling with anger and confusion, he said, "Look here, son. It is not my desire to upset you, but with the limited time we have been given together, truth will have to stand before tact."

Placing his elbows on his knees, the president leaned forward and took a deep breath. "Listen to me now. You are where you are because of your thinking. Your thinking dictates your decisions. Decisions are choices. Years ago, you chose where you would attend college. You chose your course of study. When you graduated with the degree you chose to pursue, you chose the companies to which you would send a résumé. After interviewing with the companies that responded, you chose the one for which you would work. Somewhere during that time, you chose to go to a party or a play or a ball game. There, you met a girl whom you chose to marry. Together, you chose to have a family and how large that family would be.

"When you chose the house in which you would live and the cars you would drive, you chose how much the payments would be each month. By choosing to eat rib eye steaks or hot dogs, you chose your household expenses.

And you were the one who chose not to take early retirement. You chose to stay until the bitter end. Years ago, you began making the choices that led you to your present situation. And you walked right down the middle of the path every step of the way."

Truman paused. He pulled out his handkerchief and wiped his brow. David's head was hanging, his chin on his chest. "David, look at me," the president said. David's eyes met his. "The words *It's not my fault!* should never again come from your mouth. The words *It's not my fault!* have been symbolically written on the gravestones of unsuccessful people ever since Eve took her first bite of the apple. Until a person takes responsibility for where he is, there is no basis for moving on. The bad news is that the past was in your hands, but the good news is that the future, my friend, is also in your hands."

As the president leaned forward to touch the younger man on the shoulder, he was interrupted by three quick knocks on the door. "Mr. President," came a voice from the hallway. It was Fred Canfil.

"Five-minute warning, sir. I'll wait for you out here. Mr. Churchill and the Russian are already making their way to the conference room."

"Thank you, Fred." Truman chuckled. "It seems my bodyguard doesn't care very much for Mr. Stalin. Come to think of it, neither do I, and frankly, I keep a few of my plans to myself. But I suppose he's a necessary part of this process." He stood up and began rolling down his sleeves and buttoning the cuffs.

David saw the president's jacket hanging over the back of the desk chair and went to retrieve it.

"What will you do?" he asked.

Truman buttoned his collar, straightened his tie, and eyed David warily. "Let's not play any games here, son. I think we both know what I'm about to do. Do I want to do it? Do I want to deploy this . . . this bomb? Of course not!"

He strode to his desk and gathered several notebooks. Suddenly, he put them down again and faced David. "I don't have any idea what you know about me." He paused. "I suppose I mean that I don't know what people say about me in the . . . ahh . . ." He wiggled his left hand at David as if he could conjure up the words he wanted to say. "I don't know what they say about me where you come from. For all I know, history books are full of how I feel or how I look or what kind of scotch I drink, and frankly, I don't care. But let's get something straight between you and me. I hate this weapon, okay? I'm scared of it and concerned about what it might mean for the future of our world."

"Why have you decided to use it?" David asked the question with no accusation, no judgment in the tone of his voice. He simply wanted to understand the thoughts of this common man who had been placed in an uncommon position. "Why have you decided to drop the bomb?"

Truman took a deep breath. "I am the first president since the beginning of modern warfare to have experienced combat. During the First World War, I would have given anything, paid any price, to end the death and suffering I watched my friends endure. And now, here I sit, the commander in chief with the ability—no, the responsibility—to end this war and bring our boys home.

"Believe me," he said as he slipped on his jacket, "I have examined every option. I asked General Marshall what it would cost in lives to land on the Tokyo plain and other places in Japan. It was his opinion that such an invasion would cost at a minimum a quarter of a million American lives. And that's just the invasion. After that we would literally be forced to go house to house and take the country. Did you know that during this whole war, not one single Japanese platoon has surrendered, not one?"

David watched Truman, his jaw set, but with a weariness in his face as he placed the final papers in a leather satchel. "Yes," he said. "It must be done. How could any president face the mothers and sons and daughters of these American servicemen if, after the slaughter of an invasion of Japan, it became known that there was within the arsenal a weapon of sufficient force to end the war and it was not used?"

He stared blankly at David for a moment. It was as if he were seeing something of his own future, and it scared him. Shaking his head to clear his thoughts, he said, "Still got the paper?"

"Yes, sir," David said as he held up the folded page that had never left his hand.

"Well, then," the president said with a smile, "go ahead and read it." He walked to the door, opened it, and was about to walk through when he paused, turned, and said, "David?"

"Sir?" David answered.

"Good luck, son."

"Thank you, sir," David said.

Truman turned to leave, but again reached back in to shake David's hand. "And one more thing," he said as he raised an eyebrow, "just because I use the expression 'good luck' doesn't mean that luck actually has anything to do with where you end up." With that, the president of the United States closed the door.

All alone, David glanced around the room. He walked slowly to the desk and sat down behind it in the big leather chair where Truman had been only moments before. Carefully, he unfolded the paper and began to read.

The First Decision for Success

The buck stops here.

From this moment forward, I will accept responsibility for my past. I understand that the beginning of wisdom is to accept the responsibility for my own problems and that by accepting responsibility for my past, I free myself to move into a bigger, brighter future of my own choosing.

Never again will I blame my parents, my spouse, my boss, or other employees for my present situation. Neither my education nor lack of one, my genetics, or the circumstantial ebb and flow of everyday life will affect my future in a negative way. If I allow myself to blame these uncontrollable forces for my lack of success, I will be forever caught in a web of the past. I will look forward. I will not let my history control my destiny.

The buck stops here. I accept responsibility for my past. I am responsible for my success.

I am where I am today—mentally, physically, spiritually, emotionally, and financially—because of decisions I have made. My decisions have always been governed by my thinking. Therefore, I am where I am today—mentally, physically, spiritually, emotionally, and financially—because of how I think. Today I will begin the process of changing where I am—mentally, physically, spiritually, emotionally, and financially—by changing the way I think.

My thoughts will be constructive, never destructive. My mind will live in the solutions of the future. It will not dwell in the problems of the past. I will seek the association of those who are working and striving to bring about positive changes in the world. I will never seek comfort by associating with those who have decided to be comfortable.

When faced with the opportunity to make a decision, I will make one. I understand that God did not put in me the ability to always make right decisions. He did, however, put in me the ability to *make* a decision and then *make it right*. The rise and fall of my emotional tide will not deter me from my course. When I make a decision, I will stand behind it. My energy will go into making the decision. I will waste none on second thoughts. My life will not be an apology. It will be a statement.

The buck stops here. I control my thoughts. I control my emotions.

In the future when I am tempted to ask the question "Why me?" I will immediately counter with the answer: "Why *not* me?" Challenges are gifts, opportunities to learn. Problems are the common thread running through the lives of great men and women. In times of adversity, I will not have a problem to deal with; I will have a choice to make. My thoughts will be clear. I will make the right choice. Adversity is preparation for greatness. I will accept this preparation. Why me? Why *not* me? I will be prepared for something great!

I accept responsibility for my past. I control my thoughts. I control my emotions. I am responsible for my success.

The buck stops here.

FOUR

AS DAVID READ THE FINAL WORDS ON THE PAGE, HE looked up. The office turned and seemed to shift, the edges of the room lower than its center. The desk, which had been right in front of him, appeared to stretch and curve. Standing, he pushed the chair away and stepped toward the window. He never made it. Suddenly dizzy, David felt his knees buckle, and his forward motion sent him face first to the floor. Reaching out to catch himself, David was somehow not surprised to see his hands continue through the Persian rug as if it were not there. His head, body, and legs followed into darkness.

Almost instantly, as if he had fallen through the floor into a room below, David was on his feet, alert and unharmed. He stood in a large room that was more than one hundred feet long, fifty feet wide, with a ceiling close to fifty feet high. He was caught in the middle of a group of people who were actively jostling for position in order to see a disturbance occurring somewhere to the front. The men, he could see, were bare-chested and tanned deeply from the sun. Women wore robes of brightly colored cloth, and their hair, rolled into ropes and twisted down their backs, was extremely long.

Moving with the crowd, David breathed deeply. The air smelled strongly of cedar. He noted with amazement that the walls and huge columns supporting the roof were crafted entirely from the pungent wood. The floor was fitted with massive slabs of gray, almost purple, marble.

Without warning, a gong was struck. The sound was ear shattering. Immediately, every man and woman around David ceased talking, fell to their knees, and lowered their heads. David, too stunned to do anything but stand there, suddenly had a clear view of the room.

Directly in front of him were six steps. On each side of the steps were statues of lions. Carved from dark marble, each was a masterpiece. They paled in comparison, however, to the sight at the top of the steps. Standing alone in the center of a granite pedestal was a throne made of ivory and detailed in pure gold. The back of the elaborate chair was rounded at the top and had armrests on each side. Two more lions, these made of gold, stood silent watch beside the throne.

The gong sounded again. This time, a man near the throne walked quickly to a curtain behind it and parted the cloth. Stepping through the open space was the most radiant human being David had ever seen. He wore a robe of brilliant turquoise. Rubies and gems of every sort were sewn into the hems and sleeves of the garment. Around his arms and neck were bands of solid gold. The crown on his head, also made of gold, was dusted with small diamonds. David was open-mouthed, the only person in the room still standing, staring openly at this awe-inspiring figure.

He was a large man. In his sandaled feet, he appeared to be slightly taller than David. His thick, dark hair was shoulder length, parted in the middle, and seemed to be held in place by the heavy crown. Circling to the front of the throne, he sat down and said simply, "Let us begin."

Immediately, the crowd leaped to its feet, and the disturbance began again near the throne. As he maneuvered to a better vantage point in order to see, David could hear the angry voices of two women.

"He is mine!" one of them screamed.

"No, no!" cried the other. "You are a thief!"

David eased his way to the front as the crowd started to become unruly, taking sides with the two women and shouting insults.

"Silence," the man on the throne said forcefully, and at once a hush passed over the people.

David moved to the edge of the steps. He was in plain view of the two women and the throne above them. As of yet, no one had acknowledged his presence. He felt utterly invisible. Seeing the women clearly for the first time, David noticed that one of them held a newborn baby.

Every person in the room had his eyes directed toward the throne. David felt as if he were the only one breathing. Then with a gesture of his hand, the man indicated the second woman—the woman standing alone—and said softly, "Tell me your story."

The woman bowed and said, "Your Majesty, this woman and I live in the same house. Not long ago, my baby was born at home. Three days later, her baby was born. No one was with us. Last night, while we were all asleep, she rolled over on her baby, and he died. Then while I was still asleep, she got up and took my son out of my bed and put him in her own. Then she put her dead baby next to me."

There was murmuring through the crowd as she continued, "In the morning, when I arose to feed my son, I saw that he was dead. Then I looked at him in the light, and I knew he was not my son."

"No!" the other woman shouted. "He was your son. My child is alive!"

"The dead baby is yours," yelled the woman who told the story. "You are holding my child. My baby is alive!"

David watched the women argue back and forth until the king raised his hand and silenced them all again. Carefully, the king looked into the eyes of each woman. In a measured tone, he commanded an attendant, "Bring me my sword."

David stood transfixed as the sword was brought from behind the curtain. It was very nearly five feet long— gleaming silver with a golden handle. Emeralds decorated the lower part of the shaft. The king took it in his hand, stood up, and said, "Bring the baby to me. I will cut him in half. That way each of you can have a part of him." He raised the sword as if to strike.

"Please don't kill my son!" screamed the woman standing alone. "Your Majesty, give him to her, but don't kill him!"

"Go ahead and cut him in half," the other woman snarled as she pushed the child toward the king. "Then neither of us will have the baby."

The king said softly, "I won't harm the baby. I never intended to." He pointed to the woman who was on her knees, weeping. "Give the child to her," he said. "She is his real mother."

As the woman's tears of anguish turned into tears of joy, the baby was placed in her arms, and the crowd cheered. David yelled and clapped right along with them. When the king rose from his throne, the people knelt to the ground once more, leaving David standing alone. As the king moved behind the throne toward the curtain, he paused, turned, and looked directly at David as if to say, Are you coming?

David caught the look and quickly followed him up the steps and behind the throne. Passing through the curtains, he entered a smaller but more fabulous room. Gold shields crossed with silver spears lined the walls. Pillows of linen and tanned skins were scattered in the corner near a low table covered with food of every description. Light entered the room through high windows embellished with ivory and gold.

David came fully into the center of the room. The two attendants guarding the door did not notice him, but the king, who was speaking to another man near the table, saw David and finished his conversation. "As you wish, Ahishar," David heard him say. "I am certain you, as prime minister, will make the correct decision." He moved to recline on the pillows at the table. "Please go now and instruct all the attendants to leave the hall."

The man called Ahishar was shocked. "But, Your Majesty," he said, "it is not safe to—"

"I prefer to be alone," the king interrupted. "Thank you for your concern, but at this time, it is unnecessary. Now go, Ahishar." Bowing as he left, the prime minister exited and motioned the attendants out after him.

Alone at last, David and the king stared curiously at each other. The king spoke first. "Do you know where you are?" he asked with a smile.

"Yes, sir," David answered hesitantly.

"Do you know who I am?"

"Yes, sir, I do." This time David answered the question more confidently. "You are King Solomon, sir. I recognized the story." Solomon furrowed his brow. "I mean, I recognized what happened out there." David motioned toward the curtain. "What I am trying to say is that I remember the story from when I was a child."

Solomon smiled, amused at David's confusion. "No matter," he said. "Are you hungry?"

"Yes, sir," David replied.

"Then, please, join me." Solomon pointed to an especially big pillow on which David promptly sat. "You see before you the finest food available anywhere in the world. The food, and anything else you might need, is yours for the asking."

"Thank you," David said as he reached for some fruit. "By the way, my name is David Ponder."

"Two names," Solomon noted with interest. "Incidentally, you speak my language well. Have you been schooled in Hebrew, or is your tongue also a surprise?"

"Actually," David said as he opened a pomegranate, "I was startled to find that I understood every word being spoken when I arrived. I am even more amazed that I am able to talk with you now. I never even learned Spanish, and here I am speaking effortlessly in an ancient language."

Solomon chuckled. "The dialect is not so ancient to me, my friend, but I do understand your astonishment.

Wherever you travel on this unusual journey, you will find that your mouth and ear have been granted a special ability to communicate and comprehend. This unique competence in other languages is, of course, critical to your understanding and application of the gift with which you are being entrusted."

"A gift?" David asked.

"The scrolls," Solomon answered. "I prepared this one for you only this morning." He gently placed his hand on a thin piece of leather that had been tightly wound around a small wooden rod. "It is the message that was placed in my heart for you. This is merely a part of what must be ingrained in your life before you will be able to pass the gift to others."

"How am I supposed to pass this . . . this gift to anyone?" David asked, shaking his head.

The king smiled slightly as he reached for a bunch of grapes. Plucking one from its stem, he placed it in his mouth and said thoughtfully, "That is something you may not know for yet some time. Then again, the answer could be revealed to you tomorrow. Jehovah moves mountains to create the opportunity of His choosing. It is up to you to be ready to move yourself."

David leaned forward. "I think I understand what you are saying. You mean I have to prepare for whatever is in store." Solomon nodded slowly. "Then here's a question," David said, almost sarcastically. "How do I prepare for something when I don't know (*a*) what it is or (*b*) when it will happen?" Solomon was quiet. "Sir?" David said a bit louder. He was becoming exasperated. "Look," he began again, "I'm serious. How do I prepare for an uncertain future?"

"Seek wisdom," the king said simply.

David came close to rolling his eyes. "Maybe I'm not too smart," he said, "but I'm just not catching on here. Okay, let me ask you this: How do I seek wisdom?"

"The answer I have for you will not quell your frustration with me," the king replied and then paused. "My answer is to seek wisdom."

David's mouth dropped open. He shook his head and was about to speak when Solomon interrupted.

"David," he said, "you have a condition common to most people. You hear, but you do not listen.

"Seek wisdom. *Seek* wisdom. Wisdom waits to be gathered. She cannot be bartered or sold. She is a gift for the diligent. And only the diligent will find her. The lazy man—the stupid man—never even looks. Though wisdom is available to many, she is found by few. Seek wisdom. Find her, and you will find success and contentment."

"Well," David said, "I certainly don't have success or contentment in my life right now."

"All a part of the past," Solomon noted. "Even the present is constantly becoming the past—now . . . and now . . . and now." He snapped his fingers as he talked. "The past will never change, but you can change the future by changing your actions today. It is really a very simple process. We, as humans, are always in a process of change. Therefore, we might as well guide the direction in which we change."

"How do I guide that direction?" David asked.

Solomon rose to his feet and began to walk around the room. Clasping his hands behind his back, he asked, "Do you have a child?"

"Yes, I do," David answered. "A twelve-year-old daughter."

The king said, "Are you concerned about the children with whom your daughter plays?"

"Yes," David replied. "Of course."

Solomon turned quickly and said, "You say, 'Of course.' Why?"

David wrinkled his forehead. He was trying to figure out where the king was taking this. "Well," he began, "I say, 'Of course,' because my child's friends have such an effect on her. And I mean both good and bad. We've noticed that when she is around good, respectful children, we very rarely have a problem with her behavior. But occasionally, she'll mix in with the wrong group at school, and her mother and I have to deal with the consequences at home."

"Consequences?" Solomon asked.

"Her speech patterns, her attitude, the way she dresses, how she responds to us," David struggled to find the right words. "Everything she does at her age seems to be influenced by someone else."

"How do you guide the direction in which your daughter changes?" Solomon asked.

"By keeping tabs on who her friends are," David said.

"Exactly!" the king said excitedly. "And at what age are we no longer affected by those around us? Eighteen? Twenty-one? Thirty? The answer, of course, is that we are always and forever influenced by those with whom we associate. If a man keeps company with those who curse and complain—he will soon find curses and complaints flowing like a river from his own mouth. If he spends his days with the lazy—those seeking handouts—he will soon find his finances in disarray. Many of our sorrows can be traced to relationships with the wrong people."

David got to his feet. Wiping his hands on his jeans, he said, "So this is an important step in seeking wisdom?"

"Possibly *the* most important step," Solomon responded. "Guard your associations carefully, David. Anytime you tolerate mediocrity in your choice of companions, you become more comfortable with mediocrity in your own life. If a lazy man isn't an irritation to you, it is a sign that you have accepted slothfulness as a way of life. You saw Ahishar as you entered, did you not?"

"Yes." David nodded. "I believe you said he was the prime minister."

"That is correct," the king acknowledged. "You have not met Zadok, Azariah, and Abiathar. They are my priests. Elihoreph and Ahijah are my personal assistants, Jehoshaphat is in charge of government records, and Benaiah is my army commander. All are wise and energetic men with whom I keep counsel. If it is important for a king to be careful in his choice of friends, would it not also be important for you?"

David walked to one of the gold shields on the wall and stroked it absentmindedly. "You are the wisest man in the world," he said, "and obviously the richest. Yet you said you keep counsel with those other men. Why?"

Solomon smiled patiently. "Only a fool refuses the counsel of wise men. There is safety in counsel. Sensible instruction is a life-giving fountain that will help you escape all manner of deadly traps. Find a wise man, a person who has accomplished what you wish for in your own life, and listen closely to his words." Solomon moved to the table and picked up the scroll. Placing it into a fold of his robe, he motioned to David. "Follow me," he said.

As Solomon exited the interior room, he held the curtain open for David to pass. David stepped under Solomon's arm and said, "I should be holding the curtain for you. After all, you are the king!"

Solomon laughed. "Thank you, but I appreciate the opportunity to serve *you*. When a king begins to act like a king, it is not long before someone else is king! Serving is a way we can place value on one another. A wise man is a server."

As they strode into the great hall, David indicated the throne and said, "May I touch it?"

"Certainly," Solomon replied. "You may sit in it if you wish. It is only a chair."

David placed his hands palm down on the throne. Lightly brushing the seat and armrests with his fingertips, he admired the placement of the ivory and gold. Turning, he eased himself onto the throne. Smiling sheepishly, he said, "I feel very small sitting here."

"As do I." Solomon chuckled. Then seriously, he said, "The responsibility that comes with leadership is often humbling. When I sit where you are now, I am grateful for the lessons of my father. As you might know, his name was also David. He was not only the king before me, but my mentor as well." Solomon gazed out at the empty hall, seemingly lost in thought. Continuing, he said, "My father has been dead now for many years, yet the fundamentals he taught guide me still."

Solomon removed the scroll from his garment and unrolled the skin from the wooden rod. As he passed the precious words to David, he said, "It is time for us to part, my friend. Perhaps our time together will bring more under-standing to your life's journey. I can do nothing to alleviate your struggles and would not if I were able. It is never the duty of a leader to struggle for someone else; a leader must encourage others to struggle and assure them that the struggles are worthwhile. Do battle with the challenges of your present, and you will unlock the prizes of your future."

"Thank you, Your Majesty," David said.

"Of course," Solomon replied. He smiled as he bowed slightly. "It has been an honor to assist you. Farewell." With those final words, the king walked down the steps and directly through the middle of the vast hall. As he neared the doorway at the opposite end, he clapped his hands twice. Immediately, attendants appeared to flank the king as he left the building.

Alone, David stood up and looked once more at the magnificent room. Slowly, he slid back onto the throne of King Solomon and smoothed the king's words onto his lap.

The Second Decision for Success

I will seek wisdom.

Knowing that wisdom waits to be gathered, I will actively search her out. My past can never be changed, but I can change the future by changing my actions today. I *will* change my actions today! I will train my eyes and ears to read and listen to books and recordings that bring about positive changes in my personal relationships and a greater understanding of my fellowman. No longer will I bombard my mind with materials that feed my doubts and fears. I will read and listen only to what increases my belief in myself and my future.

I will seek wisdom. I will choose my friends with care.

I am who my friends are. I speak their language, and I wear their clothes. I share their opinions and their habits. From this moment forward, I will choose to associate with people whose lives and lifestyles I admire. If I associate with chickens, I will learn to scratch at the ground and squabble over crumbs. If I associate with eagles, I will learn to soar to great heights. I am an eagle. It is my destiny to fly.

I will seek wisdom. I will listen to the counsel of wise men.

The words of a wise man are like raindrops on dry ground. They are precious and can be quickly used for immediate results. Only the blade of grass that catches a raindrop will prosper and grow. The person who ignores wise counsel is like the blade of grass untouched by the rain—soon to wither and die. When I counsel with just myself, I can make decisions only according to what I already know. By counseling with a wise man, I add his knowledge and experience to my own and dramatically increase my success.

I will seek wisdom. I will be a servant to others.

A wise man will cultivate a servant's spirit, for that particular attribute attracts people like no other. As I humbly serve others, their wisdom will be freely shared with me.

Often, the person who develops a servant's spirit becomes wealthy beyond measure. Many times, a servant has the ear of the king, and a humble servant often becomes a king, for he is the popular choice of the people. He who serves the most grows the fastest.

I will become a humble servant. I will not look for someone to open my door—I will look to open the door for someone. I will not be distressed when no one is available to help me—I will be excited when I am available to help.

I will be a servant to others. I will listen to the counsel of wise men. I will choose my friends with care.

I will seek wisdom.

FIVE

I WILL SEEK WISDOM—THE LAST WORDS. THIS time, David was ready. In anticipation of the dizziness he had felt before, he closed his eyes and tensed his whole body. David could feel the skin of the scroll in his left hand as he gripped it against the armrest of the throne. He was holding on for dear life. For a moment, nothing happened. Just as David was about to relax, he opened his eyes to see his fingers literally sliding through the ivory as if it were air. The scroll was still in his possession, and David's hands, holding so tightly to a solid object only a moment before, reflexively made fists as the throne disappeared.

The next conscious moment, David was standing amid the loudest noise he had ever heard in his life. His first thought as he tried to regain his senses was *thunder*, and he looked toward the sky. Suddenly, a hand roughly slammed into his chest, grabbed his shirt, and forcefully yanked David to the ground. "Get down, man!" the owner of the hand said as he pushed David's face to the dirt. "I don't know if you can get shot, but let's not find out, okay?"

David turned his head in panic and stared at the man who had pulled him down. He was somewhere in his mid-thirties with dark brown hair and a long, bushy mustache. He wore dark blue trousers with a faded yellow stripe down the side and a shirt of indeterminate color. The clothes, like their owner, looked as if they had not been washed in a month. He was rather thin and probably tall. It was hard to tell because he was laid out on the ground firing an old rifle over a pile of rocks. The sound David had mistaken for thunder moments earlier was the sound of cannon fire.

Bullets whined off the rocks like swarms of angry bees. All around him David heard howls of anger and pain. A man not ten feet away sat propped against a tree, shrieking in agony from a wound in his stomach, while another, missing his right leg below the knee, slowly crawled toward a friend who was already dead. The cannonballs that weren't pounding groups of men found trees nearby, severing trunks as big around as the soldiers on whom they fell.

It was so loud that David had to scream to be heard. That was not a problem. In fact, at the moment, it was the most natural thing in the world—he was terrified. David grabbed at the man's shoulder and cried, "Who are you?"

The man had turned his back to the rocks where he was reloading his rifle from the muzzle. "Chamberlain!" he yelled. "Chamberlain of the Twentieth Maine!" and he turned to fire again.

Once again the man called Chamberlain turned to reload. He lay awkwardly on his side as he bit the paper from a round and rammed it down the barrel of the gun with a metal rod. "What's going on?" David hollered. "Where are we?" David had never been so scared in his life.

"Stay down!" Chamberlain yelled in reply. "No time now. We'll talk later—I hope."

David anxiously glanced around. He could see that the rocks they were crouched behind had actually been thrown up as a makeshift wall extending more than fifty yards to his right and fifty yards again to his left. They were almost at the top of a steep wooded hill that sloped down and away from them. Chamberlain continued to fire downhill, reload, and shout encouragement to the men around him.

Just beyond Chamberlain, David saw a man thrown backward, his blood arcing into the air from a wound in his throat. He landed on his hands and knees. Slowly shaking his head, he crawled toward David. Reaching the wall, he eased over onto his back, and as his arm fell across David's leg, he looked up, smiled, and died. As David stared into the unseeing eyes, he was horrified to realize the soldier was a boy, certainly no older than fifteen.

David wasn't aware of the precise moment when the shooting stopped. He had remained huddled against the rocks, looking into the dead boy's face, until Chamberlain's hand broke his trance. The man gently brushed the young soldier's eyes, closing them, and said, "Neilson. He was a good kid." He gestured to a man, obviously dead, lying across the rock wall no more than ten yards away. "That was his father. Hiram was a bank teller from Bangor. Both joined when this regiment was formed last fall. There were a thousand of us then. The three hundred that're left are strung out along this pile of rocks."

Chamberlain stood up and offered his hand to David. Helping him to his feet, he said, "I'm Colonel Chamberlain. Joshua Lawrence Chamberlain. I know why you're here, but I don't know your name."

"I'm David Ponder, sir. Is it safe to be standing up like this?"

"For the moment," Chamberlain replied as he pulled a small twig from his mustache. "But they'll sure be back. That was the fourth time they made a try for us already."

"If you don't mind me asking," David stammered, "who are *they?*"

The colonel cocked his head and frowned. "Why, Lee's boys . . . the Army of Northern Virginia. We have fully half the Confederate battle complement facing off against us in a long line that stretches to a little town about a mile that way." Chamberlain pointed with his rifle.

"What's the name of the town?" David asked.

"Gettysburg," Chamberlain offered. "Ever hear of it?"

David nodded his head as a cold boiling began deep in his stomach. "The Civil War," he whispered.

"What?" Chamberlain asked.

"I said this is the Civil War."

"Hmmph," Chamberlain snorted. "That may be what *you* call it. Stick around for a bit. I can assure you that there is nothing civil about it. Come with me," he said, beginning to walk. "We won't have much time until they hit us again."

"Joshua!" The two men turned at the shout. "Joshua!"

It was Tom and John Chamberlain, the colonel's younger brothers. Tom was a lieutenant in the regiment, while John, a muscular young man, had been pressed into service as a medic. Both were almost as tall as the colonel and wore mustaches and sideburns that almost covered their faces. They were endowed with a cheerfulness, however, that their older brother had long since discarded. "You're a little dirtier than you ought to be, Joshua, but you're looking well. Are you all right?" John asked.

"Yes. Fine to this point. You?"

"So far, so good," John said. David followed the three brothers as they walked quickly along the wall. "Sergeant Tozier was hit but not seriously. His section took some heavy losses, though."

"How're we doing, Colonel?" The question came from a

man of about fifty. He had a bandage around his head and was busily making a wounded friend comfortable.

"You're giving it to them, soldier," Chamberlain said. "Keep pouring it on." Turning to his brothers, he instructed, "John, get over the hill and find a place for the wounded. Tom, go to the rear of the regiment and see that it is well closed up. And tell the men to thin their lines. Stretch at least half the men to the left of that big rock. The Rebs are working that way, and if they flank us . . ." Chamberlain's voice trailed away. "Well," he continued, "they just can't flank us. That's all." They turned to move away when their older brother stopped them again. "Boys," he said, "I don't like this. Keep your head down. With all of us here, it could be a bad day for Mother."

As his brothers ran off, Chamberlain turned to David and motioned for him to follow. They picked their way through the broken trees and tumbled sections of the wall, stepping over the men who were preparing to fight again and the ones who would fight no more. The colonel climbed onto the big rock he had indicated earlier to his brother and helped David up beside him. "You can see them from here," he said.

David squinted through the smoke that still lay thick in the air. Following Chamberlain's gaze, he saw the gray and pale yellow uniforms of the Confederate army massing below. They were less than 150 yards away. David could see their hats and the occasional face looking up the hill.

"Who are you?" David asked.

Chamberlain had been peering intently down the hill, but at this question, he jerked his head sharply back toward his visitor. "What? I've already told you. My name is—"

"That's not what I mean," David interrupted. "I mean who *are* you? No offense, but are you famous? The other places I appeared, it was to see someone . . . well . . . famous."

Chamberlain laughed. It was a quick, dry laugh devoid of humor. "Famous? Ten months ago I was a schoolteacher. Now, I'm a soldier. For a while anyway. Actually, it was about the time I joined up that I started dreaming about you. I knew what you looked like, how tall you were." The colonel tugged at David's sleeve. "I even knew you'd be wearing this. I've never had dreams like these before. Strange, constant, every night for months. You want to hear something spooky? Just before you arrived—there in the middle of the fight—I looked up and raised my hand. You appeared. I closed my fist on your shirt and pulled you down. When I raised my hand to grab you, I knew you'd be there. It was just like in my dreams."

"Why are you here?" David asked.

Chamberlain eyed him curiously. "Do you mean the war in general or this specific desolate hill?"

"Both, I suppose."

"Hmm," Chamberlain stroked his beard. "I joined the Union army for a myriad of reasons—same as everyone else really. We got caught up in the patriotism. We were bored. We were ashamed *not* to join. We thought it'd be quick and fun. For the most part, though, I think the vast majority of our men left their homes and families because it was the right thing to do."

Chamberlain was quiet for a moment, distracted by the men forming behind fallen trees as they spread out their line. "Colonel!" one of the men yelled. "The brush is too thick here. We can't see thirty yards!"

"Dig in and stay where you are, son," Chamberlain yelled back. "They'll be a lot closer than that!"

After a few moments of silence, David prompted Chamberlain. "Colonel?" he started. "You said you joined because it was the right thing to do."

"Yes," Chamberlain continued. "Over the centuries, wars have been fought for land or women or money. Thousands of people have died in battles caused by jealousy or an insult. More than a few times, men have fought because a king or president or someone told them to fight." Chamberlain turned squarely to face David and looked him in the eye. "David Ponder, I say to you now that this is the first time in history that men have fought to set another man free. Most of us Maine boys have never even seen black skin on a man, but if it is true that all men are created equal, then we are fighting for each other. We are fighting because it is the right thing to do."

The colonel held David's eyes for a long moment, then slowly turned to look up the line of men. "I'm not certain anymore just what I expected when I signed on for this fight, but it wasn't this." He lowered himself into a squatting position, balancing easily on the balls of his feet. Picking absently at a weed that had grown through the rock, Chamberlain said, "I was at Fredericksburg, you know." It wasn't a question. It was a statement.

"Three thousand of us attacked a rock wall just like this one. We came across a field as the sun was setting. From about fifty, sixty yards they fired. We dropped in waves. Literally sheets of men falling like a curtain on a bad play. The attack failed, but I made it to the wall. I lay there all night, too scared to withdraw, cold. I burrowed down into the corpses for warmth, listening to our men shoot, their men shoot back. *Whap!* That's the sound a bullet makes when it hits a dead body. Altogether different from the sound of a bullet in living flesh."

Chamberlain shook his head forcefully as if to drive the memory away. "Oh, well," he said as he stood up. He had pulled the weed from the rock and used it as a sword, pointing again toward the wall. "That'll never happen here. This wall won't turn 'em much longer. We don't have enough men left." He threw the weed to the ground. "I have a feeling," he said, "that if we lose this fight, the war will be over."

David stepped up beside the colonel. "Why did you choose this place to defend?"

"I didn't choose it," Chamberlain said dryly. "Colonel Vincent placed me here this morning."

"Why did he place you here?" David pressed.

"We are the extreme left of the Union army. The Eighty-third Pennsylvania is formed on our right, but to our left, nothing. We are the end of a line that runs from here all the way back into Gettysburg. That means I cannot withdraw. If the Confederate army flanks us, if the Rebs overrun us, they'll come in behind our cannons and barricades, and the Army of the Potomac will be forfeit. Eighty thousand men caught from the back on a downhill charge with no protection. And if it happens, it will have come through me."

At that very second, David heard a ghostly sound resonate from down the hill. Rising to a high, thin pitch, a thousand voices strained in a long, continuous scream. It was the Rebel yell. They were coming. David caught glimpses of the soldiers through the trees as they ran up the steep hill.

Chamberlain had turned to direct David off the rock when the cannon shell hit. Striking the base of the rock on which they were standing, the projectile threw both men into the air. As he hit the ground, David felt as though a giant vacuum had sucked all the air from his body. Before he could check to see if he'd been injured—before he could even breathe—Chamberlain had him by the arm, dragging him to the protection of the wall.

Only the cannons were firing now, David realized as he struggled to get his lungs working again. He could still hear the blood-curdling yells as the Rebels worked their way up the hill. He rolled over onto his knees and glanced over the wall. They were within sight. It seemed to David as though the Confederate army was about to step into his lap. *Shoot!* he thought. *For God's sake, shoot! They're right here!*

It seemed an eternity, but finally, David heard Chamberlain call out, "Hit 'em!" A long, rolling crack of rifle fire rang out. It began near David and ran like a fuse up the line to the right. Scores of Rebels fell on the first volley. They were more careful after that, using trees to shield them from the deadly fire, but still they came.

The firing was continuous now. To David, it sounded like thunder and firecrackers thrown into an earthquake. The man next to him grunted and fell backward, his head and face a bloody mess. To David's astonishment, the man sat up, pulled a handkerchief from his pocket, and wrapped the cloth around his head. Wiping the blood from his eyes with a sleeve, he picked up his rifle and began loading it to fire again.

Chamberlain was directing his men now and had moved some distance from David. All down the line, a few of the Rebels had reached the wall. Most of the shooting was point-blank. The colonel had drawn his pistol, and David watched as Chamberlain and a Rebel, no more than three feet apart, aimed guns at each other. The Confederate soldier went down in a cloud of red mist. Chamberlain continued to fire at targets all around him until, without warning, the Rebels pulled back.

As suddenly as they had appeared, they withdrew. Chamberlain's men cautiously stood up to take stock of their situation. David walked quickly toward the colonel who was walking away from him. The rock wall, on his left side as he walked, was draped with the bodies of blue and gray. He passed a man who was crying and cursing as he held a younger man in his arms.

Jogging as he caught up with Chamberlain, David reached out and touched his shoulder. "Colonel?" he said. Chamberlain stopped, staring straight ahead. "Colonel? I know you're very busy, and I don't want to bother you, but why am I here?"

Chamberlain slowly shook his head. "I don't know. I only knew that you would come."

"There is something I am to learn from you," David pleaded. "I am sure of it. Think—what could it be?"

The colonel smiled slightly and raised his eyebrows.

Turning to David, he said, "I am a professor of rhetoric. I am fairly certain I have nothing you would care to learn. I am a teacher with a cause in my heart and men to lead. These poor men . . . their leader has no real knowledge of warfare or tactics. I am only a stubborn man, Ponder. That is my greatest advantage in this fight. I have deep within me the inability to do nothing. I may die today, but I will not die with a bullet in my back. I will *not* die in retreat. I am, at least, like the apostle Paul, who wrote, 'This one thing I do . . . I press toward the mark.'"

"Do you have anything written that you are to give me?" David asked.

For a moment, David could see that Chamberlain did not understand his question. Then recognition flared in his eyes. "Yes," he said. "I do. I had almost forgotten."

Digging into his pocket, he pulled out a small tobacco pouch. The pouch was hand-sized, navy blue, with crossed swords, the symbol of a fighting man, embroidered on the flap. It had been sewn from stout cloth, but the rough treatment it had received had worn the pouch to a mole-skin softness. The two gold buttons that closed the flap were metal, engraved with the image of an eagle. The tobacco pouch was beaten and threadbare, but it was still handsome—regal in a sense—the possession of an officer.

Chamberlain opened the pouch and extracted a small, folded piece of paper. "I wrote this more than two months ago," he said. "We've had no tobacco for longer than that, so I slipped it in here for safekeeping." Passing the paper to David, he said, "I'm a little foggy on what I actually wrote. I woke up in the middle of the night after one of those dreams. The words you have there were rumbling around in my head as plain as day. I lit the lamp, found an inkwell, and put them to paper. I knew they were for you."

"Thanks," David said as he held the paper in his hand.

"My pleasure," Chamberlain replied. "This has all been a very curious situation. By the way, how do you get out of here?"

David held up the paper. "All I have to do is read this—" he snapped his fingers, "—and I'm gone."

Chamberlain looked around him. Noticing his brother Tom and several other men approaching, he put his hand on David's shoulder, squeezed it, and said, "If that's all you have to do, then, brother, you might want to read it now."

He turned to go, then turned back to David. Still in his hand was the small tobacco pouch. Holding it out, he offered it to David. "I'll not be getting any more tobacco anyway," Chamberlain said.

Wordlessly, David took the gift and watched the colonel walk away. Alone for a moment, everything in him wanted to take Chamberlain's advice. *Read the paper now,* he told himself. *Get out of here.* But something kept nudging him to stay, to watch.

Placing the precious piece of paper back into the tobacco pouch, David shoved the whole thing in his jeans pocket and eased up to the group of men surrounding Colonel Chamberlain. Sergeant Tozier was there, the hard-nosed old soldier who carried the battle flag. Tozier had a thick wad of torn cloth stuck into a hole in his shoulder where he had been wounded earlier. "No help from the Eighty-third," he growled. "They're shot to ribbons. All they can do is extend the line a bit. We're getting murdered on the flank."

"Can we extend?" Chamberlain asked.

"There's nothing to extend, Joshua," his brother Tom answered. "Over half our men are down."

"How are we for ammunition?"

"We've been shooting a lot."

"I know we've been shooting a lot! I want to know how we're holding out."

"I'll check, sir."

As Tom moved off, a voice came from a young soldier who had climbed a tree. "They're forming again, Colonel." Chamberlain looked up to see the boy pointing downhill. "They're forming up right now," he said, "and they've been reinforced. There're more of them this time."

"Sir!" Sergeant Ruel Thomas, out of breath, stumbled into their midst. "Colonel Chamberlain, sir. Sir . . . Colonel Vincent is dead."

"Are you sure, Sergeant?"

"Yes, sir. He was shot right at the first of the fight. We were firmed up by Weed's Brigade in the front, but now Weed is dead. They moved Hazlett's Battery up top. Hazlett's dead too."

Tom came running back. "Joshua," he said, "we're out. One, two rounds per man at the most. Some of the men have nothing at all."

Chamberlain turned to a thin man standing to his right. It was First Sergeant Ellis Spear. "Spear," he said calmly, "tell the boys to take ammunition from the wounded and dead."

"Maybe we should think about pulling out, sir," Spear said cautiously.

"We will *not* be pulling out, Sergeant," Chamberlain replied grimly. "Carry out my orders, please."

"Colonel," Tozier spoke up. "Sir, we won't hold 'em again. You know we won't."

"Joshua." It was Tom speaking again. "Here they come."

David had been listening to the exchange between the officers, fascinated by the horror of their situation, but when he heard the Rebel yells coursing up through the trees once more, his blood turned icy cold. *I've waited too late to read the paper,* he thought. *I'll never get out of here now.* As he grabbed for the tobacco pouch, a calm washed over him with that same familiar urging—wait, watch, listen, learn.

Chamberlain was standing in full view on top of the wall, his arms crossed, staring down at the advancing enemy. Sergeant Spear had returned and was standing at his colonel's feet. Tozier, Tom, and another lieutenant, a boy named Melcher, were also bunched below. David stood several feet behind the group. "Joshua!" Tom shouted. "Give an order!"

Chamberlain remained stoic. Deep in thought, he was quickly sorting the situation. *We can't retreat*, he said to himself. *We can't stay here. When I am faced with the choice of doing nothing or doing something, I will always choose to act. I am a person of action.* Turning his back to the Rebels, he looked down at his men. "Fix bayonets," he said.

At first, no one moved. They simply stared at him with open mouths. "We'll have the advantage of moving downhill," Chamberlain said. "Fix bayonets now. Execute a great right wheel of the entire regiment. Swing the left first."

Lieutenant Melcher spoke up. He was confused. "Sir," he asked, "what's a great right wheel?" But the colonel had already jumped from the rocks.

Tozier answered the question. "He means to charge, son. A 'great right wheel' is an all-out charge."

David watched in awe as Chamberlain drew his sword, leaped up onto the wall again, and screamed, "Bayonets! Bayonets!" Turning, the colonel pointed the sword directly at David and slightly bowed his head. Then he wheeled to face the overwhelming odds and slashed his blade through the air. With a power born of righteousness and fear, the schoolteacher from Maine roared, "Charge! Charge! Charge!" to his men. And they did.

Tumbling over the wall, the men who were left rose their voices to meet the voice of their leader. "Charge!" they cried. "Charge! Charge!"

David rushed to the wall, looking downhill. He was stunned to see the advancing Confederate force stop in its tracks. Almost immediately, the soldiers turned and ran. A few of the braver souls emptied their rifles before dropping them to follow the rest. About seventy yards down the slope, David caught sight of Chamberlain. He had his left hand on the trunk of a tree, and in his right he held the sword, the point of which was resting on the collarbone of a Rebel officer. The man had his hands up. It was over.

David climbed over the rocks and sat down. With his back to the wall, he pulled the pouch from his pocket. As he looked down the slope, David brushed his fingers over the silky smoothness of the material. He put it close to his face and smelled the mixture of earth, sweat, and old tobacco. Unbuttoning the flap, David removed the paper that Chamberlain had written. With a final glance down-hill and a deep breath, David opened the page.

The Third Decision for Success

I am a person of action.

Beginning today, I will create a new future by creating a new me. No longer will I dwell in a pit of despair, moaning over squandered time and lost opportunity. I can do nothing about the past. My future is immediate. I will grasp it in both hands and carry it with running feet. When I am faced with the choice of doing nothing or doing something, I will always choose to act! I seize this moment. I choose now.

I am a person of action. I am energetic. I move quickly.

Knowing that laziness is a sin, I will create a habit of lively behavior. I will walk with a spring in my step and a smile on my face. The lifeblood rushing through my veins is urging me upward and forward into activity and accomplishment. Wealth and prosperity hide from the sluggard, but rich rewards come to the person who moves quickly.

I am a person of action. I inspire others with my activity. I am a leader.

Leading is doing. To lead, I must move forward. Many people move out of the way for a person on the run; others are caught up in his wake. My activity will create a wave of success for the people who follow. My activity will be consistent. This will instill confidence in my leadership. As a leader, I have the ability to encourage and inspire others to greatness. It is true: an army of sheep led by a lion would defeat an army of lions led by a sheep!

I am a person of action. I can make a decision. I can make it now.

A person who moves neither left nor right is destined for mediocrity. When faced with a decision, many people say they are waiting for God. But I understand, in most cases, God is waiting for me! He has given me a healthy mind to gather and sort information and the courage to come to a conclusion. I am not a quivering dog, indecisive and fearful. My constitution is strong and my pathway clear. Successful people make their decisions quickly and change their minds slowly. Failures make their decisions slowly and change their minds quickly. My decisions come quickly, and they lead to victory.

I am a person of action. I am daring. I am courageous.

Fear no longer has a place in my life. For too long, fear has outweighed my desire to make things better for my family. Never again! I have exposed fear as a vapor, an impostor that never had any power over me in the first place! I do not fear opinion, gossip, or the idle chatter of monkeys, for all are the same to me. I do not fear failure, for in my life, failure is a myth. Failure exists only for the person who quits. I do not quit.

I am courageous. I am a leader. I seize this moment. I choose now.

I am a person of action.

SIX

THE NAUSEA WAS MORE PRONOUNCED THIS TIME.
When the rock wall disappeared behind David's back, he
immediately felt a swaying sensation drawing him down,
back up, and then down again. Balling his fists and duck-
ing his head, David wondered when the time shift would
be finished. The sick feeling was almost overwhelming.
Carefully, David opened his eyes and understood. The
movement he had felt was not part of the travel; he had
arrived in less than an instant. He was on a boat.

It was dark, but despite the darkness, David could see
the water in starlight. It was the ocean, he knew, for the
salty smell reminded him of vacations to the beach with
Ellen and Jenny. The motion of the boat bothered him less
as his vision adjusted to his surroundings. Feeling around
him, David discovered that he was sitting on a large pile of
coiled rope. At least he thought it was rope. It was rougher

and less uniform than any rope he'd ever used. It felt as if it were made out of grass.

Touching the rope reminded David that he still held Chamberlain's paper in one hand and the tobacco pouch in the other. Excited and somewhat amazed that the pouch had come with him, David hurriedly placed the paper in the pouch and buttoned it. Then he remembered the page from Truman and King Solomon's leather scroll. Removing them from his pocket, David placed the first two priceless writings inside the colonel's tobacco pouch with the third and shoved it back into the pocket of his jeans.

Gingerly, David rose from his place of arrival. He was stiff and somewhat sore as if he'd been still for a long time. Looking up, David saw a massive broadcloth—a sail—and smiled. He had sailed with his father as a child. Small lakes and small boats—nothing this size! "Dad would really get a kick out of this," he said aloud. Then David frowned. "Where are you, Dad?" he whispered.

Suddenly, David felt very alone and very tired. Sinking down onto the pile of rope, he lay his head back as the tears welled up in his eyes. Would he ever see Ellen again? Or his daughter? Sweet Jenny. What were they thinking now? Were they scared? Happy? Had ten minutes passed . . . or a hundred years?

"My friend! Pssst! My friend!" David felt a tugging on his sleeve and opened his eyes. It was still dark, though he felt as if he'd been asleep for some time. "My friend," a figure hissed urgently, "please, if you will, come with me." After being practically jerked to his feet, David followed the outline of a small, stocky man as he lightly stepped around barrels and ropes and poles, working his way to the center of the boat.

Struggling to keep up, David almost tripped several times until, finally, the man stopped at the base of the mast. It was a large pole, bigger around than David could have reached, rising up into the darkness. Supporting the mainsail, it was covered in ropes and buckles. Without a glance at David, the man said simply, "Up," and motioned with his hand for David to follow.

The man was almost out of sight in seconds, so quickly did he climb. David hurried to keep up, but it was like crawling through a spider's web. In only a short time, however, he felt a hand grasp the back of his shirt. The small man was very strong. He heaved David up, over the lip, and into a wooden cup built around the top of the mast. They were in the crow's nest.

The man smoothed David's shirt where he had grabbed it, then placed both hands on David's shoulders. "Welcome. Welcome, my friend," he said quietly, but with enthusiasm. "I am most honored to make your acquaintance. And your name is . . . ?"

"My name is David, David Ponder."

"Ah, Señor Ponder. May I call you David?"

"Yes, of course."

"Excellent! Are you hungry?"

"No, not really. I . . ."

"Good! We have very little to eat, and what we *do* have contains wee bugs!" David flinched. "But there is no problem," the man said. "You will see. Our journey is almost at an end."

Despite the darkness, a reflection of the stars from the water illuminated the crow's nest in a soft glow. David could see the man clearly now. He had reddish-brown hair, very curly, that fell almost to his shoulders. A triangular green felt hat was set far back on his head, the forward point jutting toward the sky. The rest of his clothes, but for a stout canvas jacket, were in tatters. The man's pants fell in strips around his ankles, and his shoes were virtually nonexistent—hard leather wrapped around his feet.

"May I ask *your* name, sir?" David asked.

"Why, yes, of course." The man put a hand to his head. "How rude of me! I am Capitán Colón. Capitán Cristóbal

Colón, master of the *Santa Maria*, at your service." He gave a little bow.

"Colón?" David asked. "Columbus? You are Christopher Columbus?"

"Yes." The man smiled, a bit confused. "Columbus is the English pronunciation of my name, but your Portuguese is flawless. I naturally assumed . . ."

David grinned. "I'm speaking Portuguese tonight only."

Columbus tilted his head as if trying to understand what David thought was humorous. "I see," he said, though it was obvious to David that he did not. Clapping his hands together and rubbing them vigorously, Columbus changed the subject. "Whatever it is that you are doing tonight," he said, "the night itself will soon be over. The sun will join us shortly!"

The rocking of the vessel was more pronounced in the high perch, but otherwise, David felt safe, almost comfortable. From this elevation, he could see below that the boat was not very large compared to the vastness of the sea in which it sailed. Less than two hundred feet in length, the *Santa Maria* creaked and groaned with the rolling of the gentle waves. Looking behind her, David could just make out the shadows of two other boats. They rode the swells about a hundred yards to the rear, flanking their leader on either side.

"The *Niña* and the *Pinta?*" David asked.

"Why, yes," Columbus answered. "Seaworthy vessels both, though not quite so luxurious as this." He flung his arms out below him, indicating the deck of the *Santa Maria*.

David suppressed a smile. "Do you know where you are?" he asked.

"Certainly." Columbus smiled. "I am right here! Do you know where *you* are?"

David glanced around. "The Atlantic?"

"Good! Good!" Columbus said as he clapped David on the back. "You are a wonderful navigator!"

David was somewhat confused and more than a little uneasy. He spoke up again. "Do you *really* not know where you are?" he asked.

"Does that have any bearing on what I can accomplish?" Columbus asked in return.

"I don't quite understand," David said.

"I have heard that question in one form or another since I was a child," Columbus began. "Do you know where you are? Do you know *what* you are? Colón, you are uneducated. Colón, you are poor. You are the son of a weaver! What do you know about the sea?" He shook his head in disgust. "'Do you know where you are?' is a question that affects me not in the least! Now, 'Do you know where you are going?'—there is a question I can answer! So, ask me that."

"Excuse me? Ask you . . . ?"

"Ask me, 'Do you know where you are going?' Ask me!"

"Okay." David shrugged. "Do you know where you are going?"

For the few minutes the two men had been in the crow's nest, they had conversed in rather quiet, measured tones. At that point, however, Columbus received the question for which he had been waiting. He boomed out the answer. Carrying across the water, it sounded like the voice of God. Throwing his hand forward, pointing into the western sky, he cried, "Yes! Yes! I *know* where I am going! I am going to a new world!"

Shivers played up David's spine as he watched the explorer point into the darkness. For a moment, neither man said a word. Clearing his throat, David broke the silence. "How long since you left Spain?" he asked.

"Sixty-four days," Columbus said as he lowered his arm, "and today we shall see land. Look behind us." David turned and saw a brightening in the eastern sky. "Dawn will be breaking soon. When it does, directly in front of the *Santa Maria* you will see land. Beautiful land with trees and fruit and animals and people who will welcome us as heroes! The water gushing from the ground will be cold and pure. It will sparkle as if sprinkled with diamonds! This will be a place for men's dreams to come true—a glorious new world claimed by Cristóbal Colón in the name of King Ferdinand and Queen Isabella!"

David leaned forward and put his hands on the lip of the

crow's nest. "That would be King Ferdinand and Queen Isabella of Spain, correct?" he asked.

Columbus nodded. "They are the financiers of this expedition. King John of Portugal, *my* king, said no to this grand opportunity, as did the kings and queens of many other countries. Nineteen years, my friend. It took nineteen years to find sponsorship. For nineteen years, I endured the agony of public humiliation for my convictions."

"Which convictions?" David asked.

"The conviction . . . ," Columbus said, his voice rising, "no, the absolute certainty that I can establish a new trade route by sailing west. West!"

Columbus grabbed David by the shoulders and shook him once as he said, "My friend! The world is a sphere! It is not flat! We are sailing *around* the earth on the smooth surface of a sphere. We will not fall off some imaginary edge!"

"Are you the only person who believes this?" David asked.

"At the moment, yes," Columbus said, "but that bothers me not in the least. Truth is truth. If a thousand people believe something foolish, it is still foolish! Truth is never dependent upon consensus of opinion. I have found that it is better to be alone and acting upon the truth in my heart than to follow a gaggle of silly geese doomed to mediocrity."

"You say it doesn't bother you in the least," David said.

"You don't care that people think you are . . . well . . . crazy?"

"My friend," Columbus said with a smile, "if you worry about what other people think of you, then you will have more confidence in their opinion than you have in your own. Poor is the man whose future depends on the opinions and permission of others. Remember this, if you are afraid of criticism, you will die doing nothing!"

David frowned. "But with so many people against you," he asked, "how did you get started in the first place?"

"Getting started, getting finished—both ends of a journey require a demonstration of passion," Columbus mused. David stared blankly at the great man. "Passion!" he said again in a forceful whisper. "Passion is a product of the heart. Passion is what helps you when you have a great dream. Passion breeds conviction and turns mediocrity into excellence! Your passion will motivate others to join you in pursuit of your dream. With passion, you will overcome insurmountable obstacles. You will become unstoppable!"

David began to ask another question, but Columbus put his hand out to silence him. "Please, my friend," he said. "Quiet for a time." David did as he asked and followed his gaze into the western sky. The sun was just breaking the horizon behind them, throwing a brilliance over the miles of open ocean. Columbus peered ahead, concentrating with all his might into the distance. For one full minute he did not move. For two minutes . . . then ten. Only his eyes shifted as he scanned the line where the water touched the sky.

After almost half an hour, Columbus straightened his back and rubbed his eyes. "Nothing?" David asked softly.

"Yes, something," Columbus answered.

"What?" David looked around, confused. "You see land?"

"Yes," the great man said simply.

David frowned. He was still straining to catch a glimpse of what Columbus claimed he saw. "Point it out to me, please."

"Señor Ponder," Columbus said. "You are looking in the wrong direction. Today, you will not see land off the bow of my ship. You will see land only by looking into my eyes."

David turned. He felt as if he'd been tricked. "So there's no land?" he said indignantly.

"Yes, there is land," Columbus replied, "and it is right there." He gestured past the bow of the ship again. "I see it as plainly as I see you. For almost twenty years I have seen it. And tomorrow, you will see it too. It will come into view just as dawn breaks, directly in front of the *Santa Maria*. Beautiful land with trees and fruit and animals and people who will welcome us as heroes! The water gushing from the ground will be cold and pure. It will sparkle as if sprinkled with diamonds! This will be a place for men's dreams to come true—a glorious new world claimed by Cristóbal Colón in the name of King Ferdinand and Queen Isabella!"

For a brief time, David did not breathe. His hair rustled in the steady breeze as he looked deeply into the eyes of the man before him. He saw there the passion and belief that had fueled this voyage of destiny. *What could I accomplish*, David wondered, *with a spirit as powerful as this?*

"El Capitán!"

David blinked. The spell had been broken by a voice calling from below.

"El Capitán, sir!"

The two men peered over the edge of the crow's nest. Directly underneath them were four men. They motioned for Columbus to join them.

Columbus pursed his lips and sighed. "Trouble?" David asked.

Swinging his leg over the lip of the wooden cup, Columbus answered, "Most assuredly. These are my officers."

David climbed through the rigging, trying his best to follow the agile descent of the seaman. When at last he reached the deck of the *Santa Maria*, voices were already being raised. The first officer, though dressed exactly like his captain, was tall and heavily muscled. His long black hair had been tied into a ponytail and laid over his shoulder so that it fell down the front of his shirt. Like the other three men, he was clean shaven. Leading the contingent against their leader, First Officer Juan Garson did all the talking. "Your officers are in agreement, El Capitán. This voyage is finished! It is time to return."

Columbus looked at the men and said, "But we are almost there! The hardest part of the journey is past! Tomorrow you will see land. It will be beautiful land with trees and fruit and . . ."

"Enough!" Juan Garson cried. "We have heard this sad refrain for too many weeks. Sir, surely, you must see that the men have reached their limit!"

Columbus smiled stiffly. "I see men who don't know the limits they can reach."

Juan Garson briefly closed his eyes as if to contain himself. "Sir! Your officers and I have decided to turn back. We are at an end."

Garson and the other men moved to go but were brought up short by the booming voice of their captain. "Gentlemen!" Columbus shouted. The officers stopped and faced him. "Gentlemen," he said with less volume this time, "might I remind you that we have less than ten days of food and water left in our stores. To reverse course is the gambit of a fool. It not only means failure but certain death as well! In God's name, men, I ask you to think! We are at sea now for sixty-four days! To which port do you return? Our only course is forward! Our only hope is to press on!"

The men stood with their heads down. They seemed not

only outmaneuvered but beaten. Garson spoke again, softly this time. "Is this realistic, Capitán? Will we find land?"

Columbus moved to put his arm around the shoulders of the taller man. "Is this realistic, Garson? I say to you 'no,' but then nothing great was ever accomplished by a realistic person! Will we find land? Yes! Yes! We will find land, but that will be the least of *your* discoveries." Columbus pointed to his first officer's chest. "You will find a heart for success that you did not know existed. You will find a Juan Garson who is able to lead men to new worlds of their own! You will find . . . greatness!"

Garson straightened and breathed deeply. "Forgive my insolence, El Capitán, I . . ."

"Forgotten," Columbus said, as he made a dismissing motion with his hand. "Go, Juan Garson. Lead your men—and believe!"

As the officers left, Columbus moved once more toward the crow's nest. David followed him up, finding it easier this time because of the daylight. Again, however, Columbus pulled David into the cup by the back of his shirt.

Catching his breath, David watched Columbus settle his back against the mast and fix his gaze again upon the western horizon. "May I ask a question?" David said quietly.

"Certainly," Columbus replied.

"What did you mean down below when you told your officer that he would find a heart for success?"

Columbus inhaled and slowly blew out his breath before answering. "Most people fail at whatever they attempt because of an undecided heart. Should I? Should I not? Go forward? Go back? Success requires the emotional balance of a committed heart. When confronted with a challenge, the committed heart will search for a solution. The undecided heart searches for an escape."

Columbus cleared his throat, coughing gently, then continued. "A committed heart does not wait for conditions to be exactly right. Why? Because conditions are *never* exactly right. Indecision limits the Almighty and His ability to perform miracles in your life. He has put the vision in you—proceed! To wait, to wonder, to doubt, to be indecisive is to disobey God."

Without taking his eyes off the water, Columbus reached under his jacket and removed a parchment. "For you," he said simply. Unfolding it, he handed it to David.

David took the yellowed paper, glanced at it briefly, and said, "You *will* find your new world."

Columbus, eyes still straight ahead, spoke quietly, "I know."

David smiled and shook his head in wonder. "How do you know?" he asked.

Columbus turned and looked at David. "I have a decided heart," he said and turned back.

For a moment, David said nothing. He felt the purest

sense of awe for this man who knew nothing, yet seemed to know everything. He opened his mouth to speak again. "But how—"

"Señor Ponder," Columbus interrupted. He placed his arm over David's shoulders. "It is time for you to read the message I was given for you. Study it carefully, for it is within these words that you will find a heart for success that *you* did not know existed. You will find a David Ponder who is able to lead men to new worlds of *their* own. You will find greatness." And with those words, the great explorer Christopher Columbus hugged David and kissed him on each cheek. "Read," he said again and smiled. "I am very busy."

David watched him ease to the edge of the crow's nest, put his elbows on the lip, and look to the west once more. The wind shifted and rattled the parchment in his hand. Sitting down, David propped his back against the wall of the cup and braced his feet on the mast. Stealing one last glance at the man who had penned the words, he read.

The Fourth Decision for Success

I have a decided heart.

A wise man once said, "A journey of a thousand miles begins with a single step." Knowing this to be true, I am taking my first step today. For too long my feet have been tentative, shuffling left and right, more backward than forward as my heart gauged the direction of the wind. Criticism, condemnation, and complaint are creatures of the wind. They come and go on the wasted breath of lesser beings and have no power over me. The power to control direction belongs to me. Today I will begin to exercise that power. My course has been charted. My destiny is assured.

I have a decided heart. I am passionate about my vision for the future.

I will awaken every morning with an excitement about the new day and its opportunity for growth and change. My thoughts and actions will work in a forward motion, never sliding into the dark forest of doubt or the muddy quicksand of self-pity. I will freely give my vision for the future to others, and as they see the belief in my eyes, they will follow me.

I will lay my head on my pillow at night happily exhausted, knowing that I have done everything within my power to move the mountains in my path. As I sleep, the same dream that dominates my waking hours will be with me in the dark. Yes, I have a dream. It is a great dream, and I will never apologize for it. Neither will I ever let it go, for if I did, my life would be finished. My hopes, my passions, my vision for the future are my very existence. A person without a dream never had a dream come true.

I have a decided heart. I will not wait.

I know that the purpose of analysis is to come to a conclusion. I have tested the angles. I have measured the probabilities. And now I have made a decision with my heart. I am not timid. I will move now and not look back. What I put off until tomorrow, I will put off until the next day as well. I do not procrastinate. All my problems become smaller when I confront them. If I touch a thistle with caution, it will prick me, but if I grasp it boldly, its spines crumble into dust.

I will not wait. I am passionate about my vision for the future. My course has been charted. My destiny is assured.

I have a decided heart.

SEVEN

DAVID FELT THE SWAYING OF THE *SANTA MARIA* AS he looked up from the parchment. Columbus turned to stare as David stood up and saw that he was no longer in the crow's nest, but seemingly had his feet planted firmly in midair, moving at an ever increasing pace away from the ship. Columbus smiled and raised his hand. David did the same and suddenly streaked away so fast that his vision perceived a thousand images of Columbus as the *Santa Maria* stretched out like strobes of light in the tail of a comet.

In the next instant, David was standing in a small room. The air smelled strongly of mildew with just a hint of lye soap. The only light in the room came from a bare bulb hanging on a wire from the ceiling. David quickly counted seven people within several steps. He frowned. Incredibly, they were motionless. A man and a woman were seated at a tiny table. Two teenagers, a boy and a girl, were sprawled on the floor, an interrupted card game between them, and the rest, two men and a woman, appeared to have stopped in midstride. Every person wore a look of terror.

David heard knocking on the wall behind him and the muffled voices of men. As he turned to look, he noticed a small girl he had missed before. She was thin and sharply featured with dark wavy hair and eyes so black that they shined. She appeared to be perhaps twelve or thirteen and wore a faded blue cotton dress that seemed at home in the dingy room.

David understood why he had not seen her at first. She was standing right next to him, so close that he had literally looked over her. This girl, too, David saw, was not moving, but as he caught her gaze, she slowly raised a finger to her lips.

The knocking seemed to run in a pattern, first high on the wall, then to the middle and on toward the floor. The muffled voices would then move to the right, and the knocking would begin again. High, center, low. For almost five full minutes, David remained still as he listened to the sounds on the other side of the wall.

Once, one of the voices began yelling something unintelligible, and they heard several people running. At that point, the woman sitting at the table reached out to hold the man's hand. Both closed their eyes. Except for the small girl putting her finger to her lips, it was the only movement David saw from any of them.

After what seemed an eternity, the knocking ceased. There was no more running, no voices, just the tense silence of the little room. And still, no one moved. For a full minute, then two. Finally, the man at the table took a deep breath and blew it out with a whoosh. "Het is oke nu allemaal," he said quietly. "It is all right now, everyone." And with that, the people in the room shook their heads and softly began talking to each other.

"This was close, I am thinking," said the teenage boy on the floor. "If there had been dogs . . ." He let the thought just hang there, never finishing the sentence.

A tall woman, her hair rolled tightly into a bun, began weeping softly. "Now then, Petronella," her husband said as he put his arms around her. "We are safe. Shhh, hush now." He turned to the boy and said sternly, "Peter, that'll be enough about what might have been. You've upset your mother and most everyone else, I expect. We'll have no more about dogs."

"I was just saying . . . ," Peter began.

"Yes," the man interrupted, "and I was just saying that will be enough!"

David watched as the man led his wife into a narrow room to his left. Before the door closed, he saw a mattress on the floor and a stack of movie-star magazines. The young girl gently moved David to a corner and whispered, "Stay here for now, but when I leave the room, follow me."

She moved toward the couple sitting at the table. The man looked tired, but even though his clothes were worn, he was clean-shaven except for a small mustache. What little hair he had left on his head was neatly combed. David thought him a rather distinguished sort. The woman sitting across from him, her hair in a bun just like the other woman had worn, was ghostly pale, as if she'd recently been ill. Nevertheless, she smiled as the girl approached.

"Papa," the girl said. "May I have your permission to go upstairs?"

The man smiled. "Time to be alone again, is it?"

"Yes, Papa."

"Then certainly you may go," he said. She gave a glance to David and moved resolutely to a stairway at the back of the room. Seeing her reach the stairs, her father spoke once more, his smile fading.

"Anne." She stopped and turned. "Keep away from the window."

"Yes, Papa," she nodded and without a sound moved up the staircase and out of sight.

David followed quickly, careful not to bump any of the people as he passed. Ascending the stairs, he saw the girl motioning for him to hurry. The staircase appeared to go directly into the ceiling, but as David soon saw, there was a hatch cover that provided an entrance to the attic.

As soon as they were inside, the girl replaced the cover

and said, "I am so excited to meet you that I almost cannot breathe!" She clapped her hands together quickly, but softly. "This is thrilling, is it not?"

"Yes," David said, grinning at her enthusiasm. He glanced around. There was not a stick of furniture or a box of anything stored in this attic, just dust and dirt. "I suppose *thrilling* would be a proper choice of words."

"I expected you, did you know?" she said. "A dream is how. I even know your name. It is Mr. Ponder. I wrote you a note just this morning. Should I get it now?"

"No, no." David chuckled. "Slow down just a minute. You have me at a disadvantage. I don't even know where I am!"

"Why, you are in Amsterdam," the child said. She took David's hand and pulled him toward a window. "Come," she said with a little smile, "I will show you the city."

Across the bare attic, there loomed a large nine-paned window. Three of the panes had been separated from the other six by a brick column. The window itself was dirty, almost as brown as the attic. "Is this the window," David asked, "that your father warned you to stay away from?"

"Yes, yes," she said as she nodded her head, "but it is all right to peek from the corner." And with that she got down on her hands and knees and exclaimed impatiently, "You too! Come now!"

David got down on his hands and knees and followed

the girl to the edge of the window where she was waiting underneath the sill. When he reached her, he turned to sit on the floor, his back to the wall. She sat with her legs folded underneath her and leaned her right shoulder to the dirty plaster. As he settled himself into a more comfortable position, David said, "I heard your father call you Anne."

"Yes," she replied. "And my sister's name is Margot. She is very quiet. She was the one playing cards with the boy downstairs. His name is Peter. Peter Van Daan."

"What is your last name?" David asked.

"Frank," she said simply. "My papa's name is Otto, and Edith is my mother. Peter's parents are Mr. Herman and Mrs. Petronella. She was the one who cried, but of course, she always cries. The other man you saw was Dr. Dussel. You did see him, didn't you? He was sitting on the floor near the door to my room, but of course, you don't know which room is mine, so maybe you didn't see him. In any case, he's not a doctor really. He's a dentist . . ."

David wasn't certain how long Anne talked. He was not really listening anyway. His mind was a jumble of thoughts and emotions. *Anne Frank*, he thought. *Anne Frank! This is the young girl whose diary I read in high school.*

". . . so Peter brought him with us," Anne continued, ignoring the stunned look on the face of her guest. "Mouschi is wonderful, though not as loving as my own dear cat, Moortje, who is still at home. Mouschi is black as coal dust. Moortje, on the other hand . . ."

I am in the annex, David thought. The annex, he knew, was a secret location consisting of several rooms connected to the back of a warehouse. Anne and her family were Dutch Jews in hiding during the Nazi occupation of Holland.

". . . don't you think?" Anne said as she looked directly at David, obviously waiting for a response.

David was startled by the pause in her nonstop chatter. He had been so caught up in his surroundings that he hadn't actually been listening. "I'm sorry. What did you say?" he asked uncomfortably.

"I said," Anne answered slowly, "that Peter is very hand-some, don't you think?"

"Peter?" David wrinkled his brow. "Oh, the boy down-stairs, yes. Yes, he is!"

"I let him kiss me sometimes. On the cheek, of course."

"Of course," David said seriously. "Anne," David began in an effort to change the subject, "how long have you been here?"

"One year and four months," she said quickly.

"Do you know today's date?"

"Certainly. Today is Thursday, October 28, 1943. We went into hiding last year on the first Sunday in July, the fifth it was." Anne glanced up at the window above. "None of us have been outside in a very long time."

"How do you get food in here?"

"Miep."

"Who is . . . ?"

"Miep is Papa's secretary. She still comes to work in the warehouse every day. After hours, she and her husband, Henk, move the bookcase in the accounting room and come through the door behind it."

"Anne," David said. "When I arrived . . ."

"Oh, yes," Anne broke in, "that was so terrifying! You appeared directly in front of me, and I was the only one who could see you! Have you done that before? Does it hurt?"

David smiled in spite of his aggravation at being interrupted. He supposed he could understand her excitement. After all, a new person with whom to talk must be thrilling after sixteen months. "Yes, I have done it before, and no, it doesn't hurt." David reached out to touch her arm as he tried again to ask his question. "Anne, when I arrived, what, or who, was knocking on the walls?"

"Nazi soldiers," Anne said. "Papa calls them Gestapo. He says they dress in black. They have come now two times. We are quiet and they go away." She turned and got up on her knees, rising carefully to put one eye in the corner of the window. "If you do this, you can see most of Amsterdam."

David rose and looked out the opposite corner. To his left, he saw a huge chestnut tree reaching almost one hundred feet into the air and casting its last shade of the day into the attic window. A clock tower stood majestically across the street. Its spires and gables were the centerpiece of the city.

"That's the Westerkerk," Anne said, referring to the clock. "I can lie here and watch the hands move." Anne laid herself out flat on the floor. "Lie down," she said. "See for yourself."

David eased himself down beside the young girl and looked up. There, framed in the window as if by divine providence, was the clock face of the Westerkerk tower. It was, he noticed, almost six o'clock in the evening. David looked at Anne, staring intently at the clock, and thought of his own daughter. She and Anne were about the same age. He tried to imagine Jenny in this situation. What would she do? How would she react? Or, for that matter, how would he?

"What are you thinking?" David asked softly.

"About the clock," Anne said. "Sometimes I wish for it to speed up, and at other times I beg it to slow down. But it never hears me. It is always the same."

David jumped as whistles and loud, angry voices blasted the silence of the street four floors below them. Anne did not move but continued gazing at the clock. "What is going on?" David asked.

"It is a razia," Anne answered with no emotion. "They are rounding up Jews. It makes me wonder about my friends. I don't know what has happened to any of them." For several moments she was quiet, thoughtful. David said nothing. Then she looked directly at him and said, "Everyone is being taken away to camps. Did you know? The Germans say that the Jews are working and living comfortably, but it is not true."

David was careful with his words. "How do you know that?"

Anne shrugged. "We all know," she said. "Letters are censored, of course, but occasionally, the truth is made known. Miep received a postcard from a friend that said the food was good and conditions were superb, but at the end of the message, he wrote: 'Give my regards to Ellen de Groot.'" She paused. "The words were Dutch, of course. The German censors did not know that *ellende* means 'misery.' *Groot* is 'terrible.' His intent was to convey a message of terrible misery."

Without warning, the Westerkerk clock tower began to chime. Six times the clapper hammered out its message of time on the lip of the massive bell. Less than seventy feet away, Anne merely placed her hands over her ears and smiled at David, who had nearly jumped out of his skin when the chiming began.

"It is only a bit too loud," Anne said, giggling at her understatement.

David smiled. "I'm glad you think it's funny," he said. "I

thought my head was about to come off! How do you sleep with that thing ringing day and night?"

"Actually," Anne said, "we don't even notice it much anymore. Mrs. Petronella is the only one of us who even makes comment. Papa says the clock is a good thing for her because it provides something to complain about every hour on the hour!"

David laughed. "What about you?" he asked. "What do you complain about?"

"I do not complain," Anne said. "Papa says complaining is an activity just as jumping rope or listening to the radio is an activity. One may choose to turn on the radio, and one may choose not to turn on the radio. One may choose to complain, and one may choose not to complain. I choose not to complain."

David stared at the sincere little girl for a moment, then said, "I don't mean any offense to what your father has taught you, but have you taken a look around here? These are pretty rough conditions for anyone, never mind a girl your age. How can you *not* complain?"

Anne tilted her head to the side as if she were having difficulty understanding. Sweeping a lock of hair from her eyes, she said patiently, "Our very lives are fashioned by choice, Mr. Ponder. First we make choices. Then our choices make us.

"Rough conditions? Yes, an ungrateful person might see

this place as too small for eight people, a diet that is limited and portions that are too meager, or only three dresses for two girls to share. But gratefulness is also a choice. I see an annex that hides eight people while others are being herded onto railway cars. I see food that is generously provided by Miep, whose family uses their ration cards for us. I see an extra dress for my sister and me while there are surely others who have nothing. I choose to be grateful. I choose not to complain."

David was amazed at the self-control that Anne seemed to possess. He tucked one leg under the other, sitting cross-legged, and shook his head as if to clear the cobwebs. "Are you honestly telling me that you are always in a good mood?"

Anne had folded her legs to mimic the way David was sitting. As she draped her dress over her knees, she laughed. "Of course not, silly! But if I ever find myself in a bad mood, I immediately make a choice to be happy. In fact, it is the first choice I make every day. I say out loud to my mirror, 'Today, I will choose to be happy!' I smile into the mirror and laugh even if I am sad. I just say, 'Ha, ha, ha, ha!' And soon, I am happy, exactly as I have chosen to be."

David was now shaking his head in wonder. "You are a very special young lady, Miss Frank."

"Thank you," Anne said. "That is also a choice."

David leaned forward. "Really," he said with his eyebrows raised. "You've got me now. Explain."

"My life—my personality, my habits, even my speech—is a combination of the books I choose to read, the people I choose to listen to, and the thoughts I choose to tolerate in my mind. Before the war, when I was a little girl, my papa took me to Het Vondel Park on a Saturday afternoon to hear the orchestra play. At the end of the concert, from behind the musicians, a hundred helium balloons of red and blue and yellow and green floated up into the sky. It was so exciting!

"I tugged on Papa's arm and asked, 'Papa, which color balloon will go the highest?' And he said to me, 'Anne, it's not the color of the balloon that is important. It's what's inside that makes all the difference.'"

For a moment, Anne was quiet and the attic still. She seemed so deep in thought that David barely breathed. Then she looked David directly in the eye, lifted her chin, and said, "Mr. Ponder, I don't believe that being Jewish or Aryan or African has any bearing on what one can become. Greatness does not care if one is a girl or a boy. If, in fact, it is what's inside us that makes all the difference, then the difference is made when we choose what goes inside."

Anne turned and looked toward the clock again. David had not noticed the darkness that had filled the attic, but now realized that only the glow of the light from the

Westerkerk tower enabled him to see Anne's face. "I must get ready for dinner soon," she said. "Come with me to my room. I have written something for you."

David followed Anne through the hatch in the attic, down the stairs, and back into the living area. "Dinner is almost on the table, dear," her mother said as the two walked by. "Five minutes. No longer."

Anne led David to a door that was situated to the right of the staircase. As they walked inside and closed the door behind them, David could see that the room was no larger than a closet. A small mattress lay on the floor with two stacks of books beside the only pillow. "Margot and I share this room," Anne said. "It is very close, but we respect each other's privacy."

David didn't see how anyone could hope to have any privacy in this tiny room. On the wall at the foot of the bed hung a simple white dress. The hem, sleeves, and neckline were stitched in small red flowers. Above the head of the bed were pictures cut from magazines and newspapers that had been glued to the wall. Pointing to the array, David asked, "Are these yours, or do they belong to your sister?"

"They are mine." Anne smiled. "Beautiful, aren't they?"

David looked more closely. There was a picture of Greta Garbo and one of Ginger Rogers. A picture of the head of the statue of David by Michelangelo was positioned over a picture of a house in the country. To the left was a black-and-white photo of a rose that someone had colored pink and a large picture of chimpanzees having a tea party. Spread all over the wall were pictures of cute, cuddly babies. "Yes, they are beautiful," David said. "What do they represent?"

"My future," Anne whispered softly as she reached out to touch the picture of the rose. "These are the people I want to meet, the places I want to see, and the things I want in my life. Laughter and love and a home with a husband, maybe Peter, and lots of babies." Suddenly, tears came to her eyes.

David reached out, his hand cupping her head and drawing her to him. Anne put her arms around David's neck as he sank to his knees. As Anne sniffled and sobbed, tears also ran down David's cheeks. He felt such deep admiration for this child. Her courage and wisdom were those of a person who had already lived a lifetime. And in a way, he knew, she had.

Anne eased away to dry her eyes on the sleeve of her dress. "I'm sorry," she said. "I didn't mean to make you uncomfortable."

"I wasn't uncomfortable, Anne," David said as he dried his own eyes. "You remind me of my daughter. Her name is Jennifer. We call her Jenny. She is about your age, and I think you and she are the two prettiest girls I have ever seen."

Anne blushed. "Thank you for saying so." She looked back at the wall and reached out to touch the rose picture again. "May I ask you a question?" she said.

"Certainly," David replied.

"If your Jenny were here instead of me, would she be afraid?"

David could feel the pulse pounding in his head. "I think that she probably would be afraid, Anne. Are you?"

Anne pulled her hand down from the rose and clasped both hands in front of her. Momentarily, she cut her eyes toward David, then back to the pictures. "Sometimes," she said. "But most often, I choose not to be. Papa says, 'Fear is a poor chisel with which to carve out tomorrow.'"

Anne turned and faced David. "I will have a tomorrow, Mr. Ponder. Margot and Mrs. Petronella, they make fun of me. They call me a Pollyanna. They say that I live in a dream world, that I do not face reality. This is not true. I know that the war is horrible. I understand that we are in terrible danger here. I do not deny the reality of our situation. I deny the finality of it. This, too, shall pass."

Anne knelt down and reached under the mattress. She pulled out a red-orange checkered clothbound book. "This is my diary," she said. "Papa gave it to me for my birthday, June twelfth." She thumbed through the pages quickly until she found what she was looking for. "These are yours," she said and carefully tore several pages from the small journal.

David took the pages from her hand and watched as she placed what he knew to be her life's work back under the dirty mattress. "Thank you, Anne."

She stood awkwardly in front of him for a long moment. "Will you tell your daughter Jenny that I said hello?"

David smiled. "Yes, I will."

Anne paused again. "I must go eat," she said. "You will be gone when I return?"

"Yes."

"Then remember me," Anne said, smiling. "I will remember you. But most of all, both of us must remember that life itself is a privilege, but to live life to its fullest— well, that is a choice!"

With those words, Anne hugged David and quickly left the room, softly closing the door behind her. David sat down on the mattress and looked up at the pictures on the wall. For several minutes he listened to the quiet murmuring of the Franks and their friends eating dinner. Then he put the pages Anne had given him in his lap. These were words he fully expected to change his life. Four small pages, written with a pencil, in the hand-writing of a little girl.

THE FIFTH DECISION FOR SUCCESS

Today I will choose to be happy.

Beginning this very moment, I am a happy person, for I now truly understand the concept of happiness. Few others before me have been able to grasp the truth of the physical law that enables one to live happily every day. I know now that happiness is not an emotional phantom floating in and out of my life. Happiness is a choice. Happiness is the end result of certain thoughts and activities, which actually bring about a chemical reaction in my body. This reaction results in a euphoria that, while elusive to some, is totally under my control.

Today I will choose to be happy. I will greet each day with laughter.

Within moments of awakening, I will laugh for seven seconds. Even after such a small period of time, excitement has begun to flow through my bloodstream. I feel different. I am different! I am enthusiastic about the day. I am alert to its possibilities. I am happy!

Laughter is an outward expression of enthusiasm, and I know that enthusiasm is the fuel that moves the world. I laugh throughout the day. I laugh while I am alone, and I laugh in conversation with others. People are drawn to me because I have laughter in my heart. The world belongs to the enthusiastic, for people will follow them anywhere!

Today I will choose to be happy. I will smile at every person I meet.

My smile has become my calling card. It is, after all, the most potent weapon I possess. My smile has the strength to forge bonds, break ice, and calm storms. I will use my smile constantly. Because of my smile, the people with whom I come in contact on a daily basis will choose to further my causes and follow my leadership. I will always smile first. That particular display of a good attitude will tell others what I expect in return.

My smile is the key to my emotional makeup. A wise man once said, "I do not sing because I am happy; I am happy because I sing!" When I choose to smile, I become the master of my emotions. Discouragement, despair, frustration, and fear will always wither when confronted by my smile. The power of who I am is displayed when I smile.

Today I will choose to be happy. I am the possessor of a grateful spirit.

In the past, I have found discouragement in particular situations until I compared the condition of my life to others less fortunate. Just as a fresh breeze cleans smoke from the air, so a grateful spirit removes the cloud of despair. It is impossible for the seeds of depression to take root in a thankful heart.

My God has bestowed upon me many gifts, and for these I will remember to be grateful. Too many times I have offered up the prayers of a beggar, always asking for more and forgetting to give thanks. I do not wish to be seen as a greedy child, unappreciative and disrespectful. I am grateful for sight and sound and breath. If ever in my life there is a pouring out of blessings beyond that, then I will be grateful for the miracle of abundance.

I will greet each day with laughter. I will smile at every person I meet. I am the possessor of a grateful spirit.

Today I will choose to be happy.

EIGHT

DAVID FINISHED READING THE WORDS ANNE HAD prepared and wiped at a tear clinging to his chin. Blinking his eyes, he folded the pages, placed them in the tobacco pouch, shoved the pouch into his pocket, and stood up. He reached out to touch the picture of the rose Anne had glued to the wall. With his finger, David traced the stem from the bottom of the photograph to its center. Touching the bloom, he smiled at the waxy feeling of the pink crayon that had been used to color the black-and-white picture.

Slowly, the rose began to distort. The edges appeared fuzzy and the shape of the bloom pulsed. David pulled his hand back and wiped his eyes. With his left elbow and fore-arm, he steadied himself against the wall. There, for a moment, he was mildly dizzy, but the feeling quickly passed.

Opening his eyes, David examined the picture again. It was still blurry but seemed to be clearing. He squinted and moved his face only inches from the flower. There! Now it was in focus. He saw the petals of the rose so sharply, so distinctly, that it seemed to have depth. Tentatively, without moving his face, David reached out with his right hand and, using just one finger, touched the rose. Startled, David's breath caught in his throat. The rose was real.

For a moment, he froze. Shifting his eyes, David saw that his left arm was now braced against an old desk. Easing himself away from the rose, he noticed that it stood in a simple crystal vase on the edge of the desk. Next to the rose sat a pitcher of water and four glasses. David stood erect and looked around. He was in a room of some sort . . . no, a tent. It was a rather large tent, he noted, made of white canvas, enclosing an area of approximately fifteen by twenty feet. The floor was dead grass, and except for the desk and three plain wooden chairs, the tent was empty.

Hearing activity of some sort, David moved to the closed flap of the tent's entrance. Carefully, he eased the loose canvas door aside several inches. About seventy-five feet away on a raised platform or makeshift stage, a man stood alone behind a podium. He was facing away from the tent, speaking to thousands of people. David saw saddled horses and carriages and wagons interspersed among the throng. Many had parasols to ward off the sun, and they had spread quilts on the ground or sat atop their wagons.

David saw that the tent and the stage were on top of a hill surrounded by large trees. Since most of their leaves had dropped and the temperature was comfortable even in the tent, David supposed he had arrived in this place during October or maybe even November. In any case, it was autumn, he decided, and judging by the sun, it was somewhere close to noon.

Beyond the crowd, David saw fields and broken forest land that stretched as far as he could see from his limited vantage point. The hills and pastures within his view gave David a strange feeling. The area seemed eerily familiar, though he couldn't quite place how or why.

Perhaps, David thought, *the speaker holds the key to why I am here.* Turning his attention once again toward the stage, David observed that the gentleman, from behind, appeared to be elegantly dressed. He wore gray pants over polished black boots, and a high white collar rose from the back of a black coat complete with tails. His flowing gray hair completed a look of distinction.

In addition, the man appeared to be quite the orator. David noted how he paced the stage and gestured dramatically with his hands. His audience certainly seemed enthralled. They had laughed as a group twice during the short time David watched from the doorway of the tent. David couldn't quite hear the speaker's presentation, for there was no microphone or sound system of any kind, and because the man faced away from him, David could catch only a word here and there.

Suddenly, the crowd thundered a loud and sustained applause. David looked closely as the speaker returned to the podium, which was on the speaker's right and slightly behind him at that moment. As the man waited for the ovation to die away, David got a clear view of his features. His hairline receded from a clean-shaven face. The man's eyebrows were bushy; his nose and ears were a bit large for his head. David didn't recognize him at all.

Disappointed and somewhat confused, David eased himself back inside the tent. For several moments he stood there, wondering where he was and who he had been watching on stage. *Is that the person I am here to see?* he asked himself. David moved to a chair beside the desk and sat down heavily. Pouring himself a glass of water, he couldn't shake the uneasy feeling that he was somehow connected to this place.

Just then, above the continuous sound of the speaker, David heard the crowd begin to murmur. For almost half a minute, the audience's talking among themselves easily drowned out the voice of the man on stage. David rose from his chair and quickly walked toward the tent door. Before he reached the entrance, however, he heard the sound of horses' hooves and creaking leather saddles just outside. Hearing voices approach, David stepped to the corner of the tent as one man walked inside.

He was a young man of about twenty-five, impeccably

groomed in a long coat and high collar. His hair was parted crisply in the middle, and his thin mustache ran in a perfect line above his lips. With the presence of a person who is accustomed to being in charge, the young man strode across the tent directly to the desk. He opened each drawer and carefully inspected the contents before closing it.

David saw him pause for the briefest moment when he spied David's glass of water. The young man picked up the glass and frowned. He was obviously quite aggravated. Shaking his head from side to side with little jerks, he took the glass to the far corner of the tent and poured the remainder of the water onto the ground. Curiously, David thought, he then placed the empty glass in his coat pocket and moved back to the desk where he proceeded to examine the remaining glasses and pitcher.

He picked up the pitcher and looked intently into the water. Then he smelled the water. Finally, he poured a small amount into one of the three glasses left on the desk and carefully tasted it. Satisfied, he then placed *that* glass into his other coat pocket, looked cautiously around the tent, and exited.

David took a deep breath. Evidently, that person was not the one he was there to see. The man hadn't even noticed him standing in plain sight. Before David had time to move, the tent flap opened again.

Bending almost double in order to fit through the

door, this man entered with his hat under his arm. As the tent flap closed behind him, the tall man straightened, glanced around, and saw David. He smiled and with two quick strides stood before David, extending his right hand. "Mr. Ponder, isn't it?" the man said with a twinkle in his eye.

David's mouth was open and his knees felt as if they might collapse. He wanted to say, "Yes, sir," or "How do you do?" or "Nice to meet you," or anything, but his throat was so dry that nothing came out. Becoming aware of the bemused expression on the gentleman's face and seeing that his hand was still extended, David did the only appropriate thing. He shook the hand of Abraham Lincoln.

"I . . . I am honored, sir," David managed to stammer.

"The honor is mine, Mr. Ponder," the president replied. "After all, it is you who has traveled the greater distance for this occasion."

Lincoln wore white riding gloves, gauntlets, that contrasted sharply with his totally black attire and made his large hands seem larger still. Removing the gloves, he walked to the desk and, after placing the gloves and his hat on the far side, asked, "Won't you join me please in refreshment?"

Seeing that the president had indicated the pitcher of water, David accepted his offer and asked, "Sir, where are we?"

Lincoln held up one long finger, then poured David a glass of water. Pouring his own glass, he drank it all, poured another, and sat down. "Bring up a chair," he said as he drew his own from behind the desk.

As David sat down, he watched the sixteenth president of the United States cross his legs at the knee and loosen his high starched collar. He was dressed well. His hair was combed, his beard neatly trimmed, and yet he still appeared somewhat . . . well, disheveled. David noticed that the president seemed oversized in all physical respects. His legs, arms, hands, even his face appeared to be too long. David smiled to himself as he realized that Abraham Lincoln looked exactly like every picture he'd ever seen of the man.

David's only surprise, after Lincoln's sudden appearance, was the president's voice. It was not a rich baritone as he had heard it portrayed in numerous movies, but a higher-pitched tenor.

Lincoln placed the glass on the desk and said, "Riding horseback always makes me thirsty, though I'm usually too embarrassed to drink in front of the horse. After all," he chuckled, "I'm not the one who has done the work!" David laughed politely. "So, Mr. Ponder, you wish to know where we are."

"Yes, sir, and please call me David."

"Thank you," Lincoln said as he slightly inclined his

head to the younger man. "David, I am here for two reasons today. First, to dedicate a cemetery. That, by the way, is where we are now . . . Gettysburg, Pennsylvania."

Shivers ran down David's back. "And the date?"

"November nineteenth, eighteen sixty-three."

No wonder this place seems so familiar, David thought. *I was here four months ago. Or was it only an hour?* He shook his head to clear his thoughts. "Mr. President, you mentioned two reasons you came here. What was the second?"

Lincoln smiled. "Why, to meet you, of course." David's eyes widened. "You are certainly more important than any remarks I might share with those in attendance today. This cemetery is about the past. You are about the future!"

David looked away. "I appreciate your confidence," he said, "but I'm not sure it's justified. At the moment, I'm just hoping there is a future. I am actually going through the worst time in my life right now."

"Congratulations are in order then! Better days are most assuredly ahead." The president then raised his water glass and exclaimed, "To us, two men experiencing the worst life has to offer."

David didn't respond. He wasn't sure whether Lincoln was teasing him or not. "I'm not kidding," he said slowly.

"Oh, let me promise you," Lincoln said with a tight smile, "neither am I." He reached to his right, across the desk, and picked up his hat. It was the tall black stovepipe that had become as much a part of the man as any image David could remember. For a time, Lincoln let his fingers play softly across the large silk band. "This is a piece of cloth I carry with me in memory of Willie, my little boy. He died only a few months ago." He took a deep breath and sighed. "Now my son Tad has taken to bed . . . deathly ill. And as you might imagine, Mrs. Lincoln did not agree that I should be here today."

"Why did you come?"

"Duty. And the fact that I knew I could choose to pray for my son while wandering about the White House or pray as I continued in pursuit of the task that has been placed before me. I am quite confident the Almighty hears my cry no matter the location. Surely, His arms stretch from Washington to Gettysburg. I also believe the good Lord would rather me pray and work, not pray and wait."

The president shifted position in the chair and crossed his arms. "You know, I mentioned a moment ago that we were two men who were experiencing the worst life has to offer. That is true in a smaller, selfish way, and I must confess my propensity toward self-serving behavior. Actually, it seems to be one of my life's most constant battles. In a larger sense, however, we are being presented an enormous opportunity for change and the betterment of ourselves."

"The betterment of ourselves? You're talking about what we call 'personal growth.' I'm not sure that I want any more personal growth," David said.

"Of course not!" Lincoln responded. "And wouldn't that be the easy choice to make? In fact, it is the most popular choice on the planet! But the question you are facing at this particular point in your life is: How powerful do you want to be?"

David tilted his head to the side. Confused, he said, "I'm lost here. In the first place, what does personal growth have to do with power? And in the second place, no offense, but I have no interest in power anyway."

Leaning forward, Lincoln said, "Mr. Ponder . . . David, if that is true, if you have no interest in power, then an incalculable amount of attention is being wasted on you. Some of it at this very moment!"

David wasn't certain whether to be insulted or not. He began to speak. "I was not the one who . . ."

Lincoln reached over and touched David's knee. Smiling patiently, but interrupting firmly, he said, "David." As David became silent, the president leaned back in his chair. With his dark eyes still on David and the smile still on his face, he said softly, "Now think with me here. Personal growth leads to power. There is a certain level of personal growth that will provide the skills necessary to feed and clothe one's family. There is another level of personal growth that will furnish influence and wisdom in sufficient quantities to be perceived a leader." Lincoln paused. He looked directly into the younger man's eyes. "But to do great deeds, great power is essential.

"Do not run from power. Gather it as you would the finest fruit. Power in the hands of a good person is like a cool drink of water on a hot summer day. It refreshes everyone with whom it comes in contact.

"You see, some people want just enough power to get by. Then there are other people who will acquire enough power to make things more comfortable for their families, and they'll include other less fortunate souls in their charity if the personal growth part of the equation doesn't become too uncomfortable. But there are a few of us, David, who have latched on to this silly idea that we can change the world. We will develop the power to ignore what is popular and do what is right. One person can attain the power to lead hundreds of thousands of people to the promised land of their dreams.

"As children, we were afraid of the dark. Now as adults, we are afraid of the light. We are afraid to step out. We are afraid to become more. But how can we lead others to a destination we have not reached? Keep searching, son. I am urging you to seek the light that to you seems so far in the distance. It will be worth the journey. You will become a lighthouse of personal growth and power, and by your example and leadership, you will prevent many a worthy man from crashing his life upon the rocks of mediocrity."

"Now I see what you're saying," David said, nodding. "So how do I engineer my personal growth? What is important in this . . . this quest?"

"Well," Lincoln began, "it has always been enlightening for me to question myself."

"About what?"

"About myself."

"You question yourself about yourself?"

"Yes," the president said with a laugh. "At least I generally know all the answers!" Stroking his beard with the back of his hand, he continued, "Seriously, questions such as, 'How do other people see me?' and 'What don't they like?' can be quite revealing if answered honestly. When you become a person whom others want to be around, you will have become a person of influence."

"Then I am to work at pleasing people?" David asked.

"Not necessarily. I am speaking primarily of honing the rough edges you might find in your physical appearance and actions such as manners and speech. Of course, I continue to find fertile ground for change in my attitude.

"But you will never please everyone, nor should pleasing everyone be your goal. For example, to seek the approval of someone who is lazy or jealous is to cast your pearls before swine. You will find that God rarely uses a person whose main concern is what others are thinking."

"Are you ever bothered by what other people say about you?" David asked.

The president quickly leaned forward with a serious look on his face. "Why?" he said. "What are they saying?"

Seeing David's shocked expression, Lincoln laughed loudly. "David, I inherited a nightmare from President Buchanan. By the time I was sworn in, seven states had already seceded from the Union, and Jefferson Davis was named president of the Confederate States of America. Just between us, Buchanan was no great help. He left Washington proclaiming himself the last president of the United States.

"As you may know, I am the first ever Republican president. I was elected by a minority of the popular vote, and even some members of my own cabinet view me as third-rate. To many of the elite in Washington, I will always be a country lawyer, a gawky, unrefined outsider. If I were to concern myself with the newspaper columns that label me dishonest or stupid, if I had my feelings destroyed every time a political opponent called me an ape or a buffoon, I would never be about the work for which I was born!"

Lincoln stood and shoved his hands into his pockets. "Sooner or later, every man of character will have that character questioned. Every man of honor and courage will be faced with unjust criticism, but never forget that unjust criticism has no impact whatsoever upon the truth. And the only sure way to avoid criticism is to do nothing and be nothing!"

As he paused for a breath, Lincoln's attention was diverted by loud, rolling applause from the gathering outside the tent. He grinned and motioned for David to come with him. "Let's see where we are in the program."

Moving to the tent's entrance, the president eased the door flap aside, affording them a clear view of the stage. The same gentleman David had seen earlier was still speaking. "Who is he?" David asked quietly.

Without turning, Lincoln answered, "That is our principal orator at this occasion. The Honorable Edward Everett. He was the president of Harvard University and secretary of state under President Fillmore. He can certainly hold an audience in the palm of his hand. Look at the faces of the people. They are transfixed."

"I am sure they are waiting for you, sir," David replied.

Lincoln smiled and carefully dropped the flap. Backing away from the entrance, he said, "I appreciate the compliment, but today I have only a few remarks. I am here for the dedication. I was invited only three weeks ago."

At that instant, the door flap was thrown aside, and the young, smartly dressed man who had been in the tent earlier entered. Lincoln gestured toward him with his hand and said, "John Hay, my personal secretary."

David froze momentarily and then held his laughter as the young man hesitated. He watched as Hay looked from side to side, then glanced around the tent and said hesitantly, "Sir?"

Recovering quickly, Lincoln asked, "How may I be of assistance, John?"

Hay wrinkled his brow, obviously puzzled, and continued to peer cautiously behind the president.

"John," Lincoln said again, snapping Hay to attention, "how may I be of assistance?"

"I . . . ahh . . . excuse the interruption, Mr. President." Now Lincoln stifled a chuckle. David had his hand over his mouth. "Well . . . sir," Hay stammered. "I wanted you to know that when Mr. Everett has concluded, the Baltimore Glee Club will sing an ode written for this occasion. The music will provide the time necessary to escort you from here to the stage."

"Thank you, John," Lincoln said as he moved to the doorway. "The beginning of the music, then, will be my cue to join you outside the tent. Until that time, sir, I trust you will maintain my privacy."

The president pulled back the door flap, an obvious gesture intended to hasten his secretary's departure. Hay ducked through the opening and turned around. Bent over, half inside and half outside the tent, Hay carefully worded his question. "Sir, excuse me, but are you saying that I should not come back inside?"

"That is correct, John."

"So, you will meet me outside the tent when you are ready to go to the stage?"

"Yes, John."

Briefly, Hay paused. Then, still doubled over in the doorway, he said, "Sir, if I may be so bold as to ask—"

"John," Lincoln interrupted.

"Yes, sir?"

"I will meet you outside the tent when I am ready to go to the stage."

"Yes, sir," Hay said resignedly and slid outside the door.

The president closed the canvas and, urging David to follow with a jerk of his head, walked quickly to the desk. As he sat down, tears were streaming down his face as he finally let his laughter burst forth. For several moments, they both laughed heartily.

Gaining control, Lincoln took a deep breath and sighed. "That was extremely close, my friend. Momentarily, I forgot that he could not see you. John is a fine young man. I hate to laugh at his expense, but if the Almighty will forgive me, the look on his face was priceless!"

David chuckled as he sat down, tipping the chair back on two legs into a more comfortable position. "Before your secretary entered, you were talking about your part in this ceremony today."

"Yes." Lincoln's smile disappeared as he cleared his throat. "Yes, today we take pause from our battles to dedicate one ugly reality of this war: a cemetery. There are quite a few of them around now, as you must know. Certainly more than I can dedicate."

Lincoln frowned and continued, "There were more than fifty thousand casualties here. They say blood and gore ran in rivulets on the ground." He was quiet for a moment, and then brightening, he said, "I have Grant now. This will not last much longer."

"Are you winning the war?" David asked.

"We weren't, I can tell you that! But after this battle, Gettysburg, last July, the outcome seems much brighter indeed."

David suddenly had a thought and asked, "Mr. President, are you familiar with an officer in your army by the name of Colonel Joshua Chamberlain? He is with the Twentieth Maine."

Lincoln cocked his head and thought briefly, then said slowly, "No, I don't believe so. Should I know this man?"

"Maybe. He fought here at Gettysburg. When you return to Washington, you might look him up." The president nodded. "I have another question," David continued, "do you believe that God is on your side?"

Lincoln looked at David thoughtfully. "On September twenty-second of last year, I signed a proclamation of emancipation for all slaves specifying that they will be henceforward and forever free. The timing of that gesture is still the subject of some debate. One of my cabinet members made it known to anyone who would listen that a vast majority of the public stood against me and my intention to sign the Emancipation Proclamation. My platform, however, is that while public opinion might sway back and forth, right and wrong do not.

"If we familiarize ourselves with the chains of bondage, we prepare our own limbs to wear them. The spirit of our government and our institutions must be to elevate people, and I am opposed to whatever degrades them. I am of the opinion that right makes might. Therefore, I signed the document, and now we will enforce its effectiveness.

"So your question was, 'Do I believe that God is on our side?' To be quite honest, I haven't given that question very much attention. I am much more concerned with whether we are on God's side."

David remembered something Lincoln had said earlier. "You mentioned Grant," he prompted. "Why will he make such a difference?"

"Because he cares as I do!" came the sharp reply. "It has taken me almost three years to find a general officer whom I don't have to watch over like a nursemaid.

Winfield Scott was my first general in chief. Then McDowell, followed by Fremont, then the disastrous McClellan. Can you imagine? In McClellan, I had a commander of the entire Union army who refused to engage the enemy!

"After McClellan, I appointed Henry Halleck. Halleck is a graduate of West Point and has even written a book on military tactics. I read it last year before his appointment. Fine book, good theory, but books don't fight wars. The man evaded all personal responsibility, lost what little composure he brought to the task, and became nothing more than a first-rate clerk.

"McClernand was next, and all he did was complain about the other generals. It was the odd week I didn't receive a long, rambling communication critical of something Sherman or Grant had done. After McClernand, I suffered through Rosecrans, then Burnside, and finally Nathaniel P. Banks.

"Naturally, the day I announced my intentions to promote General Grant, I was vilified in the press. Actually, many people have been pushing for Grant's dismissal, but I can't spare this man. He fights! I've heard it said that he drinks too much. Well, if I can find out exactly what he's drinking, I'll send a few cases to the other generals!"

David laughed at that comment. Lincoln smiled and continued, "I suppose the point of all this is that Ulysses S.

Grant wants to win as badly as I do. If you are determined to win, you will have to surround yourself with winners. Don't be discouraged by the people you might choose for your team who talk big but produce little. Grant is my tenth try. I just keep putting them in the boat to see who wants to paddle as hard as I do."

"What will you do if . . . when you win?" David asked.

"Do you mean, where will I lead this nation?"

"Yes. After the war, what will be your first priority?"

"That is rather an easy question to answer. In fact, I have spent many hours in prayerful consideration of my response. The first morning after all hostilities cease, I will greet the day with a forgiving spirit."

David was stunned. "How can you? I do not understand!"

"It's a very simple concept actually, and it is the single most important action I take on a regular basis. Forgiveness allows me to be an effective husband, father, friend, and leader of this country."

Confused, David asked, "What does forgiveness have to do with being effective?"

Lincoln thought for a moment, crossed his legs, and answered. "Have you ever been so angry or upset with someone that all you could think of was that person and the horrible way you'd been treated? You think about him when you should be sleeping, and all the things you should have said or would like to say come to mind. When you could be enjoying an evening with your family, your children aren't foremost in your thoughts. That person who offended you is receiving all your energy. You feel as if you might explode." Leaning forward, he asked, "Have you ever felt this way?"

"Yes." David nodded. "I have."

Lincoln relaxed back in his chair and uncrossed his legs. "Well, so have I. I owe business failures, marital strife, and defeats in several political races to those very feelings. But I also owe a great deal of the success I enjoy to the discovery of this simple secret."

"What secret?" David asked.

"The secret of forgiveness," Lincoln responded. "It is a secret that is hidden in plain sight. It costs nothing and is worth millions. It is available to everyone and used by few. If you harness the power of forgiveness, you will be revered, sought after, and wealthy. And not coincidentally, you will also be forgiven by others!"

David looked puzzled. "Just who is it that I am supposed to forgive?"

"Everyone."

"But what if they don't ask for forgiveness?"

Lincoln raised his dark eyebrows and smiled. "Most will not! Amazingly, many of these dastardly people who dare to occupy our minds with angry thoughts are actually wandering about in life without any knowledge of our feelings or any conviction that they have done anything wrong!"

David frowned. "I'm sure that's all true, but I still don't understand how you can forgive someone who doesn't ask for forgiveness!"

"You know," Lincoln began, "for many years, I thought forgiveness was akin to a knighthood—something I bestowed upon some poor wretch who groveled at my feet and begged my blessings. But as I matured and observed successful people, I gained a new perspective on forgiveness.

"I cannot recall a single book, including the Holy Bible, that says in order for you to forgive someone, he or she has to ask for it. Think about this concept! Where is the rule written that before I forgive people, they have to deserve it? Where is it written that to be forgiven by me, you must have wronged me no more than three times? Or seven? Or seventeen?

"The unmistakable truth about forgiveness is that it is not a reward that must be earned; forgiveness is a gift to be given. When I give forgiveness, I free my own spirit to release the anger and hatred harbored in my heart. By granting forgiveness, I free my spirit to pursue my future happily and unencumbered by the anchors of my past. And forgiveness, when granted to others, becomes a gift to myself."

David nodded slowly. "I guess I never considered forgiveness to be something under my control."

Just then, cheers and a long, sustained ovation began outside. The president pulled a pocket watch from his vest and said, "I expect that will be the end of Mr. Everett. Well, not much longer now."

David stood up.

"Sit back down for a moment, son," Lincoln commanded gently. David did so.

"David, you are at a critical point in your life's race, and there exists a person to whom your forgiveness has been withheld for far too long. By the limited authority I have been granted as your host for this short time, I must now warn you that without a forgiving spirit, your effectiveness as a husband, a father, and a leader of people will be at an end. The key to everything your future holds, the touchstone that will, for you, bring dreams into reality, is forgiveness."

David's mouth was open, and a look of confusion and faint astonishment was written in his eyes. "Who is it?" he said. Lincoln merely looked at him. "Sir? Who is it?"

Lincoln stood up and brushed off the front of his jacket and pants. David stood up and said, "Mr. President, you have to tell me who it is!" Lincoln picked up the glass of water and drained the contents. He stepped toward the door, and David put his hand on Lincoln's arm. "Listen!" David said. "You're about to go out there, and I'll never see you again. You as much as said my life would be over if I did not forgive this person. So if it's that important, tell me! Who must I forgive?"

The president looked carefully into David's eyes and said simply, "Yourself."

Tears formed in David's eyes, and he shook his head. Softly, he said, "I didn't think . . ."

"David," Lincoln said as he placed his hands on the younger man's shoulders, "your wife is not mad at you. Your child is not mad at you. Your friends, of which I am one, are not mad at you, and God is not mad at you. So, David . . . ," Lincoln stopped briefly and said with a smile, "don't *you* be mad at you. Forgive yourself. Begin anew."

"Thank you," David said as he wiped his eyes on his shirt-sleeve.

"I am honored to have been of assistance," Lincoln said. Picking up his hat from the desk, he asked, "Would you care to follow me out? You could join the crowd and listen if you wish."

"That would be great," David said. "Thanks! By the way, I'm sorry I took up all your preparation time here in the tent."

"No problem at all," the president responded. "I've been ready with these remarks for about two weeks."

"Really? You know, that's fascinating. When people study you now, or . . . ahh, in the future, one of the things we were all taught is that you wrote this particular speech on the train into Gettysburg."

Lincoln smiled. "No, I wrote the dedication for today back in Washington. I suppose the situation could have been easily confused because I was writing on the train into Gettysburg. In fact . . . ," Lincoln took a piece of paper from the inside band of his stovepipe hat and presented it to David, "I was writing this for you."

David smiled and followed Lincoln to the door. The choir was singing a hymn, and inside the tent, the two men could hear the sounds of twenty thousand people shifting and stretching. Lincoln ducked to go through the door and then, suddenly, he stopped. Turning and straightening to face David, he had a quizzical expression on his face. "You say people study me in the future?"

"Yes, sir," David answered.

Lincoln lowered his voice and narrowed his eyes. "Just between you and me, we *do* win this war, correct?"

"Yes, sir."

With a sly smile on his face and one raised eyebrow, he added one last question. "Grant?"

David grinned. "Yes, sir," he said and followed the great man from the tent.

Outside, David fell back as John Hay and several soldiers immediately surrounded the president and whisked him toward the stage. Lincoln shook hands with Edward Everett, who had remained nearby to hear the president. The choir had finished and left the stage when an emcee, dressed in a fine black tuxedo, approached the podium and sang out, "Ladies and gentlemen, the president of the United States of America, Abraham Lincoln."

With that announcement, twenty thousand people rose to their feet and cheered. David squeezed around to the front of the stage and stood with everyone else. As the applause died, they remained standing. David was just to the right and under his friend when, in a high-pitched, almost shrill voice, Abraham Lincoln spoke the words that would begin the healing of a broken nation:

"Four score and seven years ago, our fathers brought forth upon this continent a new nation, conceived in liberty, and dedicated to the proposition that all men are created equal.

"Now we are engaged in a great civil war, testing whether that nation—or any nation so conceived and so dedicated—can long endure. We are met on a great battlefield of that war. We are met to dedicate a portion of it as the final resting place of those who here gave their lives that that nation might live. It is altogether fitting and proper that we should do this.

"But in a larger sense we cannot dedicate, we cannot consecrate, we cannot hallow this ground. The brave men, living and dead, who struggled here, have consecrated it far beyond our power to add or detract. The world will little note nor long remember what we say here, but it can never forget what they did here. It is for us, the living, rather to be dedicated here to the unfinished work that they have thus far so nobly carried on. It is rather for us to be here dedicated to the great task remaining before us— that from these honored dead we take increased devotion to the cause for which they here gave the last full measure of devotion—that we here highly resolve that the dead shall not have died in vain, that the nation shall, under God, have a new birth of freedom and that the government of the people, by the people, and for the people, shall not perish from the earth."

For a moment, the crowd stood silent. Then all around him, David heard people begin to applaud. Joining them enthusiastically, he watched as Lincoln nodded to the crowd, acknowledging their appreciation, and then waved to the people farthest from the stage. Looking below him, he caught David's gaze and smiled. He then waved to the audience once more, turned, and was gone.

David picked his way through the people and walked to a large beech tree standing alone on the gentle slope of a hill. He was away from the thousands of people as he sat down in the shade of the tree. Hearing the voices of the choir as they sang another hymn from the stage, David unfolded the paper given to him by the sixteenth president of the United States and read.

The Sixth Decision for Success

I will greet this day with a forgiving spirit.

For too long, every ounce of forgiveness I owned was locked away, hidden from view, waiting for me to bestow its precious presence upon some worthy person. Alas, I found most people to be singularly unworthy of my valuable forgiveness, and since they never asked for any, I kept it all for myself. Now, the forgiveness that I hoarded has sprouted inside my heart like a crippled seed yielding bitter fruit.

No more! At this moment, my life has taken on new hope and assurance. Of all the world's population, I am one of the few possessors of the secret to dissipating anger and resentment. I now understand that forgiveness has value only when it is given away. By the simple act of granting forgiveness, I release the demons of the past about which I can do nothing, and I create in myself a new heart, a new beginning.

I will greet this day with a forgiving spirit. I will forgive even those who do not ask for forgiveness.

Many are the times when I have seethed in anger at a word or deed thrown into my life by an unthinking or uncaring person. I have wasted valuable hours imagining revenge or confrontation. Now I see the truth revealed about this psychological rock inside my shoe. The rage I nurture is often one-sided, for my offender seldom gives thought to his offense!

I will now and forevermore silently offer my forgiveness even to those who do not see that they need it. By the act of forgiving, I am no longer consumed by unproductive thoughts. I give up my bitterness. I am content in my soul and effective again with my fellowman.

I will greet this day with a forgiving spirit. I will forgive those who criticize me unjustly.

Knowing that slavery in any form is wrong, I also know that the person who lives a life according to the opinion of others is a slave. I am not a slave. I have chosen my counsel. I know the difference between right and wrong. I know what is best for the future of my family, and neither misguided opinion nor unjust criticism will alter my course.

Those who are critical of my goals and dreams simply do not understand the higher purpose to which I have been called. Therefore, their scorn does not affect my attitude or action. I forgive their lack of vision, and I forge ahead. I now know that criticism is part of the price paid for leaping past mediocrity.

I will greet this day with a forgiving spirit. I will forgive myself.

For many years, my greatest enemy has been myself. Every mistake, every miscalculation, every stumble I made has been replayed again and again in my mind. Every broken promise, every day wasted, every goal not reached has compounded the disgust I feel for the lack of achievement in my life. My dismay has developed a paralyzing grip. When I disappoint myself, I respond with inaction and become more disappointed.

I realize today that it is impossible to fight an enemy living in my head. By forgiving myself, I erase the doubts, fears, and frustration that have kept my past in the present. From this day forward, my history will cease to control my destiny. I have forgiven myself. My life has just begun.

I will forgive even those who do not ask for forgiveness. I will forgive those who criticize me unjustly. I will forgive myself.

I will greet this day with a forgiving spirit.

NINE

DAVID DUG THE TOBACCO POUCH OUT OF HIS
pocket. Carefully, he folded the paper and placed it inside
the worn canvas. His hand brushed the smooth skin on
which King Solomon had written the Second Decision.
"One, two, three, four, five, six." David counted the precious pages aloud. *I'm supposed to receive seven*, he thought.
Where will I go next?

David was tense. Waiting for the experience of leaping
across time and space had left him nervous and exhausted.
As he looked across the field, he saw Lincoln's party leaving
the cemetery on horseback. The president, with his white
gauntlets and tall black hat shining in the sunlight, cut a
dashing figure. David smiled and shook his head in wonder.

Feelings of weariness overcame David. Unable to keep
his eyes open, he put the pouch back in his pocket and lay
down. He tried to stay awake and was scared to fall asleep,
but he couldn't fight it. Visions of Ellen and Jenny swept

over him. "Where are you, Daddy?" Jenny cried. "Come home!" It was a dream, David knew, but he couldn't wake up. He tried to touch them, but they were just out of his reach. *This is crazy*, David thought. *I'm having a dream in the middle of a dream. I have to wake up!*

Ellen stood with her hands on her sobbing daughter's shoulders, comforting the child. "David, we need you," she said.

Wake up! David screamed at himself.

"I'm expecting great things from you, son." It was a man's voice. David swung around to see his father-in-law. There were tears in his eyes. "You promised me you'd take care of my daughter."

David woke up drenched in sweat. He was nauseated but terrified of closing his eyes again. "Too real," he mumbled to himself as he sat up. "That was too real." Disoriented, David saw that he was on a concrete floor surrounded by . . . paper?

Sitting up straight, he rubbed his eyes as his senses cleared. Directly in front of him was more paper. David rolled to his knees and got to his feet. He saw that these were not ordinary pieces of white paper but photographs. And every photograph was of a child. There were banded stacks of photographs placed neatly on shelf after shelf after shelf. Three big baskets holding hundreds of loose photographs stood at the bottom of one row as if waiting to be filed. These were pictures of children of all ages and colors. There were two children in some photographs and just one in many more. David saw others had three children or four, and a few held five or six.

David stepped into an opening on his left. It was an aisle of some sort, and just beyond it stood massive racks of clothing. Walking tentatively, David approached the brightly colored materials and ran his hand over a small coat. Picking up the sleeve of another garment, he recognized it as a coat as well. In fact, he determined quickly that every single article of clothing was a coat. Large ones, small ones, coats and jackets, each on its own individual hanger. "Thousands," David murmured, "maybe hundreds of thousands."

David turned back toward the photographs and gasped. Standing across the aisle gave him a peripheral view of where he had awakened moments before. Close to the pictures, he had not been able to see just how high the shelves were stacked, but looking up, he could not even see a ceiling. There were shelves of photographs one on top of another stacked literally out of sight.

There were no light fixtures in this place, or any lights for that matter, and yet, somehow, everything was bathed in a soft, even glow. To his right, the aisle continued seemingly without end. To his left, the same. There seemed to be no definite structure to the building if it was, in fact, a building. *Am I still dreaming?* David wondered.

Noticing something different on the shelves just past the photographs, David walked slowly down the aisle almost a hundred yards until he saw wheelchairs. Thousands of wheelchairs. Lined up and on shelves. Row after row of nickel-plated, gleaming wheelchairs. Just beyond the wheelchairs were beds—double, single, king, and queen. Then bicycles—all kinds, all colors.

Across from the bicycles were legal documents of some kind. David looked closer. They were automobile titles. The papers, on shelves and bundled as the pictures had been, were spread over an area as large as ten houses and, like everything else in this place, were piled higher than he could see.

Next to the car titles were shoes of every description, each pair in its own separate cubicle. Baby shoes took up a cabinet that David guessed might be sixty or seventy yards long and who knew how high. The baby shoes were followed by cabinets filled with men's and women's dress shoes, galoshes, and sneakers. Hundreds of thousands, maybe millions of shoes, David wasn't sure.

David was sure, however, that he had never been anywhere like this before. The temperature seemed perfect. There was no music, no smell. He had seen no support pilings of any kind or walls or people. *Where am I?* he thought. *What is this place, and what's with this stuff?*

He continued to walk and found new aisles, but none

with an end. He saw blue jeans and medicine and pictures of homes. There were heaters and marriage licenses, roofing shingles and food. Slowly, he worked his way back toward the pictures of the children.

On the way, he passed an area stacked with money. Cash in every currency and denomination. David put his hands on his hips, pursed his lips, and expelled all the air from his lungs. "This makes absolutely no sense at all," he said aloud. Continuing, he counted two hundred and nine steps before the money was no longer beside him.

Soon, David was back where he had begun, even though he knew he had not seen nearly everything. As he turned in a complete circle, gazing all around him, a picture fluttered down from somewhere above. It landed on the floor not far from where David stood. Picking it up, he moved to place it back on a shelf but stopped. Something troubled him about the photograph.

It was a color picture of two children, a boy and a girl each around six or seven years old. They were quite obviously brother and sister, but they looked remarkably similar to Jenny, his own daughter. Their eyes were blue like Jenny's—and Ellen's—and the blond hair lifted into the same cowlick on the front left side.

David shook his head in wonder. He couldn't take his eyes off the photo.

Faintly, almost in a part of his subconscious, David

heard something. Glancing up sharply, he looked down the aisle where he had just been and saw a figure walking toward him. The person was moving from several hundred yards away, steadily and easily. As he approached the area that held the beds and bicycles, David could see that it was a man. He was huge. David was two inches over six feet but saw that this man would tower over him.

David eased a couple of feet to his left, feeling somewhat safer close to the stacks of pictures. He saw that the man had blond, almost golden, curly hair. It was relatively short, touching his eyebrows and just brushing his ears. He wore a robe draped over his shoulders and hanging to his knees. It was white, or maybe light. In fact, this man, who was now no more than fifty feet away, seemed to be dressed in what David could only describe as shades of light.

The man smiled a greeting as he came closer, then stopped and turned to straighten a wheelchair on his right. When he did, David's mouth dropped open. The man had wings.

They were of the purest white and lay close to his shoulder blades. As the man bent to move the wheelchair, David could see that they ran the length of his body, the tips extending almost to the floor. As he stood again to full height, the wings folded in close to his back.

Closing the distance quickly between them, the man stopped and said, "Hello, David Ponder. I am Gabriel."

He was as tall as David had at first thought and built like a warrior. Heavily muscled, yet somehow gentle, he was not threatening in any way. His nose was long and straight, his lips full, and the skin on his face was smooth and devoid of whiskers. But his eyes held David's attention. They were the brightest blue he had ever seen and appeared to have been dusted with flakes of gold.

David's mouth hung open. "You're an angel," he finally managed to say.

"An archangel actually." Gabriel smiled, revealing perfectly even, white teeth. "There is a difference, you know."

"I'm sorry, I . . . ahh . . . I really didn't," David stammered. "Know, I mean. That there was a difference."

"No matter, David Ponder," Gabriel responded. "I am honored to make your acquaintance."

Indicating the photograph David still held in his hand, he said, "May I?"

"Oh . . . sure!" David said and gave it to him.

Gabriel looked at the picture for a moment, then showed it again to David. "Beautiful children, aren't they?" David nodded in agreement and watched as Gabriel placed it in the basket of loose photos.

"So I *am* dead?" David blurted out.

Gabriel wrinkled his forehead and appeared confused. "Excuse me?"

"If I'm with you, then I must be in heaven. And if I'm in heaven, I must be dead."

Gabriel laughed. "No, you are not dead. This is merely a brief stopover, perhaps the most important stopover, in your travel. This is the only destination all travelers have in common."

"Have there been many travelers?" David asked.

"Relatively few," Gabriel said, "when one considers the beginning of time as you know it and the numbers of people with whom we have dealt. But for those who are chosen to travel, an understanding of their true mission begins here, in this place. Joan of Arc, George Washington, and Martin Luther King Jr. all took a step toward destiny from where you now stand."

"Which is where exactly?" David motioned with his hands. "What is this place?"

Gabriel held up one finger. "Not quite yet," he said. "First, let us walk together."

Moving slowly away from the direction in which he had come, Gabriel led David past ceiling fans and air-conditioners, tires and blankets, watches and pictures of animals. Just as there had been photographs of children,

David saw rows and files and stacks of dog pictures, cat pictures, horses, hamsters, birds, turtles, fish, and a few animals he didn't even recognize.

Approaching a vast area stacked neatly with monstrous rolls of carpet, Gabriel stopped, turned, and without warning, asked, "Do you consider yourself a man of faith, David Ponder?"

David frowned. Momentarily thrown, he said, "I'm not sure what you mean."

Gabriel's eyebrows rose. "A simple question actually. Do you consider yourself a man of faith? Does faith guide your everyday actions and emotions? All men are driven by faith or fear—one or the other—for both are the same. Faith or fear is the expectation of an event that hasn't come to pass or the belief in something that cannot be seen or touched. A man of fear lives always on the edge of insanity. A man of faith lives in perpetual reward."

"Reward?" David said, puzzled.

Walking again, Gabriel replied, "Faith is to believe what one has not seen. The reward of faith is to see what one has believed. Do you consider yourself a man of faith, David Ponder?"

"To be honest," David replied, "I have always thought of myself as a man of reason."

Gabriel turned right, leading his guest down a wide

aisle. "Reason never makes room for miracles; faith releases miracles. And in final comparison, faith is a sounder guide than reason. Reason can only be stretched so far, but faith has no limits. The only limit to your realization of tomorrow is the doubt to which you hold fast today."

"Is it realistic for me to work and live, expecting miracles?" David asked.

Gabriel laughed. "You are quite amusing, David Ponder," he said. "What is this word *realistic?* It is never used here."

David stopped. "You *are* kidding, right?"

"Yes," Gabriel said, still smiling, "I am. But it is a fact that great leaders—great achievers—are rarely realistic by other people's standards. Somehow, these successful people, often considered strange, pick their way through life ignoring or not hearing negative expectations and emotions. Consequently, they accomplish one great thing after another, never having heard what cannot be done. That is precisely why one should never tell a young person that something cannot be done. God may have been waiting centuries for someone ignorant enough of the impossible to do that very thing!"

David's attention was momentarily diverted from Gabriel. As they walked, they passed more and more aisles of bricks, rice, computers, rocking chairs, and vast amounts of items that, as far as David could tell, had no connection.

But here was something new, an area of about one hundred feet square with a single, small pedestal standing in the middle. On the pedestal, David saw as he moved closer, was a stack of papers not even a quarter of an inch high.

It had been the light that caught David's attention. The pedestal, removed from any other item in this place, also stood in stark contrast to the soft glow that seemed to permeate every other row or shelf. A bright light focused sharply on the pedestal's papers. As David moved slowly across the empty space, he looked up and around for the light's source. "Hey, where is the light coming from?" he asked. Gabriel only smiled. Seeing he would receive no answer, David moved closer. "May I touch this?"

"Certainly," Gabriel responded.

There were forty to fifty sheets of paper, some of them obviously newer, some yellowed with age. The first was a complicated mathematical equation, as was the second. The third and several other pages showed multidimensional blueprints for different machines of some sort. Scanning quickly, David saw pages of chemical equations, some that almost appeared to be recipes, and one sheet of paper, yellow and wrinkled, that held only one word in the middle. From biology classes years before, David recognized the word as a Latin name for some sort of plant.

Holding the papers in his left hand, David turned to Gabriel and said, "I don't get it. What are these?"

"One of them," Gabriel said as he moved toward David, "I believe it was the eighth page you looked at, is the cure for pancreatic, liver, or colon cancer."

David stared at Gabriel. His hand, still holding the stack of papers, remained partially extended. "What?" he said.

"Yes," Gabriel continued, "also included there is a machine that will regenerate the optic nerve, allowing even those who are blind from birth to see. A variation of that same device is blueprinted on the following page. It regenerates spinal tissue. You are holding cures and vaccinations for muscular dystrophy, cerebral palsy, and believe it or not, the common cold. Page twenty-six is the answer to Sudden Infant Death Syndrome, and page fourteen, you might be interested to know, is a liquid formula to be swabbed at the back of a child's throat. It painlessly shrinks and removes tonsils in less than six hours."

David was stunned. Barely able to comprehend Gabriel's explanation, he slowly thumbed through the papers again. "But I don't . . . ," he started and stopped. "Am I supposed to take these?"

"No," Gabriel said.

Flushing with anger and confusion, David sputtered, "Then what is the purpose? I mean, why . . . ?" He couldn't find the words. Tears of exhaustion sprang to his eyes. Embarrassed and overwhelmed, David placed the papers on the pedestal and ignored the crack in his voice as he said too loudly, "What is going on? All these things . . . these cures . . . my daughter needs her tonsils taken out. Did you know that?"

"Yes."

For several seconds, David stared open-mouthed at the angel. Then the corners of his mouth sagged and tears streamed down his face as he tried desperately to regain some sense of comprehension. Finally, David yelled, "Do you know I can't afford the operation?"

"Yes."

The frustration of a lifetime seemed to well out of David's soul at that very moment. An agonized cry escaped his throat as he sank to a squatting position. With his left arm on his knee and his right fist ground into the floor, David balanced there and cried bitterly. He cried for Ellen and Jenny. He missed them. Would he ever see them again? Did he deserve to see them again? He cried for the people he had let down in his life—his parents, his friends, his coworkers—and he cried for himself.

After a few minutes had passed, David eased into a sitting position on the floor and sat with his knees bunched under his chin. Calmer now, he tried to catch his breath and wiped his face on the sleeve of his shirt.

Gabriel had not moved. His face was not devoid of compassion, but he offered no physical comfort or suggestion of great sympathy.

David turned his face up to the angel and asked, "Why am I here?" Gabriel held out a hand to help David to his feet. Taking it, David stood and straightened his pants.

Gabriel smiled. "Why do you think you're here?"

"I don't know," David said as he sniffed loudly.

"Then it is not time for you to know," Gabriel said. "Come."

They continued their walk past the pedestal. David took one last look at it as they moved out of sight. Instantly, he again noticed the incredible quantities of an endless variety of items. Some were ordinary. There were electrical cables and light bulbs. Some were not so ordinary. "What is this?" David asked, pointing to a piece of machinery as they passed.

"That bit of equipment," Gabriel responded, "renders any moveable object collision-proof. The design is a combination of laser and sound-wave technology effective on anything from automobiles to a jumbo jet."

David ran his fingers through his hair. "If you won't tell me what this place is and you won't say why I am here, then let me ask you a different question." Gabriel nodded. "Why are all these things here?"

Brushing his hand over one of the many vacuum cleaners they were walking by, Gabriel appeared deep in thought. "What is the difference in people, David Ponder," the angel began, "when they hit despair? Why does one person take his own life while another moves to greatness?"

"That didn't answer my question," David replied, "but I'm not sure. I've never really thought about it."

Gabriel turned, still walking, with a mildly amused look on his face. "Think about it now," he said simply.

David shrugged. "I don't know. Maybe it's a difference in circumstances."

"Circumstances are rulers of the weak," Gabriel said, "but they are weapons of the wise. Must you be bent and flayed by every situation you encounter?" David frowned. Smiling, Gabriel pressed his point: "That is a question, David Ponder. Are your emotions and resolve controlled by circumstances?"

"No, they are not," David said firmly.

"That is correct," Gabriel nodded. "Circumstances do not push or pull. They are daily lessons to be studied and gleaned for new knowledge and wisdom. Knowledge and wisdom that is applied will bring about a brighter tomorrow. A person who is depressed is spending too much time thinking about the way things are now and not enough time thinking about how he wants things to be."

David walked on for a minute in thought, then swung his arm toward an area filled with mattresses and said, "So why are all these things here?"

Gabriel glanced at his confused pupil briefly and said, "Circumstances."

David sighed audibly. Gabriel laughed and said, "Walk this way, David Ponder."

David followed the angel down an aisle lined with telephones on one side and lumber on the other. Soon, they were back to David's starting place, the area with the photographs of children. "Have I seen it all?" David asked.

"You have seen only a tiny fraction of this facility," Gabriel answered. "A lifetime of wandering would not cover it all. And sadly, it gets bigger every day."

David stopped near the baskets of loose pictures. Reaching in, he removed the one Gabriel had placed there earlier—the one with the two children David had found so familiar. "The boy's name is Jason," Gabriel said quietly. "The girl is Julia."

David wrinkled his forehead. Still looking at the photo, he remarked, "I've always liked those names. My grandfather's name was Jason. In fact, if Jenny had been a boy, Ellen and I were going to name the baby Jason. We always said we would name our second girl Julia. We wanted several children, but we never were able to afford . . ." A cold wave of nausea swept over David. Lowering the picture slowly, he gripped the side of the large basket with his other hand to steady himself. Breathing heavily, he said, "But you already knew that, didn't you?"

"Yes," Gabriel answered.

"Why is this being done to me?"

Gabriel's eyes narrowed. "Explain yourself more clearly, please."

"Why am I seeing this now?"

"Special dispensation is allowed for a traveler to gain greater wisdom and understanding."

"I don't understand."

"Obviously."

David took a deep breath. "Am I supposed to somehow understand?"

"Everything will become clear to you."

Turning to face Gabriel, David said, "What is this place?"

Flexing the wings on his back, Gabriel took a step closer to David and swept his arms out from his sides as if to welcome an honored guest. "This, my friend, is the place that never was."

David scarcely breathed as the angel took the picture from his hands. Using it to gesture around him, Gabriel said, "This is the place where we keep all the things that were about to be delivered just as a person stopped working and praying for them. The contents of this warehouse are filled with the dreams and goals of the less courageous."

David was horrified. He turned open-mouthed, casting his eyes up and down the aisle, seeing the coats and shoes, the bicycles and blankets, and remembering the pedestal. His eyes fell again upon the photograph in Gabriel's hand. Reaching out, he asked, "May I keep it?"

"I'm sorry," the angel said, placing the picture back into

the basket. "Jason and Julia do not exist. The time for their arrival has passed. The opportunity is missed. There are no second chances."

Almost immediately, David's right hand felt for the ground. With his knees buckling, he lowered himself quickly to the floor. He didn't trust himself to stand, and so he just sat there at Gabriel's feet. He didn't scream or cry. He was past tears. He felt purged of energy, barely able even to breathe.

For what seemed like an hour or more, David sat trying to gather his senses. Gabriel stood motionless the entire time. Finally, David looked up and asked in a weak voice, "What am I supposed to learn here?"

Gabriel smiled and sat down beside David on the floor. "You must know," he began, "that in the game of life, nothing is less important than the score at halftime. The tragedy of life is not that man loses, but that he almost wins."

David shook his head slowly. "Why do we quit? Why do I quit? Why do I ease off? Why do I detour everything in my life?"

Gabriel responded instantly, "As a human, you detour and ease off because you lack understanding. You quit because you lack faith."

"Understanding about what?"

"For one thing, you do not understand that constant detours do not bring a man into the presence of greatness.

Detours do not build muscle. Detours do not provide life's lessons. Between you and anything significant will be giants in your path.

"Easing off does not make the going easier. Neither does it guide one to the desired destination. Most men ease off when the going is rough. Most slow down when the road appears treacherous. These are the times when you must feel the weight of your future on your shoulders—the throbbing, unstoppable strength of destiny coursing through your veins.

"Times of calamity and distress have always been producers of the greatest men. The hardest steel is produced from the hottest fire; the brightest star shreds the darkest night."

For a while, David was silent. He seemed deep in thought. Then as if having locked away the angel's words, he said, "Gabriel, you also mentioned that I lacked faith."

"I said those who quit lacked faith."

"You meant . . ."

"I meant your race. The human race. With only a few exceptions, you lack the faith that produces greatness." Gabriel sighed. "It was not always so. Your civilization was once alive, vibrant, productive, and borne in glory. Now look at you—a wandering, questioning pack of rebels teetering on the brink of dissolution."

"What?" David said as if he could not believe his ears.

"We are living in the most advanced age our planet has ever seen!"

Gabriel shook his head sadly. "You truly have no memory or cognitive knowledge of your history. Sometimes when I sit with our Father and watch the movements of your civilization as the time shifts, I am astounded at the arrogance I see displayed in your people. On several occasions, I have asked permission to teach you a lesson, but so far, His patience has greatly exceeded my own.

"It amuses me that you would think your civilization so advanced. There once existed a culture on earth so highly evolved as to make you look like dull children. Their mathematics, metallurgy, engineering, and architecture were far beyond what you revere today. These were people of great understanding, great wisdom, and an even greater faith."

"Why have we never heard of these people?" David asked doubtfully.

"Because most of your scientists work within a parameter of time that is far too narrow," Gabriel said. "A few of them, however, have begun to suspect that this society predated the Aztecs and Incas by more than thirty thousand of your years."

"What evidence is there of that?"

Gabriel chuckled. "Not much for you at this point. To be frank, you are too far removed from those people in terms of capacity and time. Your civilization is just now arriving at the point of recognizing the scant clues still left of their existence."

"What clues?"

Gabriel paused for a moment, then said, "The engineering of Cuencan temples, still standing in what you call South America, used stones that are rectangular in shape and weigh more than one hundred tons each. The builders of Balbek in Lebanon laid cornerstones as tall as your five-story buildings. They weigh more than six hundred tons apiece.

"In both places, and many more I might add, the andesite blocks were quarried and set together so perfectly that grout was never considered necessary. Just to cut stone to the same specifications, your engineers today require diamond-tipped, laser-guided quarry saws. And still, they can't duplicate the dimensions.

"Do you remember the Abu Simbel statues in Egypt? They are one hundred twenty feet high, one hundred forty feet wide, and weigh thirty-three tons. When an international task force of your civilization's finest engineers was assembled to save them before completion of the Aswan High Dam, they decided the only possible way to move the statues was to cut them into small sections and reassemble them on higher ground. Yet the original builders quarried the rock from a source miles away and moved it in one piece.

"Their knowledge of astronomy also far exceeded your current levels. They knew that the celestial dome is fixed—that your sun, moon, and planets rotate. They knew the exact circumference of the earth and chartered it into systems of measure around the world. Your mathematicians and engineers have now seen this in surviving buildings in South America and Europe because they incorporated the figures into their architecture. And these equations were calculated perfectly. You were able to obtain these exact mathematical values only after Sputnik circled the earth in 1957.

"Truth needs no evidence, of course." Gabriel smiled. "But since you were curious, that should give you something to consider."

For a bit, David sat still. He was almost unable to comprehend the riddle of history Gabriel had shared. He had no doubt, though, that it was true. "Why are they gone?" he finally asked. "Why did that civilization disappear?"

"For the same reasons that your civilization is in peril," Gabriel said carefully. "Arrogance, ungratefulness, and a loss of faith. Your people have reached the precipice of the same cliff in an astonishingly short time."

"Is there anything that we can do to turn back?"

"Of course," Gabriel said. "And that is precisely why you are here." Gabriel stood and helped David to his feet. Reaching into the folds of his robe, the angel drew out a small scroll. Laying it across his upturned palms, he extended it to David and said, "This decision is the final portion of the whole. Take it."

As David reached for the scroll and took it in his hand, Gabriel frowned. "I am not certain why you were selected for this great honor, David Ponder, for I am but a messenger." He paused and took a deep breath. "You are the last traveler. There will not be another. You have been given a gift that has the power to change your civilization. Everything from this moment on will key upon you.

"You will study one decision at a time, each for twenty-one days. You will read it aloud twice daily during that time. First, upon awakening, and again, as the last thing you do before sleep. You must not miss a day. Each decision will become a part of your being, buried in your heart, captured in your soul.

"You will share the gift of the decisions with others. Those who absorb and apply this wisdom will rise to greatness and inspire others to the same heights. Those who ignore the power of these scrolls might seem to prosper for a time, but do not be deceived. Their lives will be only brief illusions, and when their time is finished, they will be chained to the Mirror of Regret. There, they will spend eternity examining a reflection of the person they could have become."

Gabriel placed his hands on each side of David's face. "You have everything you need, David Ponder. You know that you are not alone. You are being guided. There will never be a reason to lose faith. The future, as you choose it, is yours. But be warned. Yours *is* a future as you choose it. Our Creator has granted you the extraordinary power of the wisdom contained in the Seven Decisions. But our Creator also grants you free will. Should you choose not to ingrain this wisdom in your life, should you choose to ignore this power, the future will be lost forever."

David took both of Gabriel's hands in his own and said, "Thank you. I will make the very most of this gift."

Gabriel smiled and stepped away, out into the middle of the aisle. "Yes, David Ponder," he said. "I believe that you will." And with that, he slowly stretched his wings over his head. Raising his arms, he swiftly drew the wings to his side. Instantly, in a thunderous rush of wind, he flew up and was gone. David moved quickly to the aisle and looked up, but he still could not see a ceiling . . . or any sign of the angel.

For a few moments, David stood there, watching and thinking. Then slowly, he began a purposeful walk. Entering the area of the pedestal, David glanced around again, as if to memorize this place and what it meant. Then he eased down onto the floor where he had felt such pain only a short time ago. He unrolled the scroll of Gabriel and read.

THE SEVENTH DECISION FOR SUCCESS

I will persist without exception.

Knowing that I have already made changes in my life that will last forever, today I insert the final piece of the puzzle. I possess the greatest power ever bestowed upon mankind, the power of choice. Today, I choose to persist without exception. No longer will I live in a dimension of distraction, my focus blown hither and yon like a leaf on a blustery day. I know the outcome I desire. I hold fast to my dreams. I stay the course. I do not quit.

I will persist without exception. I will continue despite exhaustion.

I acknowledge that most people quit when exhaustion sets in. I am not "most people." I am stronger than most people. Average people accept exhaustion as a matter of course. I do not. Average people compare themselves with other people. That is why they are average. I compare myself to my potential. I am not average. I see exhaustion as a precursor to victory.

How long must a child try to walk before he actually does so? Do I not have more strength than a child? More understanding? More desire? How long must I work to succeed before I actually do so? A child would never ask the question, for the answer does not matter. By persisting without exception, my outcome—my success—is assured.

I will persist without exception. I focus on results.

To achieve the results I desire, it is not even necessary that I enjoy the process. It is only important that I *continue* the process with my eyes on the outcome. An athlete does not enjoy the pain of training; an athlete enjoys the results of having trained. A young falcon is pushed from the nest, afraid and tumbling from the cliff. The pain of learning to fly cannot be an enjoyable experience, but the anguish of learning to fly is quickly forgotten as the falcon soars to the heavens.

A sailor who fearfully watches stormy seas lash his vessel will always steer an unproductive course. But a wise and experienced captain keeps his eye firmly fixed upon the lighthouse. He knows that by guiding his ship directly to a specific point, the time spent in discomfort is lessened. And by keeping his eye on the light, there never exists one second of discouragement. My light, my harbor, my future is within sight!

I will persist without exception. I am a person of great faith.

In Jeremiah, my Creator declares, "For I know the plans I have for you, plans to prosper you and not to harm you, plans to give you hope and a future." From this day forward, I will claim a faith in the certainty of my future.

Too much of my life has been spent doubting my beliefs and believing my doubts. No more! I have faith in my future. I do not look left or right. I look forward. I can only persist.

For me, faith will always be a sounder guide than reason because reason can only go so far—faith has no limits. I will expect miracles in my life because faith produces them every day. I will believe in the future that I do not see. That is faith. And the reward of this faith is to see the future that I believed.

I will continue despite exhaustion. I focus on results. I am a person of great faith.

I will persist without exception.

TEN

DAVID TOOK A DEEP BREATH AND EXHALED LOUDLY.
Carefully, he rolled the scroll into a compact shape. Then,
standing, he fished the tobacco pouch from his bulging
blue jeans pocket. For a moment, David paused and ran his
fingers across the smooth fabric of Chamberlain's offhand
present to him.

He touched the two gold buttons holding the pouch
closed and marveled at the craftsmanship that had formed
an eagle on each. With the nail of his forefinger, David
traced the embroidery of crossed swords on the flap. *The
symbol of a fighting man*, he thought. *That's what I am. I am
not a quitter. I am a fighting man.* Suddenly, David smiled. "I
will persist without exception," he said aloud.

Quickly, he unfastened the buttons and squeezed the
small scroll from Gabriel into the pouch. It nestled beside
the words of a king and under the parchment from an
explorer. At a glance, David saw the crisp, white folded

stationery of two presidents, lying together as if filed carefully at the back of the pouch, beside a ragged piece of paper written in a warrior's own hand. On top of it all, David noticed as he compressed the contents and closed the pouch, were four small pages torn from the diary of a little girl.

"Thank you," he murmured as he put the pouch back in his pocket. He was overwhelmed by thoughts of the people he had met. Then David stopped. Mindful of a larger picture, he closed his eyes, bowed his head, and said the same words again. "Thank *You*."

Opening his eyes, David found himself standing in a vast parking lot. He grinned and almost laughed out loud at his *lack* of astonishment. He didn't know where he was yet but was curious to note that he was not afraid or even unsure of himself. Looking around, he idly wondered if he'd ever be shocked by anything again!

It was very cold and obviously nighttime, though extensive lighting brightened the area as if it were the middle of the day. The parking lot, filled with cars, was arranged around a massive steel-and-glass arena standing several hundred yards in the distance. David, feeling strangely drawn to the building, walked toward it.

Threading his way through cars and the occasional tree that landscaped the parking lot, David felt his heart skip a beat when he realized where he was. To his left, rising almost directly over the building to which he was walking, was the Reunion Tower. In the skyline beyond it, David saw the Magnolia Building with its trademark flying red horse on top.

To the right, standing above them all was the Jolly Green Giant. That is the name, he remembered, that Jenny had given this building a week after the green argon lights had been installed to run the full length of the enormous edifice. The structure, the National Bank skyscraper, had for years been the tallest building in Dallas. David was home.

I'm back, David thought as he quickened his steps. But something didn't seem right to him. Continuing to walk toward the arena, David looked again to the Jolly Green Giant. There, no more than a mile beyond it and slightly to the east, was another even taller skyscraper that David didn't recognize. It was a beautiful white granite tower that was lit from the bottom to the top.

David stopped and slowly turned around. He examined the skyline to his north, then back to the east, south, and west. There were other new buildings as well. Frowning, David put his hands on his hips and thought, *What? Dallas has grown overnight?* Walking to the car in front of him, David narrowed his eyes. It was a red Jaguar convertible but shaped unlike any Jaguar he'd seen before. Next to the Jaguar was a burgundy Ford truck and next to it a white Lincoln. They were all different somehow, flashier maybe? A new type of paint?

He turned around again, this time counting eleven buildings that he knew for a fact were not there when . . . David cocked his head, raised his eyebrows, and smiled. He looked back at the Jaguar and laughed out loud. "I get it," he said to the car. "You are at least ten, maybe twenty years newer than anything I've ever seen.

"I'm in the future," David said to himself and began walking once again to the arena. "I'm in the future." He blew out a deep breath and shook his head. "This really ought to be interesting."

Approaching the massive building, David picked his way through a line of taxicabs and stepped up onto a broad side-walk. There were a few people, well dressed and evidently somewhat late, hurriedly making their way through the turnstiles. David walked around for a few minutes, seeing the same scene repeated at every gate. He searched through his pockets, knowing he had no money, but thinking that just possibly a ticket might have magically appeared. *Stranger things have happened,* he thought wryly.

Okay, David thought as he stood looking up at the arena, *I have no ticket, I have no money, I'm freezing to death—what next?* Thinking that perhaps a ticket had been left in his name, David approached the ticket booth to the right of the nearest entryway and spoke to the woman behind the glass. "Excuse me," he said.

She wore a dark green sweater that accented her red hair. The lady was, David determined, in her early to mid-fifties. At the moment, with bifocals perched precariously on the end of her nose, she was speedily counting ticket stubs. As she paused to key in some numbers on her calculator, David tried again. "Excuse me, ma'am." She looked up. Opening his mouth to speak, David realized that she was smiling at a man walking up behind him.

"May I help you?" the ticket lady asked the man as David eased himself to the side. Watching the two interact, he thought, *So I can't be seen in the future either.*

David walked slowly around the arena again. Several times, from inside, he heard the thunderous ovations of what was obviously a very large number of people. He stopped briefly as a small unmarked and unlit side entrance opened a few yards in front of him.

A skinny little man emerged into the dim light. Obviously a janitor, he wore coveralls and carried a push broom. Setting the broom against the concrete wall of the building, the man shook out a ski cap, stretched it over his head, and reached into his pocket for a pipe. As a match flared, David could see more of the man's face. *Old,* he thought.

He was not consciously interested in the man's age. It was just his mind's simple acknowledgment of what his eyes were taking in. David started to walk again in a direction that took him within a few feet of the janitor. The old man glanced up as David approached and nodded, lifting his pipe.

"Good evening," he said. "You doing all right?"

"Fine, thank you," David responded automatically. Then, suddenly excited, he stopped. "Hey! You can see me?"

"Well, yeah. I can see you," the man said, somewhat confused. He placed the pipe back in his mouth. "I ain't blind yet, son. Just because I'm . . ." David had moved closer, and for the first time, the old man got a good look at David's face. "Holy cow!" he said. The pipe, unclenched from the man's teeth, fell from his mouth and rattled on the sidewalk. David quickly bent and retrieved it. "I didn't know you were . . . ," the man stammered. "I am very sorry, sir.

"Thank you very much," the man said as he took the pipe and immediately put it in his pocket. David wondered briefly if it was still lit but didn't ask. He was too curious about the way the old gentleman was acting. "Sir," the old man said, "if you don't mind me asking, are you just here checking everything out? There's a lot of people in there tonight that're mighty grateful to you, sir. My wife's not going to believe this! May I shake your hand, Mr. Ponder? My name is Jack Miller."

Shaking his hand, David asked, "You know who I am?"

"Don't worry," Jack said conspiratorially as he looked left and right. "I understand . . . and I ain't tellin' nobody. I'd want to sneak in here and see this, too, if they was all talking about me! You know, I didn't even recognize you at first. Shoot, with your hair dyed like that, you look like one of your old pictures. Say," he paused, suddenly concerned, "should you be walking around alone like this?"

David smiled slightly with his eyebrows raised. He was trying to take all this in. "I'll be fine," he said. "By the way, do you mind if I go in this door?"

Jack grinned. "Well, I reckon. You built the place. You go in any door you like! Follow me." And with that, the old man shoved his cap back into his pocket, stepped inside, and with a motion of his hand, encouraged David to stay close.

They walked through a short hall and made their way to a large tunnel that seemed to circle the arena underground. David was trying to comprehend the fact that somehow he had, or would *have*, something to do with the presence of this huge place. Striding through the tunnel, Jack waved several times at different groups of workers. They waved, nodded, or called his name in reply. "Your disguise is working great," Jack whispered loudly to David. "Don't nobody even recognize you!"

Well, David thought as he fought to suppress a laugh,

they don't recognize me because they don't see me. You, on the other hand, walking along, waving at everybody, and talking to yourself—you must be a sight to see!

"Hey," Jack said as he skidded to a stop. "I didn't even ask. Where do you want to go? Should I take you to your sky box?"

David shook his head. This was a little much. "I'd just like to wander around a bit by myself. Is that okay?"

Jack looked at David as if he had lost his mind. "Are you sure?" he said. "I can walk around with you if you want."

"No, that won't be necessary. But I really appreciate the offer. And by the way," David added as he stuck out his hand, "it has been an honor to meet you."

"Ha!" Jack snorted as he pumped David's hand vigorously. "An honor to meet me. Wait'll I tell my wife."

David left the old man and continued walking through the tunnel. Presently, he came upon an offshoot ramp that, he saw, led into the main arena. Entering the main floor, David was astonished by the sheer number of people. He had assumed by the size of the building that the seating capacity was very large, but he had, for some reason, never really imagined this place filled. There must have been four thousand people on the floor level alone.

Stepping away from the shadow of the entry ramp, David did a slow turn. He quickly noted the gigantic video screens hung from the ceiling. These were used to bring a large audience close to the action of any event. From his vantage point, David could see that they were certainly needed here. There were fully three decks completely surrounding the main floor, each seat filled to the very top. *Twenty-five thousand people in all?* David thought. *Maybe thirty thousand?*

David had heard cheers and applause several times from outside the arena and twice from the tunnel. The noise inside, he knew, would be deafening. At the moment, however, he was amazed at the virtual silence of the place. No one was walking around or even moving in the seats. No one coughed or cleared a throat. Every person in the arena was focusing every ounce of attention on the stage.

The stage, considering the enormity of its surroundings, was a relatively simple affair. It was elegantly decorated with greenery and six white Roman-style columns that rose from the stage floor to a height of approximately twenty feet. The stage was not positioned at the far end of the arena as one might have expected but, instead, was placed at the wide edge of the floor up against the first rising deck of people. The back of the platform was open so as not to obstruct the view from any angle. The effect was one of a theater-in-the-round.

It was only David's subconscious, however, that noticed anything about the stage itself. His primary attention was drawn to the center of the platform, behind the glass podium. Like the eyes of thousands of others in attendance, David's eyes were riveted to the man who was speaking.

Though standing on the opposite side of the arena, David almost directly faced the stage and was near enough to see that the speaker was a large man. He was at least three inches over six feet tall with a slim build and wore an expensive light gray double-breasted suit. The man appeared to be in his mid-forties and was ruggedly hand-some—striking in a sense—his dark hair contrasting sharply with his suit. And he was crying.

David stared hard at the man, then glanced at a screen nearby to confirm in close-up what he thought he was seeing. Sure enough, there were tears rolling down this big man's face as he said, "It was only six years ago. We were out of money and out of hope. With my nine-year-old daughter lying in the hospital in critical condition, I was still working twenty-hour days, but financially, it wasn't enough. There was no longer any insurance and seemingly no help.

"As I drove my beat-up car home from work that night, I couldn't stop looking at the picture of my little girl that I had lying on the seat beside me. It was a photograph of her when she was in the third grade. I began to let my mind wander around the possibilities involved in helping my family collect the only insurance that remained, the insurance on my life."

David scarcely breathed as he listened, transfixed, to this man's story that was so eerily similar to his own.

"With money to pay the bills and make a new start," he said, the corners of his mouth quivering downward and his voice cracking, "I thought that maybe someday my wife could find a new husband—my child would have a new daddy. One who wouldn't let them down. I thought that maybe I could still give my family the life they deserved.

"I pulled off the side of the road, and as I sat there alone and thinking, I took the photograph of my child and held it in my hands. I could imagine the tubes running in and out of her body. I closed my eyes and could hear the respirator forcing air into her lungs. And suddenly, I felt ashamed!

"I felt ashamed for ever thinking of leaving her, for ever thinking of quitting. Yes, I felt ashamed. But I also felt strong again because I knew that this was a point in my life to which the First Decision truly applied. I looked at my child, my blood, my responsibility in that picture, and I said, 'The buck stops here. If you can fight that hard for your life, then surely I can fight as hard for your future!'"

David had been so unnerved by the reference to the Seven Decisions and so caught up in what this man was pouring from his heart that he was startled by the sudden and thunderous ovation. People all over the arena stood and clapped, applauding the honesty and courage of this man while he stood there, uncomfortably waiting for them to finish, tears streaming down his face.

As the applause died away and the audience settled back into their seats, David saw a single empty chair on the aisle, less than fifteen rows from the stage. Walking quickly, he moved to take the seat. He eased himself down and looked back up to the podium as the speaker continued.

"It was a simple choice really. A choice made under duress. But now, of course, our lives have been transformed—financially, emotionally, spiritually—literally transformed in every way. My family has been set free. You see, it wasn't enough that I possessed the Seven Decisions for Success or even that I understood their meaning. The moment I decided to make them a part of my life was the moment that the future of my family was secured for generations."

The man paused to drink from a glass of water. He wiped his eyes with a handkerchief and moved beside the podium. Resting his left elbow on its surface, he gestured with his right hand and said, "Think with me now. It is true that most of us have a rather limited view of the world, its history, and our own ability to affect the outcome of anything beyond our neighborhoods. In terms of personal history and legacy, we tend to restrict our concern to only three—some of us four—generations.

The vast majority of us do not even know the first names of our great-grandparents!

"Some years ago now, but well within the scope of our own generation, David Ponder bestowed upon the world the gift of the *possibility* of success for anyone. Our presence here tonight is evidence of the fruit of that gift. But I am here to challenge you to grasp a future that is far beyond your present thoughts and actions.

"There comes a time in every person's life when a decision is required. And that decision, should you make it, will have a far-reaching effect on generations yet unborn. There is a thin thread that weaves only from you to hundreds of thousands of lives. Your example, your actions, and yes, even one decision can literally change the world. Let me say that one more time. One decision, that *you* make, can literally change the world."

The speaker curiously held eye contact with the audience for several seconds after his last statement. Then he slipped back behind the podium and drank from his glass again. Replacing the glass under the podium, he regarded the crowd with a chuckle. "You know," he began, "it is an amazing feeling to be doubted by thousands of people at once!" He smiled as the crowd reacted with warm laughter of their own. "Okay, I'm going to try this again! One decision, that *you* make, can literally change the world!"

And with that, the man moved to the edge of the stage

and began animatedly telling a story. David sat spellbound as the speaker moved over every inch of the platform, involving the audience in front of him, behind him, and those at the very top of the arena. The story he told, though it had happened more than a century earlier, was absolutely accurate in its detail. David knew this to be true because he had been there.

"July second, eighteen sixty-three. It was a hot, humid day, and a schoolteacher from Maine was in the fight of his life.

"His name was Joshua Lawrence Chamberlain, formerly a professor of rhetoric from Bowdoin College, presently a thirty-four-year-old colonel in the Union army. The place? Gettysburg, Pennsylvania."

The speaker then described the dangerous situation Chamberlain's troops faced that day as they tried to hold their position against General Lee's men, the Army of Northern Virginia. After five bloody attacks from the Rebels, Chamberlain realized his troops would not be able to hold them off any longer.

The speaker explained, "More than half his regiment was dead, and many of his remaining soldiers were wounded. He was outnumbered by better than five to one, and the last skirmish had taken place on both sides of the wall, face-to-face. He didn't know how they had pushed the Rebels back down the hill. Some of his men, he later wrote, had been punching the enemy with their fists.

"As they quickly surveyed the situation, it became apparent that there were less than two bullets per man remaining. For all intents and purposes, the Twentieth Maine was out of ammunition. Glancing downhill and seeing the attackers readying themselves for a final assault, looking at what seemed to be certain defeat, certain death, Chamberlain's own officers counseled retreat. 'They outnumber us,' the men cried, 'and we have nothing with which to fight. It is hopeless. It is hopeless.'

"Joshua Chamberlain stood quietly for a moment. 'Here they come, sir,' a sergeant said urgently. Chamberlain didn't respond. He was calculating the cost of freezing, remaining, staying where he was. The cost, he determined, was essentially the same as running away.

"'Joshua!' It was his first lieutenant, his brother Tom. 'Joshua!' he screamed. 'Give an order!'

"And so he did. Chamberlain knew he had not been put on this earth to fail. But failure is the only possible result of a life that accepts the status quo. We move forward, or we die! 'Fix bayonets!' he barked. And his men looked at him as if he were crazy.

"'Excuse me, sir?' the sergeant asked, and for a moment, they all just stood there and stared.

"'They're coming!' came a yell from down the line.

"'Fix bayonets, I said!' he yelled. 'And charge!' As his men scrambled to fasten their steels, Chamberlain drew his sword and jumped to the top of the wall. With the enemy now a little more than fifty yards away, he pointed his sword at them and screamed, 'Charge! Charge!' and the fighting men of the Twentieth Maine Regiment, the pride of the Army of the Potomac, poured over the wall and followed a schoolteacher into history!

"The Confederate troops, upon seeing the leader of the opposition mount the wall, immediately stopped, unsure as to what was happening. But when Chamberlain pointed his sword toward them and commanded his men to charge, they literally turned and ran. Many threw down their loaded weapons. They were certain that these were not the same soldiers they had been facing. Surely, there had been massive reinforcements. In their minds, it was *not even within the realm of possibility* that a beaten regiment would charge.

"In less than ten minutes, the ragged group of men under Chamberlain's command, without any ammunition at all at this point, captured the entire regiments of the Fifteenth Alabama and the Forty-seventh Alabama, more than four hundred men. Of course, it all happened because one man made a decision to charge.

"And one decision, that *you* make, can literally change the world."

The audience leaped out of their seats with a roar, David with them, clapping and cheering the truth, as they saw it, of the speaker's final statement. *The story of Joshua Chamberlain had inspired them, and rightly so,* David thought. It *was* an incredible event in our nation's history, and as he well knew, the speaker had been exacting in his details.

As the applause died away, David realized that the tall speaker was still on stage. In fact, he had crossed his arms and was leaning both elbows heavily on the podium. A slight smile on his face, he appeared to be patiently waiting. When the last person had settled back into his seat, and the arena was again enveloped in silence, his smile broadened. "You-all thought I was through, didn't you?"

David laughed with everyone else.

"Well, see now," he began again, "I just couldn't leave you thinking what you're thinking. And I *know,*" he said with a laugh, "what you're thinking!" He moved out to the far edge of the stage. "You're thinking, *Okay. That was a great story, but you're telling me I can change the world? Come on!* You say, 'Hey! Even Joshua Chamberlain changed the outcome of only one small part of one battle!' Oh, really? Well, consider this.

"It is an accepted fact that, at the time of the Battle of Gettysburg, the North—the Union—was losing badly. Confederate troops had taken Fort Sumter, then routed the Union army at Manassas. Lee's men won major victories at Richmond in the Battles of the Seven Days and once again at Manassas in the Second Battle of Bull

Run. The South defeated General Hooker's divisions at Chancellorsville and dealt a crushing blow to General Burnside at Fredericksburg.

"Had the South been victorious at Gettysburg, historians agree that the entire conflict would have been over by the end of the summer. The Confederate States of America were one victory away from winning the war. But they didn't win.

"The schoolteacher from Maine was awarded the Congressional Medal of Honor for his decision at Little Round Top. His commanding officers determined that the actions of this one man saved the Union army from being destroyed—this one man turned the tide of the battle. Joshua Lawrence Chamberlain turned the tide of the war.

"Do you understand what this means? If the South had won the war, there would be no America as we know it now. There would be at least two, possibly three countries existing in our place. The world would not have a country big enough and strong enough to feed the other nations of this planet. There would not be a superpower available to defend weaker societies against those that would limit their freedom. But because one ordinary man made a decision to move forward, this is a very different world we live in today.

"When Hitler swept across Europe, when Hirohito systematically invaded the islands of the Pacific, when Saddam

Hussein rolled his armies into Kuwait, there existed a *United States of America* to stand in the breach. And we were there because of one man with his back to the wall. A man who, on that hot day in July, was in fear for his very life. A man whose only option seemed to be retreat. Ladies and gentlemen, the world as it exists today is largely the result of a decision to charge—one decision made by a schoolteacher more than a hundred years ago!

"Don't you *ever* think that you can't change things! You can! You can! One decision, that *you* make, can change the world!"

Once more the entire arena was on its feet. David was stunned. As he clapped, he couldn't get over the incredible chain of events that had been set in motion by one man. *What had happened to Chamberlain?* he wondered. As the crowd quieted and resettled, the speaker continued, and David found out.

"It is a fact that people follow a man who simply says, 'Follow me.' By taking leadership, ironically, a person *deserves* leadership. As you lead others to success and a life of their dreams, the life you seek and deserve will be revealed unto you.

"Joshua Chamberlain made a decision that changed our world, yes, but his decision also held personal rewards. He led successful campaigns until the end of the war. He was cited by our government four separate times for bravery in action and was promoted to brigadier general for heroism at Petersburg, this by special order of Ulysses S. Grant. Then, only a few months later, for heroism at Five Forks, he was promoted to major general.

"Among all Union officers, President Abraham Lincoln chose Chamberlain to have the honor of accepting the Confederate surrender at Appomattox. There, he stunned the world with a show of forgiveness and respect as he ordered his troops to attention, saluting General Robert E. Lee and the defeated South.

"Back home, in Maine, Chamberlain was elected governor in what is, to this day, the largest majority in the history of the state. He was reelected three times until finally, he stepped down and accepted a role of leadership at his alma mater, as president of Bowdoin College.

"Incidentally, an interesting benefit of a person's decision to charge, one that has been somewhat overlooked by scholars and historians, is the presence of a hedge of thorns. Mentioned first in the Bible, a hedge of thorns is the divine protection placed upon a person who is destined to make a difference. Until you have accomplished what you were put here to do, you will not—you cannot—be harmed. Joshua Chamberlain, on that hill in Pennsylvania, with his decision to charge not yet made and all his victories before him, was wrapped in the protection of a hedge of thorns."

The dark-haired speaker reached into the inside pocket of his jacket and brought out a small piece of paper. Holding it up for everyone to see, he said, "I have here a copy of a letter addressed to the Honorable Governor Joshua L. Chamberlain. It arrived at the statehouse several years after the war." He unfolded the page, smoothed it out on top of the podium, and read,

"Dear Sir: I want to tell you of a little passage in the Battle of Round Top, Gettysburg, concerning you and me, which I am now glad of. Twice in that fight I had your life in my hands. I got a safe place between two rocks, and drew bead fair and square on you. You were standing in the open behind the center of your line, full exposed. I knew your rank by your uniform and actions, and I thought it a mighty good thing to put you out of the way. I rested my gun on the rock and took steady aim. I started to pull the trigger, but some queer notion stopped me. Then I got ashamed of my weakness and went through the same motions again. I had you, perfectly certain. But that same queer something shut right down on me. I couldn't pull the trigger, and, gave it up—that is, your life. I am glad of it now, and hope you are. Yours truly, A Member of the Fifteenth Alabama."

Slowly, the speaker refolded the paper as chills ran through the audience. He tucked it back into his jacket pocket and moved to the very edge of the stage. David felt the man look directly at him as he said softly, "You, too, at this very moment are living under the protection of a hedge of thorns. You might feel fear, but it is an illusion. Until you have accomplished what you were put on this earth to do, you will not—you cannot—be harmed."

Then he held his arms up in a broad gesture to the crowd. "My friends, it all comes down to this. Your story, your circumstances, your timing may not be as dramatic as those of Joshua Chamberlain, but the stakes are exactly the same. There comes a time in every person's life when a decision is required. And that decision, should you make it, will have a far-reaching effect on generations yet unborn. There is a thin thread that weaves from only you to hundreds of thousands of lives. Your example, your actions, and yes, even one decision that you make *will* literally change the world.

"A decision . . . to charge." He paused. "So do it. Change your life. Change your family's future. Change the world. Charge." The audience didn't breathe. The tall man held them with his eyes. In a softer voice, he said, "Charge." Again a pause, then a whisper, "Charge."

For what seemed an eternity, but in reality must have been only several seconds, no one moved. Then in an explosion of sound both sudden and deafening, thousands rose as one, not only cheering this man who had brought a message of hope and instruction, but also celebrating their future. The applause continued on and on until the speaker, whom David had watched disappear into the tunnel entrance, returned to the stage. He waved, acknowledging their appreciation. David smiled as the man's eyebrows raised in apparent surprise at the intensity of the ovation. He waved again, turning in all directions, and then quickly was gone.

There were a few brief announcements over the public address system, but the evening, apparently, was over. David stood to the side as the lines of men and women filed out. He looked carefully at their faces and saw determination, tears of understanding and relief, and a peace that can come only from certainty.

In less than thirty minutes, the arena was empty. After one last look, David entered the tunnel, found an exit, and walked out into the frigid night.

Walking aimlessly along the sidewalk, David watched the red taillights of cars as they jockeyed for space exiting the parking lot. He looked again at the skyline of the city, so familiar and yet so different. It occurred to David as he strolled along that he didn't have any idea as to his next move. *Am I supposed to meet someone else?* he wondered. *Look for something? Go somewhere?*

Without any conscious purpose, David veered off the sidewalk and into the parking lot. The night air was clear, and though he was cold, he felt well physically. *In fact,* David thought, *I've never felt better.* He surveyed the huge empty space; black asphalt and white lines seemed to continue forever.

It had been well over an hour since the event had ended, and all the cars were gone—except one. There, straight in front of him sixty or seventy yards away, in the shadows of a tree, sat one car. David shook his head and walked directly to it. It was one very familiar car. Small, mostly faded silver except for the right fender, which was black. It was his two-door Dodge Colt. "Uh-huh," David said aloud as he approached. "And I'll bet the heater and brake lights *still* don't work."

The car was open, and not surprisingly, the keys swung from the ignition. David squeezed himself into the tiny car, noticing the black windbreaker he'd thrown into the backseat . . . when? This morning? It was too confusing to think about. He turned the key, and the little engine sputtered to life. David reached above the sun visor, and yes, there was his watch with its cheap gold band stretched around his wallet. "Wow!" he said and smiled as he put the watch on his wrist and placed the wallet in the passenger seat beside him.

So where to? he thought as the car idled loudly. Looking around, he saw that the beautiful white skyscraper he'd noticed earlier was framed perfectly in the right rear window. "Okay," David said softly as he put the Colt into gear.

He made a series of turns out of the parking lot and soon

was headed in the general direction of the white tower. Every now and then, David could see it appear between other buildings and through trees. It was easy to locate. After all, it was the tallest building in the city.

When he found the last street that led to the object of his brief search, David stopped the car. He stared at the street sign but wasn't sure he could believe his eyes. He glanced around. It was well past midnight. There were no other cars around just then, and so he opened his door and got out. He quickly walked to the corner and peered closely up at the sign. Silently, he turned around and walked back to the car. He eased it into gear, took a deep breath, and made a right onto David Ponder Boulevard.

There, directly in front of him, was the enormous white building. Oak trees lined the boulevard on either side, and as David got closer, he was awed by a majestic fountain spraying water high into the air near the main entrance. He found himself unable to take his eyes off the architectural masterpiece, and when he reached it, he simply stopped the car by the curb and got out.

David slowly wandered across an open expanse of gray rough-hewn marble. It covered an area of at least thirty yards from the street and was laid around the entire circumference of the structure. At night, because of the reflection of the building and its ambient light, the dark stone looked wet.

He walked to a series of five revolving doors at the main entrance. They were locked. Easing to the right, David put his face to the glass and looked inside, holding his hands around his eyes to shield the glare. The whole main floor seemed to be a reception area, a lobby, that was capped by its own dome at about the fifth level. Huge palms, at least twenty-five feet tall, were growing in colossal earthenware pots. They were arranged between the doors of six glass elevators, which were all poised at the bottom, waiting for their morning passengers.

Great tapestries hung on the walls from the ceiling to the lush carpet below. The centerpiece, in the middle of this spectacular main floor, was a waterfall cascading more than forty feet from a single granite boulder. It fell into a koi pond that wrapped around the elevator shaft and ended at the foot of a large stone concierge desk that looked as if it would require six to ten receptionists. Carved into the stone, on the front of the desk facing the entrance, were the words: PONDER INTERNATIONAL.

David moved away from the glass. He was not really surprised. Excited, yes, but not surprised. He was coming to grips with the reality of his successful future. *There is a thin thread that weaves from only you to hundreds of thousands of lives,* David remembered. *Well,* he thought, *there are a few of those lives working in this building.*

David moved back to his car, stopping briefly by the

fountain. A sign there read: "Coins donated in this fountain are used in support of the Jenny Ponder Zoological Gardens, City of Dallas." He smiled and went to the car.

For a while, David drove randomly and found the streets mostly empty and the city very quiet. Finding himself near the interstate, without really thinking about it, he turned onto the freeway. He drove for more than an hour to nowhere in particular. He spotted the Ellen Ponder Children's Hospital from an overpass, exited, and sat in its parking lot for several minutes.

David drove past the empty and boarded-up building that had been Marshall's Hardware. Apparently, it had been closed for years. As if on automatic pilot, he steered into his neighborhood and saw the name "McClain" on his old mailbox. The dogwoods he and Jenny had planted beside the house had grown as high as the roof.

He saw the church they attended, passed Jenny's elementary school, and noted with a shake of his head that the chemical plant where he'd worked for so many years had changed ownership again.

Before long, with no specific intent, David found himself back on the interstate headed out of the city. He was, he knew, a very different man. When he took the Grayton exit, he was only vaguely aware that he'd been there before. His mind whirled with thoughts of Truman and his piercing, clear blue eyes. He glanced at the speedometer. It read seventy.

He remembered Solomon's throne and smiled faintly. The king had said it was only a chair!

There were no other vehicles in sight. The headlights of the little car burst through the darkness like cannon fire on a Pennsylvania hilltop. He pressed harder on the accelerator and saw certainty in a sea captain's face as the man watched the horizon. Eighty . . . eighty-five. Anne. That dear, sweet little girl. "Papa says, 'Fear is a poor chisel with which to carve out tomorrow.'"

As he flew over hills and around curves, David became oblivious to his speed. *I spoke to Abraham Lincoln,* he thought. *He spoke to me.* "The secret of forgiveness costs nothing and is worth millions." David's mind was racing at a furious pace. "You are the last traveler," the angel said. "You have been given a gift that has the power to change your civilization. Everything from this moment on will key upon you."

At that instant, David Ponder's destiny intersected with an icy bridge. Covering a small stream, the bridge was still no more than fifty feet long, and the same black ice sent the speeding car careening into a spin. Tires screeching, David's car bounced off the guardrail as he crossed the short bridge and found that he remained on the highway.

Interestingly, David did *not* fight desperately for control as the car fishtailed from side to side and finally swerved off the road. He watched the scene unfold from inside the vehicle as if in slow motion. He wanted to remember everything, especially as the car careened helplessly toward a giant oak tree. With his remaining conscious thought, David gripped the steering wheel and closed his eyes. He heard the speaker in the arena say, "Until you have accomplished what you were put on this earth to do, you will not—you cannot—be harmed!"

And then . . . nothing.

ELEVEN

"HONEY? DAVID?" DAVID'S VISION WAS BLURRY AS
he tried to focus on the person in front of him. "David, it's
Ellen. Can you hear me?"

He heard another voice, a man. "It may take some time,
Mrs. Ponder." Everyone sounded so far away.

"Daddy, I love you." Jenny?

"David. This is Ellen. Sweetheart, I'm right here."

David felt his wife's hand on his face as his eyes cleared
somewhat. He could see her hand now and her face. Her
beautiful face. "Ellen," he managed to rasp out. Oh, brother,
he had a headache! "Ellen," he said again and tried to
reach for her.

"I'm here, honey," she said as she pushed his arm down.
"Please don't move." She had tears running down her face.
"David, you've been in an accident. You're in the hospital."

"Don't cry," David said groggily. "We're going to be
okay." He began to sit up.

Ellen gently forced him back. "Yes, honey," she said. "You're going to be fine, but you have a concussion. David, please be still."

His vision and hearing seemed to come and go, closer and farther, softer and louder. "No," he said with an effort. "I don't mean me. I mean *us*. We're going to be okay, our family. Where's Jenny?"

"She's right here."

"I'm here, Daddy," she said as she came to the bed. "I love you."

"I love you too. How is your throat?"

"Hurts some, but not horrible."

David reached up to touch her silky hair. "We will fix your throat, baby. I promise. Ellen?" He called his wife's name more loudly than he'd intended, and it startled everyone in the room.

"I'm here, David. I'm right here." She was still holding his hand and had not moved from his side.

"Ellen, we are going to be okay. I know things now. I went to places that . . ."

And suddenly, he woke up. In a matter of several seconds, David's head cleared and his vision sharpened. He looked around and, seeing his wife, daughter, and a short man in a white coat huddled over him, asked, "Where am I?"

"You're in the hospital, honey," Ellen answered. "You were in an accident."

"Am I . . . ?"

"You will recover, Mr. Ponder." The short man moved forward. "I'm Doctor Green. You are a very lucky man, sir."

"I hit a tree."

"Yes, you did," the doctor replied, "And actually, that is a very significant sign in our favor, the fact that you remember anything at all. You have suffered a severe concussion. Do you remember anything else?"

"I had been at the arena."

Ellen furrowed her eyebrows. "No, honey," she said. "You had been at work. David, why were you so far out of town?"

The doctor placed his hand on her shoulder. "Mrs. Ponder," he interrupted, "there will be quite a few jumbled thoughts for a while. Confusing dreams, misplaced conversations." He smiled at David and shrugged. "That is one nasty lick to the head you have, but all in all, I can honestly say, I've never seen anything like it. The skull is not fractured. The paramedics who brought you in said you'd been thrown from the car, and yet so far, except for the concussion, we haven't found so much as one broken bone. Yes, sir. I'd say that you are one extremely lucky man."

As the doctor went on about what to expect as he healed and which medicines would be prescribed and why and how long he could plan on staying in the hospital, David watched his wife and child. He was a lucky man, he knew, but a curious disappointment settled over him like a fog. A dream. It had all been a dream. A confusing dream, the doctor had called it.

". . . and of course, we just take our time with these things," the doctor was finishing. "So, why don't we leave for a little while and let your dad get some rest?" he said to Jenny.

"I'll take Jenny home, honey," Ellen said. "Mom and Dad have come in to help so they're at the house. As soon as I drop her off, I'll be back." Ellen carefully kissed David on the cheek and turned to leave. "I love you," she added.

David saw that the doctor had already slipped out of the room. A tear rolled down his cheek. "I love you, too, Ellen. I'm sorry for all this."

She moved back to the bed and positioned herself over him so that she could look directly into his eyes. "David, you have nothing to be sorry about. Jenny and I love you and trust you and want you back home. Do you remember telling me a few minutes ago that our family was going to be okay?" She smiled. "Well, you were right."

David lay alone in the small hospital room. Ellen had kissed him again before she left. He listened to the click of her heels and the squeak of Jenny's tennis shoes fade away down the hall. A *dream*, he thought. He sighed deeply.

He wasn't sleepy. His body throbbed and his head still hurt, but he wasn't sleepy. He looked above the sink beside the bed to find the source of a quiet beeping. It was a monitor of some kind. On the other side of the bed, a tube snaked its way from a plastic bag of solution hanging on a pole down to his arm, where, David was certain, a needle meant for some large animal had been mistakenly inserted into him.

There was a small cot over in the corner. Had Ellen been sleeping there? How long had he been here? A television was attached to the wall across from him. There was an extra door that led to what he assumed was the bathroom, and except for a chair under the television, that was it. *Nothing to look at,* he thought. So he looked at the ceiling.

It had all seemed so real. He had been there! He just *knew* he'd been in Potsdam. He had been in Amsterdam and with Columbus on the *Santa Maria*. He hadn't been in a car accident—he'd been in two! But no one would ever believe him, David knew, and considering his surroundings, he wasn't sure he believed it himself.

Anyway, David thought, *it wasn't the experience that was important, was it? What did I learn? Even if it had been a dream, did the Seven Decisions for Success have less value?* David smiled when he realized that by concentrating just a bit, he could recall the key phrases and basic philosophy of each principle.

Not trusting himself to remember them for long, David

found a pen and writing pad on the small table beside him.
He raised himself into a sitting position and wrote:

1. The buck stops here. I am responsible for my past
   and my future.

2. I will seek wisdom. I will be a servant to others.

3. I am a person of action. I seize this moment. I
   choose now.

4. I have a decided heart. My destiny is assured.

5. Today I will choose to be happy. I am the possessor
   of a grateful spirit.

6. I will greet this day with a forgiving spirit. I will
   forgive myself.

7. I will persist without exception. I am a person of
   great faith.

David reread what he had written and nodded his head.
He was tired. He would work more on this later—remember
more later. He placed the pen and paper on the table next
to him. David intended to reconstruct every decision and
commit them to his heart as Gabriel had told him to do. He
took a deep breath, sighed, and corrected himself . . . as he
had dreamed Gabriel had told him to do.

No matter, David thought as he stared at the ceiling. *My
family will be fine. Our future is assured. I will make it so.* The

pebbled surface of the ceiling, reflecting tiny points of light, reminded David of stars. He closed his eyes. Maybe he was sleepy, after all.

Just as he was about to drift off, David heard the slight whoosh of the door opening. A nurse entered. "I am so sorry," she said. "I didn't mean to wake you."

"No problem," David said. "I wasn't really asleep."

"You just keep resting then," she said kindly. "I'll leave this right here and get out of your way." She had a dark plastic bag in her hand, and she moved to place it in the chair.

"What is that?" David asked.

"Personal effects. Wallet and stuff. Shoes. Everything you were wearing when you had your accident. They brought it up from Emergency."

"Could I have the bag over here, please?" David asked. "I'd like to put on my watch."

"I can do that," the nurse said as she put the bag on the edge of the bed beside David. "And your watch is in here," she smiled. "We have to inventory everything, you know, and I saw it myself."

"Thank you," David said as she left the room.

He opened the bag and pulled out his shoes. His socks were stuffed in one and his boxers in the other. They were resting on his sweatshirt and jeans, which someone had neatly folded. David dropped the shoes and clothes to the floor on the other side of the bed.

David's wedding band had fallen out with the clothes and was resting on the white sheet. He placed it on his finger and reached back into the bag for his watch, found it, and stretched the band onto his wrist. His key ring was in the bag. And his wallet. *Wasn't my wallet on the seat beside me?* David tried to remember. *Oh, well,* he thought. *Thanks to someone for getting it out of the car.* He put the wallet on the table.

Lifting the plastic bag to move it from the bed, David felt a slight heaviness. Realizing he'd missed something, he stopped and reopened it. At first, he didn't see anything. But there, stuck in the corner, was a small dark object, almost the color of the plastic bag.

Scarcely daring to breathe, David felt his heart pound as he reached through the folds of plastic and removed a small tobacco pouch. Tears welled up in his eyes as he held it up in the light.

It was navy blue and had been sewn from stout cloth, but the rough treatment it had received had worn the pouch to a moleskin softness. It was beaten and threadbare, but it was still handsome, regal in a sense, the possession of an officer. The two gold buttons that closed the flap were metal, engraved with the image of an eagle. And there, just above the buttons, embroidered on the flap, were crossed swords—the symbol of a fighting man.

ACKNOWLEDGEMENTS

I WOULD LIKE TO THANK POLLY, MY WIFE AND BEST friend, for the patience shown during endless conversations about this project; David Brokaw for his support and belief in me; Scott Jeffrey for his creative presentation strategies; Mike Hyatt, Pamela Clements, Blythe McIntosh, and the team at Thomas Nelson who didn't just contract for a book, but caught a vision! Thanks to Jenny Baumgartner for her editing skills, and the people skills she used on me as she edited! An extra measure of gratitude to Belinda Bass for the extra time and care she took in designing the cover.

Special thanks go to Sandi Dorff, Isabel Garcia, Alex McCurley, Susie White, Paula Tebbe, and Julie Plato—the people who, in support of my life, made this book possible. And finally, a very special thanks to Danita Allen, who shaped the story and my words from the beginning.

BIBLIOGRAPHY

America's Civil War. Leesburg, VA: Primedia Enthusiast Publications History Group, January, 1999.

Becker, Walt. *Link*. New York: William Morrow and Company, Inc. NY, 1998.

Chamberlain, Joshua Lawrence. *Bayonet Forward, My Civil War Reminiscences*. Gettysburg, PA: Stan Clark Military Books, 1994.

Chamberlain, Joshua Lawrence. *Through Blood and Fire at Gettysburg*. Gettysburg, PA: Stan Clark Military Books, 1994.

Compton's Interactive Encyclopedia. Cambridge, MA: The Learning Company.

Desjardin, Thomas A. *Stand Firm Ye Boys From Maine*. Gettysburg, PA: Thomas Publications, 1995.

Dyson, John. *Westward with Columbus*. New York: Simon and Schuster, Inc. New York: 1991.

Encarta. Redmond, Washington: Microsoft Corporation, 1997.

Frank, Anne. *The Diary of a Young Girl*. New York: Doubleday, 1995.

Gies, Miep. *Anne Frank Remembered*. New York: Simon and Schuster, Inc., 1987.

Hobson, Alan. *One Step Beyond*. Banff Alberta Canada: Altitude Publishing, 1992.

Mason, John. *An Enemy Called Average*. Tulsa, OK: John Mason, 1990.

Mason, John. *Conquering An Enemy Called Average*. Tulsa, OK: Insight International, 1996.

Mason, John L. *You're Born an Original Don't Die a Copy*. Altamonte Springs, FL: Insight International, 1993.

McCullough, David. *Truman*. New York: Simon and Schuster, Inc., 1992.

Muller, Melissa. *Anne Frank—the Biography*. New York: Henry Holt and Company, 1998.

Persico, Joseph E. *My Enemy My Brother, Men and Days of Gettysburg*. New York: Macmillan Publishing Company, 1977.

Phillips, Donald T. *Lincoln On Leadership*. New York: Warner Books, 1992.

Pullen, John J. *The Twentieth Maine*. Dayton, OH: Morningside House, Inc., 1957.

Shaara, Michael. *The Killer Angels*. New York: The Ballantine Publishing Group, 1974.

The Living Bible. Wheaton, IL: Tyndale House Publishers, Inc., 1971.

Wills, Garry. *Lincoln at Gettysburg, The Words That Remade America*. New York: Touchstone, 1992.

World Book Encyclopedia. Chicago, IL: World Book, Inc., 1993.

Mastering the

SEVEN DECISIONS

That Determine Personal Success

To Maryann and Jerry Tyler of Roswell, Georgia

I am so grateful for the love, wisdom, belief, patience, and example you have shown me throughout the years.

CONTENTS

PREFACE

When *The Traveler's Gift* was released in 2002, no one knew what to expect. After all, even the bookstores could not decide upon the section in which the book would be displayed. Neither, evidently, could the media.

As ABC's *Good Morning America* promoted the book, it began to appear on every bestseller list in the country. *The Traveler's Gift* was on the *New York Times* list in the fiction category. At the same time, *Wall Street Journal* listed it as *non*-fiction. It was "self-improvement" at Barnes & Noble, "literature" on Amazon.com, "religion" in *Publisher's Weekly*, and "general content" in *USA Today*. Finally, the *New York Times* changed *The Traveler's Gift* to their "advice" list, back to their "fiction" list, and lastly to the "business" list, where it stayed for seventeen weeks.

Publisher's Weekly, in a mistake they had never previously made, reviewed *The Traveler's Gift* twice. And (you guessed it) the reviews disagreed! The first review noted that the book was bland and uninteresting. Then, the very next week, another review—highlighted this time—called me "an author to watch" and said that I had done "an exemplary job" and that the book "would ring true with a broad spectrum of readers!"

I was not really surprised by the confusion. Twenty-five years of researching these Seven Decisions have not made them easier for me to label. They do, however, prove their value every time I personally put one to work or observe them in the lives of others.

Can you imagine? Every single time I have harnessed or watched someone harness these decisions, they work! Why? Because they're principles . . . and principles always work.

What you are about to read is not a work based on seven ideas or seven theories. These are not seven habits. They aren't even mine! I didn't invent or discover them. I merely identified them and have spent more than two decades proving their value.

So, as you read, be aware that principles work every time—and they work whether you know them or not. You've heard "ignorance of the law is no excuse"? Well, ignorance of principle is no protection from the principle. Just because one doesn't understand gravity does not mean that the principle won't affect him if he stumbles off a cliff.

You hold in your hands more than twenty-five years of personal research. I have come to the conclusion that the principles of personal success—parenting, relationships, financial achievement—are floating around just like the principle of gravity. Therefore, why shouldn't we learn them and harness them to create the future of our choosing?

Get ready to have fun . . . and let's get started!

—ANDY ANDREWS
Orange Beach, Alabama

INTRODUCTION
Creating the Life You Choose

Discovering the Seven Decisions

In *The Traveler's Gift*, David Ponder finds himself in a difficult predicament: he's lost his job, his twelve-year-old daughter is sick, and he can't afford to pay for treatment. After a devastating car crash, Ponder is teleported to an adventure of discovery where he meets seven prominent historical figures, each of whom gives Ponder a separate decision he can make that will change his life.

We're not all so fortunate to be offered an escape from the pain and drama of life. I know I wasn't. I grew up in a typical middle-class family—my parents loved me, I loved them, and life was great . . . until I turned nineteen. Then, in a one-two punch that sent me reeling, my mom died of cancer and my dad was killed in a car accident.

Obviously, I was devastated. My confusion and grief quickly turned into anger. I didn't have a lot of extended family or friends to lean on for support; therefore I managed to take a terrible situation and make it infinitely worse. Because I was filled with bitterness and unanswerable questions, a series of bad choices led me to a life of homelessness (at least a decade before "homeless" was even a word). No one from whom to borrow fifty dollars, no house, no car, no job, and, seemingly, no future.

Often spending nights under the state pier in my newly adopted hometown of Gulf Shores, Alabama, and in and out of the garages of unknowing homeowners, I bitterly remembered an old adage from childhood: "God will put a man after His own heart where He wants him to be." I remember thinking, *Thanks, You put me under a pier.*

Feeling desperate and helpless, I couldn't shake this one question, and it relentlessly plagued my mind: *Is life just a lottery ticket?*

How does person A end up with a healthy family and a job he loves, while person B ends up living under a pier? Does life come down to the luck of the draw? *If life is indeed a lottery ticket,* I thought, *and this is my ticket, perhaps I might just quit.* These were my first thoughts of suicide.

Man, I would have felt lucky to be teleported somewhere . . . anywhere! Instead, I was doing odd jobs, like cleaning fish and washing boats, and I had a lot of time on my hands that I often passed at the library. My free library card was my ticket to a new dimension—a world of endless possibilities, filled with extraordinary heroes from all walks of life.

Over the next couple of years, I read between two and three hundred biographies of happy, successful, influential people who, in their unique ways, changed the world. Some of these individuals amassed fortunes, but money wasn't what inspired me about them. I wanted to find people who enjoyed contentment, happiness, and success in life as parents, friends, business owners, or leaders.

Somewhere in that library, my self-pity turned to passion. I was on a mission to find out how they did it. What was special about *them*? How did they end up so lucky? Did they do something specific? Follow a formula? Was it their religion or social standing? I wanted to believe that life wasn't just a lottery ticket, influenced by a roll of the dice. I read that Albert Einstein didn't like the idea of random chance—the notion that God played dice—so who was I to disagree with Einstein?

Seek, and Ye Shall Find

Ask, and it shall be given you; seek, and ye shall find; knock, and it shall be opened unto you.

—MATTHEW 7:7 KJV

The first fifty biographies I read included Winston Churchill, George Washington Carver, Joshua Chamberlain, Will Rogers, Joan of Arc, Abraham Lincoln, and Viktor Frankl. I began to notice patterns—common threads that appeared to be woven through each historical account. These great men and women perceived the world in a similar way and were driven by similar belief systems with similar principles that guided their actions and interactions with the world.

I hunted intensely for clues, curiously discovering seven factors—seven clearly identifiable principles—that were embodied by each person, revealed in a diverse range of biographical accounts.

In some cases, these seven principles were inspired by arduous circumstances; in others, the individual seemed to learn the principles as children.

I wondered if I would be able to live these principles daily, even though I hadn't learned of them early in life. What if *I* mastered them? Would *my life* be worth writing about one day?

That day I became a lab rat in my own experiment that continues to this very moment. Over the next twenty years, I spent every day integrating the Seven Decisions into my life, and talking about them with others. I've had friends say, "Well, you have certainly been successful because of these Seven Decisions." I suppose one's perception of my success depends upon one's definition, but I can tell you this: *for some reason, I have become one of the greatest audiences to success the world has ever seen.*

For various reasons, I've had the opportunity to spend time with four different U.S. presidents. I've talked quietly with Bob Hope by his backyard swimming pool. I've walked through the woods with General Norman Schwarzkopf. I've hung out on buses with Garth Brooks, Kenny Rogers, and Randy Travis, and spent time backstage with Cher and Joan Rivers in Las Vegas. I've eaten lunches with Bart Starr, walked golf courses with Nancy Lopez, and eaten breakfast privately in Dublin with the director of the FBI while Gerry Adams, leader of the Irish Republican Army, waited for us in the next room.

Being a firm believer that the quality of our answers is determined by the quality of our questions, I have used these opportunities to ask what I believe are some great ones. I wanted to ask questions that would either confirm what I already knew or lead me to a broader definition of the truth. I asked questions like these:

- What's the first thing you do when you're depressed?

- What's the most important decision you've ever made in your life?

- What's the worst decision you've ever made in your life?

- If you were to give an eighteen-year-old one specific piece of wisdom, what would it be?

- What's the smartest thing your parents ever did?

- What's the last thing you do before you go to bed?

- What difference did someone make in your life as a child?

Over and over again, I've confirmed that the Seven Decisions weave their way through the lives of successful people.

When *The Traveler's Gift* was published in November 2002, these Seven Decisions gained a very large audience. My experiment with these Decisions has expanded to include well over a million individual experiments by men and women worldwide who are integrating the Seven Decisions into their lives. Each week I'm blessed with stories from all kinds of people who related to David Ponder's plight and experienced a turnaround in their lives as a consequence of living the Seven Decisions.

Seven Principles, Seven Decisions

Remember these Seven Decisions work *every time*. In fact, they are affecting your life right now whether you are aware of them or not. As we'll discuss, our thoughts carve a pathway to our success or failure. Our thoughts are determined by how well we understand these principles, so we'll go into some depth to explain and demonstrate these Seven Decisions in order to help you find distinctions that will enable you to create the future of your dreams!

You've heard "ignorance of the law is no excuse"? Well, ignorance of principle is no protection from that principle. Just because a person is unaware of a particular principle doesn't mean that principle is not affecting his life. After all, the principle of gravity worked long before the apple fell on Sir Isaac Newton's head. But once Newton understood the principle, mankind was able to harness the power of that principle to create airline flight, suspension bridges, and space travel.

Similarly, the principles of successful parenting, relationships, and financial achievement also work every time. And they can be harnessed by us all. By learning and applying them, obviously, we can create the future of our choosing!

Consider the impact of one principle, such as consistently taking responsibility for our own lives. How would one's life experience improve? Now, as powerful as one principle might be, imagine the power of seven principles stacked together! The result of grouping these seven life-changing principles into a common force bypasses minor, incremental changes to create an exponential explosion. Your life and the lives of those around you will be transformed as a consequence of mastering the Seven Decisions.

Before we begin in depth, here are the "Seven Decisions That Determine Personal Success":

ONE: THE RESPONSIBLE DECISION

The buck stops here. I accept responsibility for my past. I am responsible for my success. I will not let my history control my destiny.

The Responsible Decision shows us how to stop blaming other people and outside circumstances for where we are in life. Instead, we can chart our life's course, allowing our lives to become testaments to the true power of choice.

TWO: THE GUIDED DECISION

I will seek wisdom. God moves mountains to create the opportunity of His choosing. It is up to me to be ready to move myself.

The Guided Decision helps us discover invaluable counsel through books, people, and service. We learn to evaluate the network of influential people in our lives, to seek wisdom from the knowledge of others, and, perhaps most important, to commit to a life of service.

THREE: THE ACTIVE DECISION

I am a person of action. Many people move out of the way for a person on the run; others are caught up in his wake. I will be that person on the run!

The Active Decision is a wake-up call. Taking consistent action is crucial to the realization of a successful life. We're often amazed, even baffled, by the accomplishments of highly successful people, yet many of their accomplishments occur because of relentless action.

FOUR: THE CERTAIN DECISION

I have a decided heart. Criticism, condemnation, and complaint are creatures of the wind. They come and go on the wasted breath of lesser beings and have no power over me.

With the Certain Decision, we learn to break through fear and judgment to pursue our dreams with determination and focus. With a decided heart, we set our course and assure our destiny.

FIVE: THE JOYFUL DECISION

Today I will choose to be happy. My very life is fashioned by choice. First I make choices. Then my choices make me.

The Joyful Decision is perhaps the most misunderstood of all the Decisions. The Joyful Decision demonstrates that happiness is a choice, and if you're not happy right now, it's a consequence of your own choosing, not the circumstances of life.

SIX: THE COMPASSIONATE DECISION

I will greet this day with a forgiving spirit. I know that God rarely uses a person whose main concern is what others are thinking.

The Compassionate Decision can heal your heart, mind, and soul. Harboring anger and resentment poisons our minds and hinders our ability to live the other six Decisions with any measure of effectiveness. Forgiveness frees our spirits.

SEVEN: THE PERSISTENT DECISION

I will persist without exception. Reason can only be stretched so far, but faith has no limits. The only limit to my realization of tomorrow is the doubt to which I hold fast today.

The Persistent Decision reveals a critical "twist" to the notion of persistence: Persisting "without exception" is key to achieving extraordinary levels of success in any area of life. When we consistently make the Persistent Decision, our success is boundless.

Real-Life *Travelers*

To this day, I love reading biographies.

In the late 1980s, I took a more active approach to my Success Study. In addition to reading biographies and interviewing some extraordinary souls, I asked myself, *What if I could contact successful people—even those I don't know—and ask them to share with me their secrets to success and their strategies for overcoming rejection and failure?*

I began to compile a collection of what has become hundreds of personal letters from successful people in media, sports, business, art, and politics. Modern-day icons like General Chuck Yeager, Norman Vincent Peale, Dale Earnhart, Sugar Ray Leonard, Bobby Bowden, Elizabeth Taylor, Mike Eruzione, and Orville Redenbacher all shared a few of their victories and many of their greatest defeats with me.

Not surprisingly, the principles from the Seven Decisions echoed throughout the letters, further confirming the study. To deepen your understanding of each Decision, I've combed through hundreds of these letters and provided edited versions of seven letters that I feel best personify each Decision to share with you.

The Qualities of Leadership

General George S. Patton, who served in both world wars, said, "Be willing to make decisions. That's the most important quality in a good leader."

As you read about the Seven Decisions, you will find that I did not use the word *leadership* very often, but everything discussed in this book reinforces the principles of leadership. The Seven Decisions will help you become the leader you were meant to be.

Leadership, or your ability to lead, is absolutely crucial to having the life you want. However, in my opinion, leadership as a course or study is overblown, overcomplicated, and a stumbling block to a lot of people. You do not have to read a thousand books on leadership to become a competent leader.

The secret to leadership is simple. You have within you the qualities you need to lead people— you only need to recognize them and begin using them. Our beliefs create our success or failure. Begin thinking differently about the leader you already are, and you alter your destiny.

It's amazing to me how many people come up to me after I've talked on the Seven Decisions and lament, "I'm really not a natural leader."

Great leaders are rarely realistic by other people's standards. Somehow, these people, often considered strange, pick their way through life, ignoring or not hearing negative expectations and emotions. Consequently, they accomplish one great thing after another, never having heard what cannot be done.

I say, "Oh yes, you are! You are absolutely a natural leader."

Most people think, *Well, I don't have leadership qualities.*

Yes. Yes, you do!

It is important you understand this before we move into the Seven Decisions.

Leadership essentially boils down to two things: your perspective or beliefs about yourself, and a quality we can call "likeability." Likeability can be defined as the ability to build rapport so that others listen to you. We listen to the people we like.

You're already a natural leader. Everyone has led someone, even if that someone is a child. Leadership, to a great degree, is simply relating your beliefs or opinions to others with conviction and then sticking to that conviction even in the face of criticism or dissent.

How many times have you been hanging with friends and somebody says, "Where do you want to eat?"

"I don't know. Where do *you* want to eat?"

All it takes is for one person to say, "McDonald's. Let's go to McDonald's."

The group likely responds, "Okay."

Have you ever noticed that there's one person in your group who inevitably decides what movie the group will see? Or at what restaurant the group will eat?

There are basically two reasons for this: first, everybody likes this person, and second, this person says something! He expresses his opinion. Everyone usually acquiesces. You may not consider that leadership, but that's exactly what leadership is!

These Seven Decisions are a basic course in becoming a person others want to be around, and then increasing your influence. They'll make you a more influential leader than any book on leadership skills, persuasion, closing techniques, or sales scripts, and they'll help you find a platform for applying all you've learned.

Books and seminars on sales, leadership skills, and closing techniques are important, but without the implementation of these Seven Decisions, they honestly do not matter. You can know the "right" answer, have every word memorized, and know every statistic by heart, but if other people don't want to be around you or don't respect you, all the right answers in the world really don't matter. The Seven Decisions are the foundation for any other business improvement education. Although you will rarely find the word *leadership* as you move through these Seven Decisions, keep in mind that these principles will help you become the leader your children, spouse, co-workers, and friends deserve.

How to Read This Book

I've written this book for one purpose: to help you master the Seven Decisions that determine personal success. Most of us don't have the time to read several hundred biographies in order to clearly understand how successful people from all walks of life have lived these seven principles. *Mastering the Seven Decisions* is your personal "owner's manual" for crafting the life you want with a greater level of fulfillment.

Reading *The Traveler's Gift* is not a prerequisite for benefiting from this book (though I do believe the story will create greater excitement for the journey you are about to take). For your convenience, the actual Seven Decisions David Ponder received from the seven historical figures are included. For each Decision, you'll be presented with a series of exercises I often use in "The Seven Decision Seminar." These exercises will help you further integrate the Decisions into your daily life.

A word of caution: Most of us tend to read passively. We sit back or lie down and scan the pages in a trancelike fashion.

Although this style may be appropriate for pleasure reading, it is not the optimal style for processing this information. (Wouldn't it be nice if this information could be absorbed through osmosis by placing the book on our heads while we sleep at night?)

To support your comprehension of this information, a more active reading style would serve you better. What does this mean?

- Rereading certain sections that resonate with you
- Highlighting, underlining, and marking up the pages as you read
- Completing the exercises in a pad or a journal (possibly more than once)
- Consistently practicing the multiple-day exercises

Consider that these Seven Decisions aren't difficult to comprehend. In fact, one of the reasons many people don't consciously live the Decisions is because they appear too simple. *Surely the answers to life must be more complex than this!* This sentiment leads us to discount simple truths.

You may decide to read this book straight through before doing the exercises, or you may go "deep" with each Decision, completing each exercise before moving on to the next section. Whatever your preference, please make sure you do the exercises. Reading the text is simply not enough. Completing the exercises, even repeating them, will help you master all Seven Decisions. *Mastering the Seven Decisions* is an experiential learning course, reference manual, and companion for your journey toward the life you want.

Also, I'd recommend completing the exercises in a bound notebook or journal, rather than on scraps of paper, in order to have an ideal companion for future reference. I suggest investing in a leather-bound journal—something in which you will enjoy capturing your lifelong dreams, goals, creative ideas, memories, and life lessons.

The Power of Consistency

Lasting success is attainable by all of us. It's likely you've made each of the Seven Decisions at least once in your life. Although simple to understand, the Decisions aren't necessarily easy to carry out; however, the secret to lifelong success is in the *consistent* application of the Seven Decisions.

Our tendency is to try something a few times, and if it works, it gets reinforced and we continue to do it; if it doesn't work, we abandon it. In psychology, this is called the Law of Effects—we tend to keep doing things we're rewarded for doing. The opposite, however, is also true: we tend to avoid what punishes us or gives us pain.

Consciously applying the Seven Decisions consistently can be challenging at first. After all, although we may not love our life, it is at least familiar—and familiarity tends to breed comfort (even if that means being comfortable with massive debt, an unfulfilling job, or a contentious relationship).

It is helpful to view "decision making" not as a skill but as a muscle. Consider weight training: When you first try lifting a weight you're not accustomed to lifting, say fifty pounds, it's difficult. Even if you complete a few reps, it's likely your body will later feel sore from stretching the muscle. For many of us, the challenge of lifting that fifty pounds and the soreness that follows is enough to keep us out of the gym. If, however, our commitment transcends our temporary discomfort, we will repeatedly lift the fifty pounds until it's easier, causing the pain and soreness to disappear as our bodies adapt. In time, through consistent effort, mastery is achieved: lifting fifty pounds is a breeze because it is within your domain of competence.

The consistent application of the Seven Decisions brings about what can only be likened to miracles: what was once labeled "impossible" becomes reality. Opportunities that once eluded you are now attracted to you. Dysfunctional relationships transform into harmonious ones. Life, which was once a struggle, now becomes an exciting adventure. Where you once perceived limitations, you now see possibilities. You go from "pushing" your way through life to "allowing" life's gifts to present themselves. You become a person others want to be around—a mentor, guide, and leader. The changes that arise have an infectious effect on those close to you: your spouse, family, friends, and co-workers, and even people you meet in the elevator or supermarket, are all uplifted by the person you have become by living the Seven Decisions.

The rewards of embracing the Seven Decisions are beyond measure—it's important to keep this in mind during the initial, arduous stages of the journey. This is, after all, where difficulties are likely to arise. Trust that the Decisions won't fail you. Through the consistent application and diligent effort of these Seven Decisions, you will discover abundant success!

THE RESPONSIBLE DECISION

The buck stops here.

The Responsible Decision for Personal Success is a key—it represents the beginning. Taking responsibility for your past will segue you into an extraordinary future of your choosing.

From *The Traveler's Gift*

If decisions are choices . . . and our thinking dictates our decisions—then we are where we are because of our thinking.

—PRESIDENT HARRY S. TRUMAN

235

The Responsible Decision

In The Traveler's Gift, *President Harry Truman presents David Ponder with the first Decision that determines personal success:*

The buck stops here.

From this moment forward, I will accept responsibility for my past. I understand that the beginning of wisdom is to accept the responsibility for my own problems and that by accepting responsibility for my past, I free myself to move into a bigger, brighter future of my own choosing.

Never again will I blame my parents, spouse, boss, or employees for my present situation. Neither my education nor lack of one, my genetics, or the circumstantial ebb and flow of everyday life will affect my future in a negative way. If I allow myself to blame these uncontrollable forces for my lack of success, I will be forever caught in a web of the past. I will look forward. I will not let my history control my destiny.

The buck stops here. I accept responsibility for my past. I am responsible for my success.

I am where I am today—mentally, physically, spiritually, emotionally, and financially—because of decisions I have made. My decisions have always been governed by my thinking. Therefore, I am where I am today—mentally, physically, spiritually, emotionally, and financially—because of how I think. Today I will begin the process of changing where I am—mentally, physically, spiritually, emotionally, and financially—by changing the way I think.

My thoughts will be constructive, never destructive. My

mind will live in the solutions of the future. It will not dwell in the problems of the past. I will seek the association of those who are working and striving to bring about positive changes in the world. I will never seek comfort by associating with those who have decided to be comfortable.

When faced with the opportunity to make a decision, I will make one. I understand that God did not put in me the ability to always make right decisions. He did, however, put in me the ability to *make* a decision and then make it right. The rise and fall of my emotional tide will not deter me from my course. When I make a decision, I will stand behind it. My energy will go into making the decision. I will waste none on second thoughts. My life will not be an apology. It will be a statement.

The buck stops here. I control my thoughts. I control my emotions.

In the future when I am tempted to ask the question "Why me?" I will immediately counter with the answer "Why *not* me?" Challenges are a gift, an opportunity to learn. Problems are the common thread running through the lives of great men and women. In times of adversity, I will not have a problem to deal with; I will have a choice to make. My thoughts will be clear. I will make the right choice. Adversity is preparation for greatness. I will accept the preparation. Why me? Why *not* me? I will be prepared for something great!

I accept responsibility for my past. I control my thoughts. I control my emotions. I am responsible for my success.

The buck stops here.

Playing the Blame Game

If you want to hear a great fight, just turn on talk radio. They're relentless, those show hosts.

One side says, "These people need to accept responsibility, and until these people accept responsibility . . ."

The other side replies, "But it's not their fault. They're not to blame. Don't you understand . . . ?"

Both sides present a persuasive argument, but both sides are wrong.

Who or what do we blame? We blame our parents. We blame the weather. We blame the economy. We blame the president. We blame our spouses. It's amazing who we think of to blame.

Where I am today, we tell ourselves, *is a consequence of what other people* (our parents, for example) *and circumstances have done to me.* In blaming other people and events, we weaken our power. We argue, "It's not my fault . . ." As soon as we subscribe to this line of thinking, our chances for any kind of success dramatically decline.

When I was at my all-time low—homeless, living under a pier—I remember somebody telling me, "Well, you chose this." At first, that infuriated me. I remember thinking, *I didn't choose this. If my parents hadn't died, if there had been more insurance, if someone had helped me, if only . . .*

The problem with this line of thinking is that if we don't accept responsibility for where we are right now, we have no hope of changing our future. I promise you: if it's the president's fault, if it's our neighbor's fault, if it's our spouses' fault, if it's the government's fault, if it's the weather's fault, then we truly are stuck! What are you going to do about the president? What are you going to do about the weather? What can you do about your neighbor? I'll tell you: *nothing!* But if you can find the answer to your problems in the mirror—if the solution lies within you—well, there's boundless hope, because you can start working on yourself today!

What most of the people on talk radio don't seem to understand is that responsibility is not about blame or making someone feel bad about their situation. Responsibility is about hope and control. You feel more hopeful when you spread this vastly different perspective about responsibility—you can control your future! Who among us doesn't want a better future? These Seven Decisions can give you a better tomorrow by affecting the choices you make today.

Your day of reckoning is important. You must come to the self-realization that even though you couldn't control any of the crazy things that have happened in your life, your choices in response to those things are what has led you down this path you don't like.

We have the power to make choices that lead us to places we don't like. And that's great news! If we can make choices that lead us to places we don't like, then doesn't it stand to reason that we can also make choices that will lead us to a place we *do* like? If where we are today is not in our control, then how can tomorrow's fate be better? The game, then, becomes simple: *make better choices.*

We make our own way. Now that you're completely aware of this, you can claim it, make the decision to take responsibility, and begin living the Responsible Decision: *I am responsible for my past and my future.*

Why is that important? Until we accept responsibility for where we are, we have no basis for moving forward in our lives.

The Power of Thought

The Responsible Decision is all about owning our power. In a way, our choices have made us what we are today. And fundamentally, our *thinking*—the internal lens through which we see the world—creates a pathway to success or failure. To accept responsibility for our choices includes becoming aware of and accepting responsibility for our thinking. This clarification gives us the basis for moving on.

People sometimes question this idea. "Now, how does my thinking create a pathway for success or failure?" Despite what you may believe, outside influences are not responsible for where you are in life mentally,

The bad news is the past was in your hands, but the good news is that the future, my friend, is also in your hands.

physically, spiritually, emotionally, or financially. You alone have chosen the path to your present destination.

Decisions are an outward expression of our thinking. Most people agree that their decisions have guided them to where they are. If you want to create a pathway to the success you've dreamed of rather than the reality you're currently experiencing, change your thinking.

You are where you are because of how you think. If you're in a bad place financially, physically, emotionally, socially, or spiritually, what does that tell you? Think about it: Nobody sets out to fail. Nobody says, "I'm going to make every bad decision I can possibly make."

Instead we say, "I'm going to figure this out. I'm going to do the right thing."

And yet, we often end up in a horrible place in spite of ourselves! How does this happen? In many cases, our thinking got us here.

The primary way our thinking must change is to realize *we are responsible for where we are.* If we are responsible for where we are, we have hope! If we are responsible for where we are, then we can be responsible for where we're going. By disowning responsibility for our present, we give our power away and deny ourselves an incredible future.

We are often tempted to think, *Well, this is not my fault.* The words "It's not my fault" should never again come from your mouth! They have been symbolically written on the gravestones of unsuccessful people ever since Adam and Eve took the first bite of that apple.

Until we take responsibility for where we are, there's no basis for moving on. By taking responsibility, we have hope.

Responsible Thinking

What thoughts do you have on a regular basis that may be leading you to an unhappy state of mind? Very often these thoughts take the form of defeated questions. For example: Why am I so fat? is not a question that will help you understand what steps to take to change your situation. However, How can I enjoy sculpting my ideal body and reclaiming my energy? will move you in the direction you want to go.

What questions do you habitually ask that are hindering your growth?

In a notebook or journal, list the unsupportive thoughts you often think. Then, cross out each thought and restate it in a way that empowers you to obtain what you actually want.

Catching the Prize

In the 1920s, a well-known, wealthy industrialist controlled a vast portion of our country's prosperity, and with his wealth, he purchased a zoo. It wasn't a public zoo, or even a private zoo; it was his personal zoo, located on his estate, for the pleasure of this one man and his family. National dignitaries were occasionally allowed to view the animals. In the days before zoo-breeding programs traded animals, his zoo was one of the most complete collections the zoological world had ever known. (During this time, zookeepers traveled to various countries, mounted safaris, and captured the animals to bring them back.)

One day, he heard about a rare and beautiful type of gazelle from Africa that wasn't showcased in any zoo in the world. He became obsessed with the idea of becoming the first to have one of these animals in his collection.

He mounted an expedition to Africa, including food, supplies, and men to carry the tents. When they landed on the African shores, the man contacted the natives to learn about this animal and its whereabouts. Over and over he was told, "You'll never catch one. They're too fast and too strong. You can shoot and kill them from a distance—but you'll never get close enough to take one alive."

When faced with the opportunity to make a decision, I will make one. I understand that God did not put in me the ability to always make right decisions. He did, however, put in me the ability to make wrong decisions right.

He told a reporter who was on the safari with him, "Don't listen to them; I'll get as many of them as I want! And it won't be a problem."

When his men located a herd, he poured sweet feed—a blend of oats and barley rolled in molasses—on the ground in an open area in the middle of the night and left. The next night, he scattered the feed again. For two weeks, he spread the feed, night after night.

The animals, of course, came in and ate it. On the first night of the third week, he scattered the feed and sank an eight-foot post into the ground twenty feet away. The next night, he scattered the feed and sank another post into the ground twenty feet in the opposite direction. Every night, he added a post. Then he started putting boards between the posts while scattering the feed.

Six weeks rolled by. He continued adding posts and boards until he had a corral built around this feed. Every night these animals found the gaps between the posts until, finally, he watched the entire herd squeeze through the final gap. He moved in behind them and nailed the last board into place. The animals were trapped inside the corral.

He chose the animals he wanted to take residency in his zoo and let the others go.

When he was asked how he knew how to catch them, he said something that chills me to the bone: "I treat animals the same way I treat people: I give them what they want. I give them food and shelter. In exchange, they give me their beauty and their freedom."

Trading Freedom

Are you trading your beauty and freedom to help someone else's dreams come true? Way too many people trade out their freedom for security, and they don't even realize it. There's a difference between *an opportunity you seize* and *a trap you walk into*. Being aware of the choice and the trap is the key.

The buck stops here. You're responsible for your past and your future. The bad news is that the past was in your hands, but the good news is that the future is also in your hands.

You trade away your freedom every time you blame your parents, your spouse, your boss, or a colleague for your present situation. You trade away your freedom every time you blame your education (or lack thereof), your genetics, or the circumstantial ebb and flow of everyday life.

If you allow yourself to blame these uncontrollable forces for your lack of success, you'll be forever caught in the web of the past, a victim to your fears and frustrations. You cannot let your history control your destiny. By choosing to take responsibility, you can avoid living reactively—selling out your future to circumstances you choose not to control.

You're where you are today—mentally, spiritually, emotionally, financially, and, in many ways, physically—because of decisions you've made. Your decisions have always been governed by your thinking. Therefore, you are where you are today mentally, physically, spiritually, emotionally, and financially because of the quality of your thoughts, the perspectives you have about life, and your beliefs about yourself and others. In other words, your thinking. Do you truly desire a significant change in your life? Change your thinking!

Taking Personal Inventory

To take responsibility for your life, you must first take a "personal inventory" of where you are right now. In your journal, on a scale from one to ten—one being miserable and ten outstanding—rate how you feel you're doing in each of the following categories: emotionally, physically, financially, spiritually, socially, professionally, and with your family.

Overcoming Fear of Failure

When a person considers the Responsible Decision, he or she will likely confront the fear of failure. A new realization sets in: *If I'm in control of my life, if I fail, then it really is my fault!*

God didn't give you the discernment to make right decisions all the time. He did, however, grant you the ability to make wrong decisions right. Don't allow the rise and fall of your emotional tide to deter you from your course. Your life should not be an apology; it should be a statement—an extraordinary demonstration of the possibilities within all of us.

Another way of looking at failure is to ask yourself how you can use it to catapult your success. Is hitting rock bottom really the signal for your turning point? Although it doesn't feel like it, yes, you bet it is! Why? Because great ideas and inspiration often come from rock bottom.

My mind will not dwell in the problems of the past—it will live in the solutions of the future.

Thomas Watson, founder of IBM, said, "That's where success lies—on the far side of failure."

When things don't go as planned, it generally means you need to make a course correction. We've all heard how Thomas Edison responded to the notion that he failed ten thousand times in creating the light bulb: "I didn't fail. I just discovered ten thousand ways not to make a light bulb."

When you view your "failures" as opportunities for growth and discovery, you free yourself from the fear of failure. How can you fail when your "failures" are merely lessons you learned on your way to success?

Learning from Failure

What has been your biggest failure so far in your life's adventure?

Think about it. What came out of that experience? What did you learn? How is your life now different or better as a consequence of this "failure"?

Write down in your journal what you learned from this failure.

Og's Initiative for Success

I want to tell you the story of a man whose failures took him to the brink of destruction and back, paving the way for massive success. You may recognize the name Og Mandino even though he passed away in 1996. His seventeen books still grace the shelves of most bookstores in America. This man was an incredible influence on my life, although I wasn't acquainted with him personally.

Og Mandino was told by his mother—his champion and cheerleader—that he could be a successful writer. She died before he went to college. Aimlessly, Og joined the army after high school and fought in World War II. (He was a bombardier in the same squadron as Jimmy Stewart.)

Og returned to the United States after the war and discovered there wasn't much employment for bombardiers with only a high school education. The next ten years of his life were a living hell for him, his wife, and their daughter. He struggled to sell insurance, and it seemed that no matter how much he worked, his young family drifted deeper and deeper into debt.

Like so many frustrated individuals, he responded by hiding from his problems. After a long day of sales calls, he would stop by the bar and get a drink. One drink turned into two, two turned into three, and three into six. Eventually, when his wife and daughter could no longer endure his behavior or his words, they left him. The following two years of his life were a blur: He traveled the country in an old Ford, doing odd jobs to earn enough money for another bottle of wine. He spent countless nights in the gutter, literally—"a sorry wretch of a human being," as he put it.

One cold winter morning in Cleveland, he almost took his life. He paused at the window of a dingy pawnshop, gazing inside at a small handgun with a yellow tag attached: $29. He reached in his pocket and pulled out three ten-dollar bills. *I could afford a couple of bullets. I'll go back to that room where I'm staying, and I'll never have to look at myself in the mirror again.*

For whatever reason, Og did not kill himself. Years later, he joked about it, saying he was such a spineless person at the time, he couldn't muster the courage! As the snow fell that day in Cleveland, he turned from the pawnshop and wandered to a public library.

Og entered the self-help section and began to read fervently. For several months, he spent almost every afternoon and evening in the library, reading book after book until he found one called *Success Through a Positive Mental Attitude*, by W. Clement Stone, the chairman and founder of Combined Insurance of America. He was so impressed by the idea that he could think his way to a different future that he began to apply the principles to every part of his life.

In the future when I am tempted to ask the question, "Why me?" I will immediately counter with the answer, "Why not me?" Challenges are gifts, opportunities to learn. Problems are the common thread running through the lives of great men and women. In times of adversity, I will not have a problem to deal with; I will have a choice to make.

After becoming a successful insurance salesman for W. Clement Stone, he did what his mother had always wanted him to do—and what he had always wanted to do too—he became a writer for Stone's company's young magazine, *Success Unlimited*. He eventually became the editor of *Success Unlimited* and grew it from an in-house publication to a national publication with 250,000 subscribers.

One day, several months after he became the magazine's editor, he was short one article, with only a few days until press time. There was nothing suitable in the files. Since Og was a golf nut, he worked all night on a piece about golfer Ben Hogan, who had gone from being nearly left in a wheelchair after a terrible automobile accident to winning the U.S. Open.

Og ran the article in *Success Unlimited*, and several weeks later he received a letter from a New York publisher who had enjoyed the Hogan article. He offered Og the opportunity to submit a manuscript for review by the publishing house. Believe me, as an author, this is the kind of letter we dream about receiving!

Eighteen months after receiving that letter, Og's first book, *The Greatest Salesman in the World*, was published. When my mom and dad passed away, and I ended up sleeping under the pier, my own life at a total dead end, it was that book along with its little corollary, *The Greatest Secret in the World*, that I read over and over again.

It is absolutely amazing to see what has happened since that book's first printing of 5,000 copies. Soon, total sales reached 350,000, and then 500,000. Thirty years after its initial publication, it continues to sell more than 100,000 paperback copies *each month*, with more than 40 million copies of Og Mandino's books sold worldwide.

Most of Og's writings were about people in tough situations who overcame their problems and achieved extraordinary success. His failures became his inspiration for helping other men and women hang in there until the tide turned. Og Mandino has been gone for years now, but because he was willing to build on his failure, his legacy lives on, and he continues to inspire millions of people.

The Impact of Our Decisions

To fully understand that you are where you are as a result of your decisions, do the following:

Choose an area of your life from the Taking Personal Inventory exercise on page 244.

1. Reflect on the choices you've made in the past that may have contributed to your current situation. If you chose finances, consider the decisions that contributed to your current financial situation. For example, perhaps you had the choice of starting a business or staying in your current job. Or maybe you could have contributed more to your IRA or pension plan. The purpose of this exercise isn't to make you feel bad for past decisions but to trace your decisions to where you are right now. Remember, every decision *not* to do something is still a decision.

2. List at least five decisions (big or small) you have made or didn't make over the last five years that have contributed to where you are in that area of your life.

Do you notice any pattern? Are you beginning to see how you have greater power to influence your results than you may have previously realized?

A Defeated Washington

It has been more than two hundred years since George Washington walked among the admiring patriots of early America. Commander-in-chief of the Continental army during the American Revolution and the first president of the United States, Washington left a legacy ingrained into the fabric of our country for over two centuries. Interestingly, Washington never wanted to be president; he treasured his private life with his wife, Martha. His willingness to sacrifice his own desires for future generations laid the foundation on which the American dream was birthed.

Washington's courage, determination, character, and especially his sense of responsibility, inspired his countrymen. He consistently made the Responsible Decision.

The complex task of establishing a nation was wrought with challenges and missteps for Washington. Fortunately, the mistakes he made in his latter years bore little resemblance to the grave blunders the father of our country made during the dawn of his military career. These "lessons" cost many brave and honorable men under his command their lives, and nearly resulted in his own demise. As providence would have it, Washington was able to accept responsibility, learn from his missteps, and turn his early defeats into what we see today as a victorious life.

In 1754, as a young major in the Virginia militia, Washington was ordered to lead 350 raw recruits through the wilderness to French-occupied Fort Duquesne at present-day Pittsburgh. Traveling four miles per day, the militia camped at a spot some forty miles from Fort Duquesne and erected a fort named Necessity.

They advanced on the enemy until seven hundred French soldiers and their Indian allies clashed with Washington and his men, driving them back into Fort Necessity. The fort didn't live up to its name. Its location made it impossible to defend because it was surrounded by hills that were the perfect hiding place from which French and Indian fighters could attack. The enemy took its time, firing on Washington and his men from behind rocks and trees. Many of Washington's men were drunk, and the casualties began to mount. In nine short hours, with thirty dead, seventy wounded, and many more deserting, the battle was over.

Defeated, Washington was forced to give over his sword and sign hastily drafted articles of surrender by candlelight in a driving rainstorm. George Washington, the future "father of our country," lost his first battle, his first fort, and his first command in one fell swoop. Because of this humiliating defeat, the French controlled the entire Ohio Valley, and Indians freely attacked settlers all along the frontier.

As Washington limped back to Virginia to his beloved Mount Vernon, he resolved to learn from this miserable failure. He made no excuses. No "Well, they had more men than we did" or "Well, my men were drunk and not as skilled." Instead, Washington learned to use the guerrilla warfare strategies of the Indians.

During the American Revolution, Washington remembered his earlier lessons at the Battles of Trenton and King's Mountain. The settlers attacked the proud British forces from the cover of rocks and trees, routing them and humiliating them before achieving total victory for the new nation.

When we take responsibility, we realize that failure can be a classroom for the most profound lessons for success.

Crafting Your Ultimate Vision

Many people complain about where they are in life; however, very few people know where they want to be. In the Taking Personal Inventory exercise on page 244, you rated each major area of your life from one to ten. Do you know what a "ten" would look like for you?

As you've heard before, if you don't know where you're going, it's quite challenging to get there. Or, as Yogi Berra put it, "If you don't know where you're going, you'll end up someplace else."

Think about the overall lifestyle you want to create, and craft the Ultimate Vision for your life—what will it look like when it's a "ten"? Here are a few questions to consider:

1. What will your relationships be like—within your family, socially, and professionally?

2. What will your finances look like? What will your business affairs look like?

3. What will your overall emotional patterns look like? Will you be a master of your emotions? How will you know when you're *truly* happy?

4. In what areas of your life will you grow the most? What will you attract into your life as a consequence of your growth?

5. How will you handle yourself in difficult situations?

6. How will you grow spiritually?

Embracing the Gift of Adversity

Back in the day when I was reading all of those biographies, besides discovering seven common denominators, I realized an additional factor found in every single case: each person had to battle *adversity*. In fact, problems seemed to be a common experience of great people throughout time.

That's right: The stories of wealthy, influential, successful world-changers are constantly riddled with adversity. Each one was presented with the challenge of accepting responsibility for his decisions and circumstances—and each one did. But I'm sure they were tempted to play the victim, as most of us are, and ask, *Why me?*

When my parents died and I ran out of money—when things went from bad to worse—my constant refrain was, *Why me? Why is this happening to me?* I woke with *Why me?* I went to bed with *Why me?* I walked around all day long thinking, *Why me?*

My life began to change when I understood that adversity is a common experience of great people. Instead of feeling sorry for myself, I began to get excited. I realized that adversity is more like a toll bridge than an insurmountable roadblock on the way to success. My problems

Never again will I blame my [past] for my present condition . . . I will look forward. I will not let my history control my destiny.

became less invasive—I no longer felt as though they were *always* going to be there. Unfortunately, many people run from their problems, not realizing that they're necessary stops on the road to the life they want.

I began to wonder, *Is adversity what helps people become great?* Overcoming adversity strengthened my problem-solving skills, and demonstrating a positive response to adversity magnetically drew people to me.

Adversity prepares you for greatness. Challenges are gifts. Problems present opportunities to learn and grow. In times of adversity, you don't have a problem to deal with; you have a choice to make.

Why you?

Why *not* you!

Why shouldn't *you* be prepared for something great?

Realizing Your Future Identity

Now that you've identified your Ultimate Vision, ask yourself, Who do I need to become to realize this vision? Albert Einstein said, "A problem cannot be solved by the same consciousness that created it." Like it or not, you are where you are because of *what you are* right now. As a human spirit with enormous potential, you are bound only by your self-imposed limitations.

Review your Ultimate Vision. Answer the question, Who do I need to become to realize this vision?

How will you need to treat other people? How will you need to treat yourself? What will you need to read and study? What lessons will you need to learn? With whom will you need to surround yourself? What will you need to think and believe about yourself? What will you need to believe about those around you?

Capture as many ideas as you can in your journal.

Real *Traveler* Profile:
Jimmy Dean

I first met Jimmy Dean at a Nashville television studio where we were taping a show. I always enjoy talking with him—I love his good humor, and he tells some of the best jokes I've ever heard!

In 1928, Mr. Dean was born into poverty on a farm in Plainview, Texas. He began his musical career performing in nightclubs and on the radio. In the '60s he became a nationally known personality through his popular television shows on CBS and ABC, and he was Johnny Carson's first guest host on *The Tonight Show*. His Grammy-winning country music album *Big Bad John* sold more than six million copies. Ironically, it was a benefit at which he performed for a faded country music star that led Jimmy Dean to a career change that took him to even greater financial success. Jimmy told me that he left the concert that night thinking, *By gosh, no one is ever going to have to do a benefit for Jimmy Dean!*

Within the year, Jimmy diversified from the entertainment world, launching a successful food line including the most popular sausage in the country. In 1985, Jimmy Dean Foods merged with the Sara Lee Corporation to achieve combined annual sales exceeding a half billion dollars. He was inducted into the Texas Country Music Hall of Fame in 2005, and an exhibit of his life is on display at the Texas Country Music Museum in Carthage, Texas.

Read how Jimmy Dean personifies the Responsible Decision:

Dear Andy:

In your letter, you addressed my "success and wealth." To me, success and wealth have always been a state of mind. My grandfather, W. J. Taylor, was the most successful and wealthy man I ever knew, and I doubt seriously that he ever made more than $10,000 in any given year in his life. But he was the best farmer in Hale County, Texas. He knew that. He had the straightest fences, the cleanest end-rows. He had the neatest barn and the neatest house. He raised nine kids, he had a great relationship with the man upstairs and a wonderful inner peace. To me, this is success and wealth.

Many look at me and say, "He's the luckiest S.O.B. that ever lived." It is true—I have had much good fortune, but things were not—and are not—always easy. I have probably had almost as many rejections as acceptances, but I have ascertained that, were it not for the rough roads, you would never appreciate the super highways.

Being knocked down is part of life—getting up is also part of life, and I have very little use for people who cannot bounce back from the bludgeonings of temporary setback. Being able to handle temporary setbacks (notice I did not say defeat—the word *defeat* is not in my vocabulary), overcome them, and stand tall is what entitles you to the sweet bows of victory.

We, unfortunately, in this wonderful country have created an element that condones giving up. In my opinion, when our great President, F.D.R., decided it was proper that we compensate people for non-productivity, it was the gravest mistake that ever happened.

The good book says, "You'll earn your bread by the sweat of your brow," as it should be. I have no use for anyone who can help themselves and does not. Reminds me of once when I told my youngest son, Robert, that I was a self-made man, and he said, "That's what I like about you, dad, you take the blame for everything." It's just that this country has been so wonderful to me, I would like it to remain the land of opportunity for my great, great grandkids.

I feel instead of every day creating another organization for the weak, we should create organizations that make people want to stand on their own two feet and say, "I believe in me." We cannot create a muddle of mediocrity that makes people feel the world owes them a living.

Every time I talk like this, someone will invariably say, "Easy for you to talk like that; God gave you talent." Damn right he gave me talent; he gave everyone a talent. My greatest fear is that with all our federal aid, state aid, city aid, county aids, etc. that they're going to be many wonderfully talented people who will never be forced to find out what their talent is.

Sincerely Yours,

—JIMMY DEAN
JD: BMM

THE GUIDED DECISION

I will seek wisdom.

Your past cannot be changed, but you will change your future by changing your actions today. The Guided Decision teaches us to actively seek wisdom to help us craft lives of extraordinary achievement.

From *The Traveler's Gift*

God moves mountains to create the opportunity of His choosing. It is up to you to be ready to move yourself.

—KING SOLOMON

The Guided Decision

In The Traveler's Gift, *King Solomon presents David Ponder with the second Decision that determines personal success:*

I will seek wisdom.

Knowing that wisdom waits to be gathered, I will actively search her out. My past can never be changed, but I can change the future by changing my actions today. I *will* change my actions today! I will train my eyes and ears to read and listen to books and recordings that bring about positive changes in my personal relationships and a greater understanding of my fellow man. No longer will I bombard my mind with materials that feed my doubts and fears. I will read and listen only to that which increases my belief in myself and my future.

I will seek wisdom. I will choose my friends with care.

I am who my friends are. I speak their language, and I wear their clothes. I share their opinions and habits. From this moment forward, I will choose to associate with people whose lives and lifestyles I admire. If I associate with chickens, I will learn to scratch at the ground and squabble over crumbs. If I associate with eagles, I will learn to soar great heights. I am an eagle. It is my destiny to fly.

I will seek wisdom. I will listen to the counsel of wise men.

The words of a wise man are like raindrops on dry ground. They are precious and quickly used for immediate results. Only the blade of grass that catches a raindrop will prosper and grow. The person who ignores wise counsel is like the blade of grass untouched by the rain—soon to wither and die. When I counsel with myself, I can only make decisions according to what I already know. By counseling with a wise man, I add his knowledge and experience to my own and dramatically increase my success.

I will seek wisdom. I will be a servant to others.

A wise man will cultivate a servant's spirit, for that particular attribute attracts people like no other. As I humbly serve others, their wisdom will be freely shared with me. Often, the person who develops a servant's spirit becomes wealthy beyond measure. Many times, a servant has the ear of the king, and a humble servant becomes king, for he is the popular choice of the people. He who serves the most grows the fastest.

I will become a humble servant. I will not look for someone to open my door—I will look to open the door for someone. I will not be distressed when no one is available to help me—I will be excited when I am available to help.

I will be a servant to others. I will listen to the counsel of wise men. I will choose my friends with care.

I will seek wisdom.

Seeking Wisdom

Most people mistake wisdom for education, like a high school diploma or college degree. Seeking wisdom is not the same as gaining knowledge: Knowledge is a precursor to wisdom. Wisdom includes an intuitive element, an insight gained from personal experience that serves us as we make choices in our lives. Seeking wisdom should be a continual process. The humility of the wisdom seeker is a defining characteristic of influential, wealthy, successful people.

Wisdom is available to all, waiting to be known. It can't be bartered or sold; wisdom is a gift only for the diligent, because only the diligent can find it. The lazy person doesn't look in the first place.

God moves mountains to create the opportunity of His choosing, but it's up to you to be ready to move yourself.

There are three simple things you can do daily to chart your lifelong search for wisdom: *read, take the counsel of others,* and *serve others.* They may seem obvious, yet tragically, much of our society has ignored these simple, critical distinctions despite their availability.

Words of Wisdom

First, read.

I know—you're thinking, *Read? That's it?*

Yes. Read.

Read books. Magazines and newspapers inform and entertain, but wisdom is generally not found there.

We're encouraged to read books as children, but as adults, we've forgotten this vital piece of advice. What do you call a child who reads two books a year? *Slow.* What do you call an adult who reads two books a year? *Normal.* Amazingly, the national average for books read by American adults is *less than two books a year.*

You wouldn't believe how many times I've had people brag to me, "I determined when I got out of college that I would never read another book again. And I have been true to my word. I read magazines and newspapers, but I've never read another book. I haven't read a book in twenty years."

And they're proud of it! I smile, nod, and sadly think to myself, *They are not on the path for my personal search for wisdom.*

These are not folks with whom I can afford to become close. their search for wisdom ended years ago.

You, my friend, obviously already know that few things impact you like time alone with a good book, highlighter in hand. And the highlighter or pen is critical. We're not sitting with the book in our hands, passively waiting for some profound words of wisdom to leap from the page; rather, we're *actively* seeking wisdom. Even now, as you read these words, be on the lookout for something that will *change everything.* One idea has the power to transform your life forever, but you must first recognize it.

If you don't think you can take the time to read, you can always listen to audio books. Whenever I say something like this at a seminar, people often tell me, "You don't know what my life is like. I have a job. My wife has a job. I have kids. I'm the president of the social club. You're telling me you want me to read books and listen to recordings?"

The past will never change, but you can change the future by changing your actions today. It is really a very simple process. We, as humans, are always in a process of change. Therefore, we might as well guide the direction in which we will change.

People think they have to clear the house and their calendar, sit down at the table with a pen and paper, and watch that little CD go round and round while they take notes. You don't have to pay attention like that. All you have to do is press the play button. Listen while you're cooking, mowing the lawn, or driving the kids to school. Listen while you're in the shower. Listen while you're sleeping. You'll get it. After all, consider the number of commercial jingles or television show theme songs you have inadvertently memorized. If anything is going to be programming your subconscious mind, why not *choose* the programming? Why not choose something that can change your family's future for generations?

There are many choices, with literally millions of books and audio programs that can be purchased on the Internet or through your local bookstore. To find your next treasure, discuss your interests with a friend you admire, find out what has done well in the marketplace, or read reviews on online bookstores such as Amazon.com. Oftentimes, I find out about a great book because it's referenced in another book I'm reading, as if I'm led from one book to the next in a continual strand of wisdom.

If you're looking for something on leadership, you might want to check out John Maxwell. My favorite of his works is *21 Irrefutable Laws of Leadership*. Og Mandino wrote a library during his lifetime that has changed the lives of millions of people. *The Greatest Secret in the World* changed my life. I read that book at least four hundred times. People have often commented, "You gotta be kidding me. A book? You read a book four hundred times? I mean, what is it you didn't understand?!"

I'm not reading just to read, to add to my gun belt of books read. I am reading on a search for wisdom. If you desire wisdom, read.

Constructing Your Personal Library

Wisdom in the words of successful men and women throughout history can be found in books. You are who you spend time with, and you are what you read. There's nothing wrong with reading magazines for entertainment, but wisdom is generally found in nonfiction books or fiction with a specific point or purpose.

Oftentimes, we "accidentally" get conditioned into reading only nonfiction books that are related to our primary field of interest (i.e., what we do for a living). Sometimes it's useful to explore subjects that seem to have nothing to do with your occupational endeavors and let your mind make its own connections.

For example, perhaps you've always been interested in studying creativity, painting, aquatic life, theoretical biology, quantum mechanics, sewing, basket weaving, gardening, personal finances, branding, real estate, architecture, leadership, sales, or consciousness research. Any topic can prove useful if you're open and ready to receive the connections.

In your journal list ten subjects you've always been curious about. Within the next twenty-four hours, go online or visit your local bookstore or library to pick up a few titles that spark your interest.

The Power of Fellowship

As humans, we're always changing. The past doesn't change, but you can change your future by changing your actions today. Change is inevitable, so we might as well guide the direction in which we change.

So how can you guide the direction of your change? Besides reading, you must choose your companions wisely.

We all know how important the right peer group is for kids. Most parents are desperately concerned about the friends with whom their own children hang out—we understand that our kids are likely to turn out just like those friends. If our children's companions are doing drugs, having sex, or using profane language, our kids are obviously at a greater risk for exhibiting similar behaviors.

We're concerned about our children's choice of companions, and yet we ignore this principle as adults. At what age does this principle cease to work in someone's life? Do we become immune to the influence of others at age eighteen? Twenty-one? Or maybe it's no longer a factor at age thirty-five or forty?

You know the answer: it's always a factor. If you are surrounded by people who use bad language, your language will tend toward that. If you hang around people with certain viewpoints, you will be persuaded by those views. If you spend time with people who are lazy, you will tend to laziness. If you are comfortable with people who make excuses, you will tend to make excuses as well.

When you tolerate mediocrity in your choice of companions, you're going to become more accepting of mediocrity in your own life. Here's something to consider: if a lazy person isn't an irritation to you, it's a sign you've accepted laziness as "normal" in your own life.

Guard your associations carefully. Anytime you tolerate mediocrity in your choice of companions, you become more comfortable with mediocrity in your own life.

If a lazy man isn't an irritation to you, it's a sign that you have accepted slothfulness as a way of life.

It's critical to choose your friends with care. I often ask people, "What is a true friend to you?"

More than 80 percent of the time, I hear, "A true friend is someone who accepts me as I am."

My friend, this is dangerous garbage to believe. A *true friend is someone who accepts you as you are?* The kid who works the drive-thru at your local fast-food restaurant accepts you as you are—because he doesn't care anything about you. A true friend holds you to a higher standard—he or she expects you to do what you said you were going to do, when you said you were going to do it. A true friend makes you better by his or her presence.

When you were growing up, do you remember playing tennis or Ping-Pong with your father? I'm betting he didn't let you win all of the time, because he knew if he did, you wouldn't get any better. This works with the companions you choose too. Choose allies who are better than you. If you want to get better at tennis, play somebody who will beat you, because it improves your game.

This concept works in business too. Surround yourself with people who are better than you. Want to become wealthier? Spend time with people who are wealthier than you. Want to become wiser? Invest time with people who have wisdom in spades. And seek their counsel.

For a great deal of my life, I hung out with a quiet guy who didn't talk until somebody asked him a question. When I understood the principle of seeking wisdom, his way of being became clear to me: My friend had an abundance of wisdom, but you had to draw it out of him. He wasn't keeping it from anybody, but he was humble. I really had to hammer him with questions. *Why this? Why that?* Only a fool refuses the counsel of wise men. As a businessperson, as a parent, as a student, there is safety in wise counsel.

A friend of mine had a history of bad decisions. I would ask him, "Now, just out of curiosity, who did you talk to about this before you made that decision?"

He would look at me like I was out of my mind and say, "Well, nobody."

And I'd reply, "So, you didn't ask anybody? You just . . . kind of . . . decided?"

He gave me a familiar look and basically said, "I'm an adult, and I know what's best for me. I can make my own decisions."

When we take counsel from ourselves, all we can receive is what we have . . . what we know . . . what we are.

Taking the counsel of wise men and women helps us avoid bad decisions and puts us on the pathway to a more successful life. When we add someone's wisdom to our own, we greatly increase the probability of our success.

Harnessing Your Inner Circle

The Guided Decision teaches us that, to a large degree, we are who we spend time with.

1. In your journal list everyone you consider to be in your "inner circle"—those closest to you who influence your life, including family members, friends, and colleagues.

2. The Guided Decision teaches us that our peers either stretch us or burden us. Next to each name, put an arrow to denote which direction the person is leading you. (This can be a difficult exercise for many of us because we form attachments to even those "friends" who hinder our progress. Be honest as you evaluate who you spend time with.)

3. Do you see any patterns? Are there a few people with whom you spend time who generally sour your life experiences? Or do you invest most of your time with those souls who challenge you, uplift you, and help you to become more?

Your Board of Directors

I personally don't make any decisions on my own without counsel from others I respect. And post-living-under-the-pier, I have a pretty good track record of good decisions. Logically, wouldn't you be more likely to make good decisions if you're surrounded with high-level thinking from others? I leverage the insights, experiences, and decision-making abilities of intelligent people—and select three or four to be on my personal board of directors to help me make decisions. What are the chances I'm going to screw up big time when I have the counsel of wise people in my life? Find people you can rely on and from whom you can seek counsel. This is a critical component of seeking wisdom!

The acquisition of wisdom is greatly expedited by harnessing the wisdom of others. People sometimes think, *I don't have the money to hire a board of directors. That's too expensive!* They miss the point. The idea is to surround yourself with wise people. My "board members" don't actually know they're on my board of directors. I don't necessarily let them know they're influencing my decision making.

It's easy to create a personal board; simply find people who are smarter than you, are more skilled than you, and have more fruit on the tree in key parts of their life.

My wife, Polly, and I have several couples on our board of directors who have been married longer than us. Polly and I have been married almost twenty years, and both of these couples have been married more than thirty-five years. For more than three decades, they have been happy and loyal to each other. I look at them and wonder, *How have they done it?* Naturally, we want them on our board of directors.

Polly and I do the same thing with people who have already raised the kind of children we want to raise. I stock my personal board of directors with people who are wiser, better writers, healthier—those who have created for their families the life I want for mine.

Creating Your Board of Directors

With whom might you cultivate a relationship (or make better use of an existing one) to create your own personal board of directors? You may choose specific "advisors" for various areas of your life. Naturally, you wouldn't want a "health advisor" who smokes or sits around all day watching television. We must become masters at knowing where to seek the appropriate counsel.

In your journal, list the names of potential board members and the area of your life in which they would advise you. Don't limit yourself to the people in your inner circle; brainstorm who you'd love to have on your board of directors, even if you don't currently have a relationship with him or her.

Remember, you don't even have to tell these people they're on your board—it can be your own little secret. And sometimes, the information you receive will be more to the point and pure without your director aware of the pressure of "mentoring"!

Beware of the Danger Point

When we reach a certain level of success with these Seven Decisions, it is also typical to come upon a danger point. We must always remember: we are where we are because of our best thinking, and if we want to keep improving, we must transcend that level of thinking, whether we intuitively know where to improve or are receiving good counsel from our inner circle of friends. It gets dangerous when, following an abundance of success, we begin to think, *I've got it covered. It's wired. It's done. I understand. And now I'm free to make all the decisions myself.* Our actions begin to say, *I'm wiser and smarter than anyone else.*

As you become more successful, you'll find the path less traveled. There will be fewer people available to you who are stronger and wiser than you; but you can find them. Of course, you can benefit from almost

God moves mountains to create the opportunity of His choosing. It is up to you to be ready to move yourself.

everyone if you're a committed student of wisdom. Somebody doesn't have to be wealthier than you to be smarter than you. Everybody is superior to us in some or many ways—we can learn from anyone.

The danger point occurs when we begin to think too highly of our own wisdom and start ignoring the counsel of others. Remember Napoleon? He went down in history as an emperor, a leader of men, and someone who conquered what was considered the world at that time. But here's the story most people have never heard . . .

An Afternoon in Waterloo

In June 1815, Napoleon was about to defeat Wellington at Waterloo and, in fact, *did so.* (In *The Hinge Factor*, Eric Durschmied lays out a detailed sketch of the Battle of Waterloo and outlines how Napoleon defeated Wellington. If you really want to understand how Napoleon pulled off this incredible feat, I highly recommend this book.)

In February 1815, Napoleon fled from Elba, where he had been exiled by the Allied governments, signaling the start of what they called the "100 Days Campaign." During this time, nobody slept well in the capitals of Europe for fear of Napoleon. Once

Napoleon reached Paris, he organized an army to sweep across Europe. His old generals were either dead or had switched allegiance. DaVoe had been killed at Meringo; LaNey at Esperge; Janeaux shot himself. It didn't matter to Napoleon because he believed he was capable of independent command. He was a military genius. After all, everyone told him so.

Just after daylight, Napoleon was having breakfast with his generals at the emperor's headquarters at Roson Farm. One of the generals worried about Wellington's strong position, being situated at Monte St. John. The emperor scoffed, "We have no possibility of defeat!" And, of course, he didn't! Napoleon had 72,000 men and 246 cannons compared to Wellington's 67,000 men and 156 guns.

Napoleon rode a small gray horse and was dressed in a gray topcoat with a dark purple silk vest and white trousers over boots that came just past his knees. As he was about to send his troops into battle, the emperor turned to his general, Michael Nae, and said, "If my orders are well executed, we shall sleep tonight in Brussels." All day long Napoleon sent wave after wave of infantry into Wellington's forces. At the end of the afternoon, General Nae and the Fourth Corp of Cavalry—his greatest group of five thousand riders—were ready. The sun shimmered off five thousand swords and lance tips, pennants fluttering in the wind as the emperor reviewed the situation one last time. One bold sweep, he knew, would separate the enemy from their guns. Then, he would cut them down. *Yes, it would work.* A well-executed cavalry attack was more devastating than the actual losses sustained by the enemy. Because of this, he would not divide his divisions; rather, he would attack in a single broad front. It was 4:03 p.m.

The French Cavalry advanced in Eshilon, supported by the artillery. The division was in the center of the attack. The emperor's riders headed directly for the British batteries. And when the British guns opened up with their double-shotted canister, thousands of round pellets fired as Nae pointed his saber forward to signal *La Charge!*

Five thousand horses broke into full gallop, the ground trembling from the pounding of hooves. "Viva l'emperor!"

On the other side, Colonel Cornelius Frazier, battalion commander for Wellington, saw an unbelievable sight: a steel tide advancing on his position! *They'll roll right over us!* he panicked. How many rounds could his gunners loosen off? Napoleon's men, led by General Nae, riding two ranks deep, knee to knee, headed straight for Cornelius Frazier's deadly balls of fire.

Wellington's canisters tore into limbs and turned horses inside out. Riders went down, but nothing stopped the charge. At the sound of the bugle, five thousand spear tips appeared in front of their horses to form a battering ram of pointed steel.

Another blast from the enemy's guns tore into the line of riders. Every gun, every battery on the hill, was blasting away, but nothing stopped the heroic charge of these five thousand men of the Fourth Cavalry.

The gunners managed to loosen off one more round of canisters as riders and horses piled up on each other like cards. Five minutes into the battle, General Nae was out in front, watching gunners drop their sponge-staves and flee their cannons. His men ran over them and captured the cannons. They had driven the English from their artillery, they had captured their guns, and Napoleon had defeated Wellington at Waterloo.

Napoleon's Blunder

It's a great story, isn't it? And it's absolutely true. *Now, wait a minute!* you must be thinking. *I thought Napoleon lost at Waterloo!*

Well . . . he *did* lose. But first, he won. You just never hear about the win because the loss overshadowed everything else.

Consider the situation: Here's a guy who's achieved so much success that he's not listening to anybody, not even his generals, much less the colonels, sergeants, or privates. He's so obsessed with his idea of victory that he refuses counsel from anybody.

And now for the blunder: Both the French and the English artillery carried muzzle-loading, bronze, twelve-to-sixteen-pound cannons, fired by setting a glowing fuse or a machete to a narrow firing touchhole that was drilled through the solid bronze. When troops would overrun an opponent's cannon, they took headless nails and drove them down into that touchhole, rendering the cannon useless. Napoleon's troops had asked before the battle, "Where are the nails? We're about to go into battle without nails!" Their confusion was ignored.

Napoleon's men were on the battlefield with no nails. They had guns, horses, swords, lances, and artillery pieces, but no nails. This historic event was decided by a fistful of nails.

Napoleon absolutely defeated Wellington. He ran Wellington over. But the battle raged back and forth, until finally a group of Wellington's men got their cannons back, and then another group . . . Suddenly, the cannons were being turned back upon Napoleon's force, firing into them, and Napoleon had to stand there on the hill with his hands behind his back, watching his men who had defeated Wellington's forces be blasted to pieces—all because they didn't bring nails into the battle. A handful of nails would have put those cannons out of action, and history books today would contain the record of Wellington's defeat.

When you counsel with only yourself, you make decisions only according to what you know. By counseling with wise men and women, you add their knowledge and experience to your own, dramatically increasing your chances for success and decreasing the possibility of failure.

Learning to Serve Others

In addition to reading books and taking the counsel of wiser friends, the third way to chart a course toward wisdom is by serving others—find a way to help another human being. This doesn't mean you have to do something grandiose or even something you consider incredibly useful. Serving others could be opening the door for someone. Carry their luggage, pour their coffee, hold their chair. By serving others, we value them, and this increases our own value.

Perhaps not coincidentally, when we serve others, we increase the possibility that they would share their wisdom with us. When billionaire and shipping tycoon Aristotle Onassis was in his last years, a reporter asked, "If you lost all your money, what would you do to gain it back?"

He replied, "Well, it would be a process, of course. But the first step on the process of gaining a fortune, I would consider, to be serving others."

A wise man will cultivate a servant's spirit, for that particular attribute attracts people like no other.

The reporter just dropped his jaw and exclaimed, "What do you mean, *serving others?* I thought people served you!"

He said, "People serve me, but it is only because throughout my life, I've served others. You ask, 'How would you create a fortune?' and the first step would be to serve others. I would put myself in a position, by serving others, to be around people who could help me, guide me, and share their wisdom and experience with me."

Then he added: "I would get a job, maybe two, maybe three. I would save my money. I would live as simply as I possibly could, and when I'd saved up five hundred dollars, I'd go eat in a restaurant that cost five hundred dollars for a meal. Then I would work more, live simply, and save my money until I saved five hundred dollars, and I would go eat again in a restaurant that costs five hundred dollars."

The reporter was beside himself at this point, and replied, "I'm really not getting this. You're trying to create a fortune, yet you're blowing five hundred dollars on a dinner?"

Onassis replied, "It has nothing to do with the food I eat, but the associations that I create. You see, to get to where I'd want to be, I would need the wisdom and relationships with the people who eat regularly in expensive restaurants. And so, when I go into the restaurant, I make eye contact, I introduce myself, I shake hands. As I enter, I say, 'Hello.' As I leave, I say, 'Goodbye.' Somewhere down the road, I'm going to run into those people, who will say, 'Oh, yes, I saw you in . . .' Or 'You were the man at the next table when we ate at . . .'"

He concluded, "It all has to do with the associations you create with the people whom you are around. People will want to help because you were there to hold a chair or hold a door for them."

Alfred Vanderbilt's Servant Spirit

Alfred Vanderbilt was recognized everywhere he went. The Vanderbilt family was one of the wealthiest, most prominent families in the world. The family's wealth began with Alfred's father, Cornelius Vanderbilt, who in the early nineteenth century began amassing a fortune in the shipping and railroad industries.

Alfred stood out among his siblings. He was the only one in

the family who insisted on beginning his business experience at the bottom as a clerk in one of his father's offices. His siblings demanded management positions. The public respected Alfred Vanderbilt and never forgot him. His father never forgot him either, as evidenced by the division of his father's wealth: Each of Cornelius's sons and daughters was willed $7 million, but Alfred received $76 million. In his father's view, Alfred would steward the money with a servant's spirit. Cornelius Vanderbilt knew that servants often become kings and, consequently, the wealthiest among us.

Alfred Vanderbilt shared his wealth with a servant's spirit. During World War I, Alfred wasn't content with charity in the form of purchasing wagons and giving them to the Red Cross— he intended to drive them himself. He was known as a kind man, known for his kind heart to the poor.

Alfred Vanderbilt's legacy was as a servant (his story is an integral part of my second novel, *The Lost Choice*). His actions during his life's final moments aboard the RMS *Lusitania* testified to his servant's spirit. When the *Lusitania* sank in May 1915, the newspapers memorialized Alfred's servant's spirit: His last act on earth was to tie life jackets to baskets for babies, and he gave his own life jacket to a woman. Though Alfred owned many estates with swimming pools, he had never learned to swim. Alfred Vanderbilt maintained a servant's spirit to the very end.

Cultivating the Servant's Spirit

What can you do to begin or continue cultivating a servant's spirit? Can you volunteer at your local church or community center? Can you visit the elderly at your local hospital?

Can you spend more time with your family? Can you schedule a call to a family member just to make him or her smile? Can you commit random acts of kindness, such as paying the toll for the car behind you?

Brainstorm a list of ideas, and commit to doing at least one in the next five days.

Fuller's Life Experiment

In 1927, at age thirty-two, Buckminster Fuller stood on the shores of Lake Michigan, intent on committing suicide by throwing himself into the freezing waters. His first child had died. He was bankrupt. He was discredited. He was jobless. He had a wife and a newborn daughter, yet he felt hopeless.

In an epiphany, he realized that his life belonged not to himself but to others. He chose that moment to embark upon an experiment to discover what a little, penniless, unknown individual might be able to do on behalf of humanity. He thought, *If my life belongs not to myself but to others, then what can I do for others? What will become of a life of service?* Over the next fifty-four years, he proved time and again that his most controversial ideas were practical and workable.

Do battle with the challenges of your present, and you will unlock the prizes of your future.

Imagine! A man who is bankrupt, discredited, jobless, and about to commit suicide. And he decides to make his life an experiment! *My life doesn't belong to me; it belongs to others. So I will give it to others.* What happens to a man with nothing who decides to give his life in service?

During the course of this experiment, he was awarded twenty-five U.S. patents, authored twenty-eight books, and received forty-seven honorary doctorates in the arts, sciences, engineering, and humanities. He received dozens of architectural and design awards, including the Gold Medal from the American Institute of Architects and the Gold Medal of the Royal Institute of British Architects. He created work that remains in the permanent collections of museums around the world. He went from a man who was bankrupt, discredited, and about to commit suicide, to a successful speaker who circled the globe fifty-seven times, reaching millions through his lectures, interviews, and work. He decided, *I will live a life of service*.

Creating wealth, even *choosing* wealth, begins with a servant's attitude.

The Legacy Experiment

What if your life was an experiment? What is the legacy you would like to leave? How will you serve generations to come?

Your choices will determine the answers to this question. Capture your living legacy right now in your journal.

Real *Traveler* Profile: Bob Hope

Everyone has heroes. One of mine happens to be Bob Hope. Bob Hope was an extraordinary entertainer, starring in more than fifty-six movies and more than five hundred Bob Hope Specials. He entertained American military personnel all over the world for more than half a century! His commitment to our country, the tireless schedule he kept, and the freshness he worked to bring to his comedy are only a few of the things I admired about this man.

Here's a personal correspondence from *Bob Hope:*

Dear Andy,

You know I've been awfully lucky these last fifty years in show business, but I had my other tough moments. For instance . . .

Around 1928, I went into Evansville, Indiana, to do an act. I was having some breakfast so I looked at the paper to see what kind of billing I had at the theatre and it said, *Ben Hope*! So I took the paper and I rushed into the theatre. I said to the manager, "What's the idea of spelling my name that way?"

"What name?"

"Ben Hope! What kind of thing is that?"

"Well, what is your name?"

"Bob Hope."

"Well, who knows?"

I guess at that time nobody knew and nobody cared, but I got a pretty good break because at least I was working a few places.

Now about six months before that, I was standing in front of the Woods Theatre Building in Chicago. I had been getting ten dollars a show, but I couldn't even get that. Nobody knew me. My name was Lester Hope so I decided to change it to Bob Hope 'cause it sounded more chummy, but I still starved. I couldn't book a date.

I wasn't eating very well and my laundry was piling up. I was just about ready to go home to Cleveland to get a full meal and my laundry cleaned when this friend of mine walked up.

He was a very successful Vaudevillian, Charlie Cooley, and he said, "How you doing?"

"I'm starving."

"Come with me."

And he took me up and introduced me to Charlie Hogan, his booker. He booked small theatres in and around Chicago. He said, "I can give you one day at the West Inglewood Theatre, will twenty-five dollars be all right?"

Well, I gulped, because I'd only been making ten a show at that time. That was the date that got me rolling.

Andy, we all have our slack moments and they're interesting to look back on. It sort of levels you off a little bit.

I'll see you down in Port Arthur.

Good luck,

—BOB HOPE

THE ACTIVE DECISION

I am a person of action.

The Active Decision for personal success is crucial to you right now. Becoming a person of action is a choice, not a process. You either are a person of action or you are not. It's time to state your case: what are you?

From *The Traveler's Gift*

My future is immediate. I will grasp it in both hands and carry it with running feet. When I am faced with the choice of doing nothing or doing something, I will always choose to act!

— COLONEL JOSHUA LAWRENCE CHAMBERLAIN

The Active Decision

In The Traveler's Gift, *Joshua Lawrence Chamberlain presents David Ponder with the third Decision that determines personal success:*

I am a person of action.

Beginning today, I will create a new future by creating a new me. No longer will I dwell in a pit of despair, moaning over squandered time and lost opportunity. I can do nothing about the past. My future is immediate. I will grasp it in both hands and carry it with running feet. When I am faced with the choice of doing nothing or doing something, I will always choose to act! I seize this moment. I choose now.

I am a person of action. I am energetic. I move quickly.

Knowing that laziness is a sin, I will create a habit of lively behavior. I will walk with a spring in my step and a smile on my face. The lifeblood rushing through my veins is urging me upward and forward into activity and accomplishment. Wealth and prosperity hide from the sluggard, but rich rewards come to the person who moves quickly.

I am a person of action. I inspire others with my activity. I am a leader.

Leading is doing. To lead, I must move forward. Many people move out of the way for a person on the run; others are caught up in his wake. My activity will create a wave of success for the people who follow. My activity will be consistent. This will instill confidence in my leadership. As a leader, I have the ability to encourage and inspire others to greatness. It is true: an army of sheep led by a lion would defeat an army of lions led by a sheep!

I am a person of action. I can make a decision. I can make it now.

A person who moves neither left nor right is destined for mediocrity. When faced with a decision, many people say they are waiting for God. But I understand, in most cases, God is waiting for me! He has given me a healthy mind to gather and sort information and the courage to come to a conclusion. I am not a quivering dog, indecisive and fearful. My constitution is strong and my pathway clear. Successful people make their decisions quickly and change their minds slowly. Failures make their decisions slowly and change their minds quickly. My decisions come quickly, and they lead to victory.

I am a person of action. I am daring. I am courageous.

Fear no longer has a place in my life. For too long, fear has outweighed my desire to make things better for my family. Never again! I have exposed fear as a vapor, an impostor who never had any power over me in the first place! I do not fear opinion, gossip, or the idle chatter of monkeys, for all are the same to me. I do not fear failure; for in my life, failure is a myth. Failure only exists for the person who quits. I do not quit.

I am courageous. I am a leader. I seize this moment. I choose now.

The Decision to Act

Without action, none of the other Decisions are useful. People often respond to the notion of action with, "Oh, yeah, I know. I need to take action."

We know! We've all been told, "You have to do something, whether it's right or wrong. It's better to do something than nothing."

Remember that *we* make something happen. Ironically, what's the first thing most people do when they get depressed? What's the first thing people do when they're experiencing hard times? They lie down on the couch, turn on the television, and metaphorically say, "Hit me!" Just like a deer in the headlights.

Always remember that our encouragement, opportunities, knowledge, and information will come from other people—and most of them aren't sitting on the couch when we're depressed! We have to get out and do something.

There are people in your life every day, watching to determine who you are. Be a person of action! Seize moments; choose immediacy. You weren't given the ability to make right decisions all the time, but you were given the ability to make a decision and make it right!

It drives me nuts when I hear people say, "But I can't *always* do my best work." If you can't do your best work, than do your second-best work. But whatever you do, move! Get going!

When faced with a decision, many people say they are waiting for God. But we must understand that in most cases, God is waiting for us!

A person who doesn't move is destined for mediocrity. As I said before, when faced with a decision, I often hear people say, "I'm waiting on God."

I promise you, in most cases, God is waiting on you! Yes, God feeds the birds, but He doesn't throw the worms in their nests. He's given you a healthy mind to gather and sort information, and the courage to come to a conclusion.

Successful people make their decisions quickly and change

their minds slowly. Unsuccessful people make their decisions slowly and change their minds quickly.

Be a person of action. Be daring and courageous! And don't let fear get the best of you.

Fear is nothing but a misuse of the creativity God instilled in you. Fear may have outweighed your desire to make things better for your family. Never let it happen again! Take back your power and expose fear as a vapor—an impostor that never had any power over you in the first place. Never fear opinion, gossip, or the idle chatter of monkeys. Never fear failure—failure is a myth. Failure exists only for those who quit. *You don't quit.*

History Remembers the Bold

The prevailing attitude in our society seems to be "Wait and see." "Don't make a mistake." "Slow down." "Be careful." How significant, then, could it be to actually *do* something? Remember the old Indian proverb? "Man who stand on top of mountain with mouth open wait long time for roast turkey to fly in."

History chronicles the bold and the timid, but it's the bold we remember. The bold capture our imagination, inspiring us as we move through our own lives. We remember people like Susan B. Anthony, Henry Ford, the Wright brothers, Florence Nightingale, and modern giants like Lee Iacocca, Bill Gates, Oprah Winfrey, Warren Buffet, and Jack Welch. These bold people, with the courage of their convictions, seize the moment. They demonstrate that difficulties disappear and obstacles vanish in the face of unwavering courage. The bold capture our hearts and souls because they have followed their hearts to become who they are, providing a shining path for us to follow.

During the Olympics, we're enamored with the courage of the

bold. And it's not necessarily the ones who win the events that inspire us but the ones who compete with their hearts, at an uncommon level. We recognize the hero within ourselves when the athlete gives everything he has, including his last breath, and finishes, limping off the field of battle.

Do you remember what Ulysses S. Grant, the eighteenth president of the United States, looked like? You probably do. Did you know that he never held any political office other than president of the United States? And yet, we remember him very clearly.

Do you remember what Rutherford B. Hayes looked like? What about James Garfield, Chester Arthur, or Grover Cleveland? Do you remember Benjamin Harrison or William McKinley? Probably not. And yet, amazingly, each of these men was president of the United States after Ulysses S. Grant. Grant's been dead more than a hundred years, yet you recall what he looked like and may even have a good idea of his personality.

Many people move out of the way for a person on the run; others are caught up in his wake.

Grant was general-in-chief of the Union army during the Civil War. But did you know he wasn't the first one? Or the second or the third or the fourth or even the fifth? He was the *tenth* general-in-chief Lincoln appointed to that position during the Civil War. Why do you remember him? Because he was a person of action.

Winfield Scott was Lincoln's first general-in-chief. Next came McDowell, followed by Fremont, then the disastrous McClellan. In McClellan, Lincoln had a commander of the entire Union army who refused to engage the enemy! After McClellan, Lincoln appointed Henry Halleck, a graduate of West Point and a published author on military tactics. Lincoln read the book—a fine book with good theory—right before he appointed Halleck. Lincoln found out books don't fight wars. Halleck evaded all personal responsibility, lost what little composure he brought to the task, and eventually became nothing more than a clerk.

McClernon was next, and according to Lincoln, all he did was complain about the other generals almost weekly in a long, rambling communication critical of something Sherman or the other generals had done.

After McClernon, Lincoln appointed Rosecrans, then Burnside, and finally Nathaniel P. Banks. Naturally, the day Lincoln announced his intentions to promote General Ulysses S. Grant, he was vilified in the press. Even after Grant was appointed, the press was pushing for Grant's dismissal, but Lincoln couldn't spare him because Grant was thoughtful, he moved forward, and he was bold in his tactics. He was a person of action. One of the big criticisms of Grant at the time was that he drank too much. Lincoln said privately, "Well, if I can find out what he's drinking, I'll send a few cases to the other generals."

Overcoming Fear

Fear debilitates action. Where has fear hindered your progress? Has fear kept you from pursuing a job promotion, diving into a new career, going after a big account, reinventing your business, or innovating? Fear of failure, humiliation, or making mistakes hinders our creative impulses and our ability to create extraordinary changes in the world.

Step 1: To overcome fear, we must first identify it. Identify five places in your life and business where fear has hindered your progress.

When the tiger is charging you, two choices arise: stand motionless in fear to be mauled, or attack the tiger and see what happens. In standing motionless your fate is certain. In attacking the tiger a myriad of possibilities exist, including the tiger becoming afraid (or simply thinking you're insane) and running away. The point is, we must push through our fears to grow and become more.

Step 2: What if fear was no longer a factor? State an affirmative decision for each of the fears you listed in Step 1. What actions are you committed to taking (on a consistent basis) to make your fears irrelevant? Create a list of action steps for moving beyond each fear.

The Way of the Hero

Calvin Coolidge stated, "We can't do everything at once, but, by God, we can do something at once!" Changing the world begins with a single act.

Do you remember the story of a twelve-year-old from Tacoma, Washington, named J. J. Rousch? J. J. was a hero. He had stopped a fire in his aunt and uncle's house in Midland, just outside of Tacoma. The national news called him a hero, and J. J.'s parents and his aunt and uncle certainly agreed. But J. J. didn't really think he was much of a hero because he didn't really think about what he was doing.

When smoke poured from his aunt and uncle's house, he

reacted. Following his mother's orders, J. J. grabbed a sixty-five-pound fire extinguisher from his grandma's house nearby, and this twelve-year-old rushed over to the house on fire, grabbed a ten-pound object outside the back door, and hurled it through the kitchen window. As his mother used the extinguisher on the fire, the boy grabbed a garden hose, kicked in the front door, and battled the flames with water. When the firefighters arrived, the blaze was out.

An army of sheep led by a lion would defeat an army of lions led by a sheep!

Curiously, there were people who witnessed this event who simply watched because they didn't really know what to do. As J. J. said later, "All I thought was, 'Oh, wow, a fire.'"

Then he kicked the door in and battled the flames while everybody else was wondering what to do. "I'm not really a hero. I didn't really think of myself as a hero. I didn't really think at all," J. J. said.

But that is precisely why this twelve-year-old boy is a hero— because he didn't stop to think; he just acted.

Remember the story of the Kentucky Boy Scout from Bowling Green? Matt Knight was practicing with his cross-country team at a park when he stopped to tie his shoe. From across the park, he heard the screams of Susan Beth Meeks, an eighth grader who had fallen into a pipe at the end of the drainage ditch. Her foot was lodged under a rock, forcing her head underwater while she struggled to escape. Matt found her, slid into the pipe, ducked his head under the water, and pushed her out. Matt said later that he was nervous as he jumped into the pipe with the struggling girl, "but I had to do something, so I did."

For Matt's act, he received the Honor Medal with Crossed Palms from the Boy Scouts of America. Since the medal's creation in the 1930s, only 166 people have received it. He then went to the White House and met the president of the United States, who congratulated him on his heroism. Certainly, Susan calls him her hero, but to Matt, he was just acting rather than wondering what to do.

Action is a choice. Interestingly, Matt, a sophomore in high school, made the choice to act long before the crisis. In subsequent interviews, he said, "I had thought about what would happen if I was ever faced with an emergency. I determined right away I would do whatever came to mind to solve the problem."

So are you ready for your moment? Have you decided what you will do when your moment arrives? We've heard over and over again that success happens when preparation meets opportunity.

The Deathbed Exercise

Write a glowing, incredible eulogy you would like to have read aloud at your funeral. Here are some key questions to help:

- What was your life's work about?

- Who was affected as a result of your actions?

- Who was made a better person because of you?

- What were the three biggest events that happened because of you?

- For what will you be remembered?

- How was the world different because of you?

Write your eulogy in your journal; then type and print it. Carry it with you wherever you go.

1. Share your eulogy with the three most important people in your life. Ask them for their feedback and suggestions on what needs to happen for you to become the person in the eulogy. Practically speaking, to make your eulogy a reality, where do you begin?

2. Put your eulogy into a Microsoft PowerPoint presentation to help you visualize what you want to do. Your mind often thinks in pictures, and having a visual presentation of your eulogy will help you keep it in mind.

This exercise will help you clarify what you want your life's accomplishments to be and help you build momentum to achieve it.

Becoming a Person of Action

You are a person of action. Too many people, when faced with a choice, lie down on the couch and watch TV. We live in a deer-in-the-headlights world where people facing tough situations basically say, "Roll over me."

The Active Decision affirms: "I am a person of action. I seize this moment. I choose now!" Beginning today, you are going to create a new future by creating a new you. There's no reason to dwell in the pit of despair or moan over squandered time or lost opportunities. You can't do anything about the past. Your future lies before you. Grasp it with both hands and run with it! When you're faced with the choice to do nothing or do something, you will always choose to act. Seize this moment. Choose now!

Leading is doing. To lead, you have to move forward, to be ahead of other people. By being a person of action, you'll inspire others and become a natural leader. People move out of the way for a person on the run, and other people are caught up in the runner's wake. Your activity creates a wave of success for people who follow. Your activity, actions, and movements must be consistent, for consistent action instills confidence in your leadership. People follow a person on the move. Leaders encourage and inspire others to greatness. They watch what you do. *An army of sheep led by a lion would defeat an army of lions led by a sheep every time.*

Embracing the Power of Action

In the Realizing Your Future Identity exercise in the Responsible Decision, you identified the person you need to become in order to realize your Ultimate Vision. Now, you need to identify the steps to take today, tomorrow, and in the weeks, months, and years to come to help move you toward that self-actualized person.

Quickly scan what you wrote for both the Crafting Your Ultimate Vision and Realizing Your Future Identity exercises. Next, capture ten things you can do in the next twenty-four hours to move you in that direction. A simple action such as picking up the phone and reconnecting with an old friend can help you build tremendous momentum toward your desired destination.

Who can you call? What can you research? What book do you need to read? What action can you take to help move you toward your Ultimate Vision? List ten actions you are committed to taking in the next twenty-four to forty-eight hours.

Chamberlain's Charge

Andrew Jackson, our seventh president, said, "Take time to be deliberate, but when the time for action arrives, stop thinking and go in!"

Did you know that one guy 140 years ago made a move that changed how our nation operates within this world? This one man's story was told in *The Traveler's Gift*, but it bears retelling here.

On the hot, humid day of July 2, 1863, Joshua Lawrence Chamberlain, a thirty-four-year-old schoolteacher from Maine and former professor of rhetoric from Bowdwin College, was in the fight of his life. He stood at the far left edge of a group of eighty thousand men strung out in a line across fields and hills, stretching all the way to a little town called Gettysburg, Pennsylvania.

Earlier in the day, Colonel Vincent placed Chamberlain and the men of the Twentieth Maine at the end of the line, saying, "Whatever you do, you can't let them through here." Chamberlain couldn't withdraw and he knew it. If the Confederate army over-ran them, the rebels would barricade the high ground, and the Union's Army of the Potomac would forfeit. In essence, eighty thousand men would be caught from behind on a downhill charge with no protection. To win, the rebels would have come through Chamberlain. Chamberlain knew he could not retreat.

At 2:30 p.m., the first charge came from the Fifteenth and Forty-seventh Alabama, running uphill as fast as they could and firing at Chamberlain's men, stationed on a rock wall they had thrown up

Successful people make their decisions quickly and change their minds slowly. Failures make their decisions slowly and change their minds quickly.

earlier that day. Chamberlain's men pushed them back and did again on a second and third charge. On the fourth charge, Chamberlain took a bullet to his belt buckle. He fell over, got back up, and kept fighting. Again, they pushed the Confederate troops down the hill.

At that point in our nation's history, battles were fought with artillery and ammunition, and you could see your enemy's faces as they surged up the hill. Chamberlain and his men had stacked up a rock wall of pie-plate-sized rocks 110 yards long. On that fourth charge, the rebels almost breached the wall.

Chamberlain, while waiting for the next charge, thought, *I'm a professor of rhetoric. I'm fairly certain I don't have anything anyone would care to learn at this point.*

He recalled, "Later, I felt sorry for my men. Their leader had no real knowledge of warfare or tactics. I was only a stubborn man, and that was my greatest advantage in this fight. I had, deep within me, the inability to do nothing."

Chamberlain continued, "I knew I may die, but I knew that I would not die with a bullet in my back. I would not die in retreat. I am, at least, like the apostle Paul, who wrote, 'This one thing I do, I press toward the mark.'" The attack came again. On the fifth charge, the men of the Fifteenth and Forty-seventh Alabama broke the wall open. They were fighting on both sides of the wall. Chamberlain's men couldn't reload. They were almost out of ammunition anyway, so they were swinging guns at each other and hitting with their fists. Somehow, Chamberlain's men pushed the enemy back again.

After pushing the enemy down the hill five times, Chamberlain's brother, Tom, came running up with Sergeant Tozier, an old, hard-nosed soldier. Tozier had a thick wad of torn shirt stuck into a hole in his shoulder where he had been wounded.

"No help from the Eighty-third," he said. "They're shot to ribbons, and all they can do is extend the line a bit. We're getting murdered on our flank."

"Can we extend?" Chamberlain asked.

His brother, Tom, said, "There's nothing to extend! More than half our men are down."

Chamberlain's company had started in Bangor, Maine, six months earlier, with a thousand men. They'd started that morning with three hundred. Now they were down to eighty.

"How are we for ammunition?" he said.

"We've been shooting a lot," was his answer.

Chamberlain said, "I know we've been shooting a lot. I want to know how we're holding out. What kind of ammunition have we got?"

As his brother went to check, the twelve-year-old lookout who had climbed a tree yelled, "They're forming up again, Colonel."

Chamberlain looked up to see the boy pointing down the hill. "They're forming up right now. And they've been reinforced. Sir, there's a lot more of them this time."

"Sir!" Sergeant Thomas stumbled into their midst, out of breath. "Colonel Chamberlain, sir. Sir! Colonel Vincent is dead."

"Are you sure, soldier?"

"Yes, sir," he said. "He was shot right at the first of the fight. They were firmed up by Weeds Brigade up front, but now Weeds is dead. They moved Hazlett's Battery up top. Hazlett's dead."

His brother came running back. "Joshua," he said, "we're out! One, two rounds per man at the most. Some of the men don't have anything at all."

Chamberlain turned to a thin man standing at his right. It was First Sergeant Ellis Spear. "Spear," he said, "tell the boys to take the ammunition from the wounded and the dead."

Chamberlain's men started wondering where they were going and what was going to happen. Spear replied, "Maybe we should think about pulling out, sir."

Chamberlain retorted grimly, "We will not be pulling out, Sergeant. Carry out my orders, please."

"Colonel!" Sergeant Tozier spoke up. "Sir, we won't hold them again. You know we won't."

"Joshua!" It was his brother. "Here they come. Here they come!"

Chamberlain stepped on top of the wall in full view, crossing his arms and staring down at the advancing army. The Fifteenth and Forty-seventh Alabama with their pale, yellow-gray uniforms, now reinforced by a Texas regiment, moved up the hill, and that high-pitched shriek—the rebel yell—coursed up toward Chamberlain and his men. Sergeant Spear had returned and was standing at Chamberlain's feet. Sergeant Tozier, Chamberlain's brother, and another lieutenant were huddled below. His brother said, "Joshua! Give an order!"

Chamberlain just stood there, deep in thought, quickly sorting the situation. *We can't retreat,* he thought. *We can't stay here. When I'm faced with the choice of doing nothing or doing something, I will always choose to act.* He turned his back on the advancing rebels, looked down at his men, and said, "Fix bayonets!"

Can you imagine being given that command? At first, no one moved. They just stared at him with their mouths open. "We'll have the advantage of moving downhill," Chamberlain said. "Fix the bayonets now and execute a great right wheel of the entire regime! Swing left first."

The lieutenant spoke up first, confused. "Sir," he asked, "what is a great right wheel?" But the colonel had already jumped from the rocks and was moving to the next group of men.

Sergeant Tozier answered his question. "He means to charge, son. A great right wheel is an all-out charge."

His men watched in awe as Chamberlain drew his sword. He leaped up onto the wall again and screamed, "Bayonets! Bayonets!"

And, turning, the colonel pointed his sword directly downhill. He wheeled and faced these overwhelming odds, slashed his blade through the air, and with a power born of courage and fear, the schoolteacher from Maine roared, "Charge! Charge! Charge! Charge! Charge!" to his men.

I have deep within me the inability to do nothing. I may die today, but I will not die with a bullet in my back. I will not die in retreat. I am, at least, like the apostle Paul, who wrote, "This one thing I do . . . I press toward the mark."

The eighty remaining fighting men of the Twentieth Maine tumbled over the wall after Chamberlain into history. An incredible example of a leader who refused to fail, Chamberlain knew that we move forward or we die. As they rolled over that wall and ran downhill, they lifted their voices to match the voice of their leader. "Charge!" they shouted. "Charge! Charge!"

When the Confederate troops saw Chamberlain, the leader of the opposition, mount that wall, they immediately stopped, unsure of what was happening. And when Chamberlain pointed his sword toward them and commanded his men to charge, they turned and ran. Many of them threw down their loaded weapons. The rebels were certain that these were not the same soldiers they'd been facing. *Surely these men had massive reinforcements*, they must have thought. *A beaten regiment wouldn't charge!* In less than ten minutes, Chamberlain had his sword on the collarbone of a captain in the Confederate Army. "You, sir, are my prisoner," he said.

The man turned a loaded pistol around and handed it to Chamberlain and said, "Yes sir. I am."

In less than ten minutes, that ragged group of men under

Chamberlain's command, without any ammunition, captured, more than four hundred soldiers of the enemy.

Historians have determined that, had Chamberlain not charged that day, the South would have won at Gettysburg. If the South had won at Gettysburg, historians say, the South would have won the war. Now, I always thought that if the South had won, we would be the North and South, but historians say that had the South won, we would now have a continent that looks more like Europe, fragmented into nine to thirteen countries. Which means that, had Chamberlain not charged when Hitler swept across Europe in the 1940s, the United States of America wouldn't have existed to stand in the breach. When Hirohito systematically invaded the islands of the South Pacific, there would not have existed a country big enough, powerful enough, strong, populous, and wealthy enough to fight and win two wars on two fronts at the same time. The United States of America exists today because of one man who made a decision to charge. One man decided that he was a person of action.

Early to Bed, Early to Rise . . .

I encourage you to become an early riser. Thomas Jefferson woke up early every day. He said, "Whether I retire to bed early or late, I rise with the sun."

One of our country's founding fathers, Thomas Jefferson had an appetite for action. He said, "Do you want to know who you are? Don't ask. Act. Action will delineate and define you." He also said, "Determine never to be idle. It is wonderful how much may be done if we are always doing." Another one of Jefferson's great quotes: "I'm a great believer in luck; and I find the harder I work, the more I have of it."

Thomas Jefferson knew that action made the man. He managed

more than ten thousand acres as a farmer. He became a surveyor and a successful land speculator. He owned a profitable nail factory. He was an extraordinary horseman who was still riding two months before his death at eighty-three. He was an accomplished architect who designed his own home and the homes of many of his friends.

He founded the University of Virginia, designed the campus, hired the professors, and wrote the curriculum. He was a respected and published naturalist, horticulturist, and meteorologist. He was a chess player, an accomplished singer, and a violin player—he is believed to have owned a Stradivarius. He was the president of the American Philosophical Society for twenty years, as well as a regent and alumnus of William and Mary College.

He was a diligent correspondent, and more than twenty-eight thousand of his letters survived. He was fluent in Latin, Greek, French, and Italian. He studied Anglo-Saxon, German, and American Indian dialects. He was a voracious reader and book collector, with a library of twenty-seven hundred volumes by age forty. He was the creator of the Library of Congress, the U.S. Patent Office, and the U.S. Monetary System.

Jefferson was a practicing lawyer and two-term governor of the Commonwealth of Virginia. He was the U.S. minister to France for five years and the first U.S. secretary of state. He was both vice president and president of the United States, and he authored what many consider the most important document ever written: the Declaration of Independence.

There was a fifty-year period in Jefferson's life during which the sun never caught him in bed. He rose as soon as he could read the hands on the clock next to his bed. George Washington Carver also rose early. He said he did so he could talk to God and find out what His instructions were for the day. Benjamin Franklin crafted the maxim, "Early to bed and early to rise makes a man healthy, wealthy, and wise." This is more than just a quote; it's really true!

Challenge yourself to wake up early until it's a habit. Waking up before the rest of the world is a doorway to new and creative ideas. It's a biblical principle too. Romans 13:11–12 says, "Knowing the time, that now it is high time to awake out of sleep . . . . The night is far spent, the day is at hand: let us therefore cast off the works of darkness, and let us put on the armour of light" (KJV).

30-Day Early-to-Rise Challenge

I present you with the "30-Day Early-to-Rise Challenge"—an activity that will change your life if you follow through with it. For thirty days, get up at least an hour before the rest of the house. (Go to bed earlier if you need to, but you'll probably find you don't need to.)

Your objective when you wake up in the morning is to come up with several new ideas that inspire and motivate you. Keep a pen and a journal nearby and jot down the first twenty ideas that come to mind. Write quickly. Chalkboard. Brainstorm. Circle the idea that is most important to you. To set that idea in motion, quickly brainstorm five specific actions you can take within twenty-four hours and do them.

Over thirty days you'll have come up with thirty new ideas. Any one of these can take your life in an incredible new direction.

(Don't panic! I'm not saying this is something that you have to do for the rest of your life. You can occasionally sleep in after the thirty days.)

The Butterfly's Effect on Change

The beautiful thing about taking action is that each action you take changes things. Every time you do something, it matters, and I can prove it. When you grasp this concept, you will begin to truly appreciate your value as well as the value of others in the world. Every single thing we do matters—forever. And yet, most of us don't see this. Instead, it seems that some people are more important than others, and some of us are not needed at all. And some people believe they can do things all by themselves.

I love convincing the CEO of a major corporation that the man or woman answering the phones isn't just the receptionist but the "director of first impressions" for the entire company. The CEO could vacation for three or four weeks and we might not even know he or she is gone, but if the director of first impressions takes the after-noon off, the business might shut down! We are all important.

Fear no longer has a place in my life. I have exposed fear as a vapor, an impostor that never had any power over me in the first place! I do not fear failure, for in my life, failure is a myth. Failure exists only for the person who quits. I do not quit.

Have you heard of the butterfly effect? The butterfly effect was a doctoral thesis written in 1963 by Edward Lorenz. According to him, the butterfly effect posited that the butterfly could flap its wings and set molecules of air in motion that could eventually create a hurricane on the other side of the world. The butterfly effect was laughed out of the New York Academy of Science because everyone saw it as ridiculous.

But it *was* interesting. The theory hung around as urban legend until the mid-nineties, when physics professors proved the butterfly effect was accurate and viable. In fact, the butterfly effect worked with every form of moving matter, including people. Like the law of gravity, the butterfly effect was given the status of a law because it worked every time. It is now known as the law of sensitive dependence upon initial conditions.

Joshua Chamberlain is an excellent example of the butterfly effect. One man who made one move 140 years ago, and the effects of his actions are still rippling through all of our lives today.

The Protective Field of Purpose

It occurs to me that as you read this, you might be going through the worst time in your life. If that's the case, know that it's normal. *We are all either in a crisis, coming out of a crisis, or headed for a crisis.* It's just part of being on this planet. Things may feel horrible right now, but you are still here. And if you're *here*, you haven't finished what you were put here to do.

The greatest part of your life—your purpose—has yet to be lived. There is more fun to have! There's more success to experience. There's more laughter to enjoy. There are more children to teach and more friends to influence and help. And if what you were put here to do hasn't been completed, you can't be harmed. There is a protection around you just like there was around Chamberlain. When the bullet found its mark on Chamberlain, it hit his belt buckle. He got proof (just like you'll see proof) that until you accomplish what you were put here to do, you will not and cannot be harmed.

Chamberlain would later serve four terms as governor of Maine. During the third term, he received further confirmation of the divine protection that surrounded him. A letter arrived at the state house addressed to Governor Joshua Chamberlain from a member of the Fifteenth Alabama:

Dear Sir,

I want to tell you of a little passage in the battle of Round Top, Gettysburg, concerning you and me which I am now glad of. Twice in that fight I had your life in my hands. I got a safe place between two rocks and drew bead fair and square on you. You were standing in the open, behind the center of your line, fully exposed. I knew your rank by your uniform and accents, and I thought it a mighty good thing to put you out of the way. I rested my gun on the rock and took steady aim. I started to pull the trigger, but some strange notion stopped me. Then I got ashamed of my weakness and went through the same motions again. I had you perfectly certain. But that same strange something shut right down on me. I couldn't pull the trigger and gave it up. That is, your life. I am glad of it now and hope you are.

Yours truly,
A Member of the 15ᵗʰ of Alabama

There will be protection around you as you act and move and become what you were meant to be. You may never see it, but I can promise you this: there is no need to live the rest of your life—any part of your life—in fear.

Capitalizing on Your Strengths

We each excel in certain areas. Some of us are fast runners. Some of us are sharp thinkers. Others might be better at managing finances. Some are confident communicators. Some are caring, loving, and uplifting. Some are loyal. You get the idea.

We don't want to only identify areas we need to improve; we

want to capitalize on our God-given strengths! If we capitalize on our current strengths, we can create momentum and take on the challenges that await us.

Clarify what you're great at—what you do best and enjoy most. What's your "hot zone"? What are your current areas of mastery? List your strengths in your journal.

Adams's Choice

John Adams was more than just our second president—the accomplishments of his life massively shaped our world. He was a servant who proclaimed, "If we do not lay ourselves out in the service of mankind, whom should we serve?"

John Adams had a purpose far beyond his own life. He believed that it wasn't words or reactions but *actions* that make the person. There was a new law going around the colonies that could have easily ruined Adams: the colonists refused to purchase stamped paper while the British governor refused to acknowledge legal documents without the stamps. Although this basically cut off Adams's income as an attorney, he stood with the colonists even when some fellow "patriots" stood only when it didn't affect their pocketbooks. To Adams, his stand was critical because it was aligned with the words of Thomas Jefferson in one of the most potent documents ever created— the Declaration of Independence: "And for the support of this declaration with a firm reliance on the protection of divine providence, we mutually pledge to each other our lives, our fortunes, and our sacred honor."

What can you learn from the example of one of our greatest

presidents? Greatness comes at a cost. What will you have to give up to get what you want? Will it be time? Will it be petty habits or limiting beliefs? Will you have to give up your fears? Remember: thoughts don't change anything until they are acted upon. Action changes everything.

Adams saw himself as more than just a Harvard-educated man, a great lawyer, a husband to Abigail, or a president to a nation. Adams saw himself as a shaper of the future. He knew his actions would affect many; therefore he acted and spoke in a manner consistent with this understanding. What if you believe today that your actions will affect millions of people? How will you act and speak? How must you act and speak now to make not only your dreams but the dreams of millions come true? John Adams knew his role. He said, "I must study politics and war, that my sons may have liberty to study mathematics and philosophy." He was giving something for the future. He didn't really want to study politics and war, but in his mind he had to so his children would have the freedom to study what they wanted.

Your Roles in Action

John Adams knew his role: "I must study politics and war that my sons may have liberty to study mathematics and philosophy."

How do you see yourself? Write down three roles that you feel identify who you are and what your life is about (visionary businessman, extraordinary father/mother, etc.).

What specific actions can you take that are linked to each of these roles?

Real *Traveler* Profile:
Stan Lee

If you have ever read a comic book or seen a comic hero–based action movie, you've most likely experienced the vivid imagination of Stan Lee. The former chairman of Marvel Comics and Marvel Films and now co-founder of POW! Entertainment, Stan Lee is perhaps the most influential personality in the comic book industry. Legendary characters like Spider-Man, the Incredible Hulk, the Fantastic Four, and the X-Men were all conceived in Lee's brilliant mind.

It's easy to assume that such an extraordinary innovator would have little trouble starting his career. "Hey, this guy created Spider-Man. I'm sure he didn't have any trouble getting work." The path of the *Traveler*, however, is always checkered with failure and adversity.

Here's a personal correspondence from Stan Lee:

Hi, Andy,

I've rarely followed anyone else's advice in my lifetime, so I don't know why you would want to follow mine, but for what it's worth, here's a thought you might want to to play with . . .

You neither learn nor grow by your successes, only by your failures. Failure is the grease that keeps the world's engines running. It's the adrenaline that sparks the human condition, that keeps us grasping and groping and growing. But, you have to know how to deal with failure—and, most importantly, how to free yourself of its yoke. Case in point . . .

For the first twenty years of my career in comic books, I tried in vain to sell a comic strip to the major newspaper syndicates. I wanted to be right up there with the guys who created Dick Tracy, Terry and the Pirates, and Flash Gordon. But, for that entire twenty-year period, I received rejection after rejection. Talk about failure—I was its poster boy! Did I quit? Did I figure I was wasting my time? Did I give up? Damn right I did! [NOTE: Actually, Stan is just being poetic. He didn't give up; he just changed his approach to getting what he wanted!]

I then devoted all my energies to making my comic books as good as they could be. [Stan Lee chose the Active Decision, which led to a turning point.] And what happened? After I stopped wasting time collecting rejection strips from newspaper syndicates and started concentrating on what I did best, Spider-Man, the Incredible Hulk and all our other Marvel heroes made it big. They became world famous.

And then it happened! The syndicates came after me! No more writing countless letters or endlessly knocking on doors—now I could pick and choose which syndicate I deigned to allow to represent me!

That taught me an unforgettable lesson. I'm just sorry it took me twenty years to learn it. Persistence is a great virtue. Whatever it is you're trying to accomplish, you should never give up while there's a shred of hope left. But . . .

You must also be perceptive enough to know when something just isn't going to work. There has to be a time when you let it go and look for other opportunities—the world is filled with them. Not everybody makes it in every endeavor. Not everybody gets to grab the gold ring in a chosen field. Just as it's important not to give up so long as you have a fighting chance, it's equally important to know when to stop wasting time trying for an impossible goal. It's sometimes better to switch gears, change your direction, and find another challenge, one which has a better chance of success.

The trick is not to get hooked on failure. You don't need that monkey on your back. If something doesn't work, jump off the track, take another train. There's a big, wide world out there; you've got countless options—don't neglect a single one! Just like me. I suddenly realize that this letter may not be making it, so I'm smart enough to quit—right now!

All the best,

—STAN LEE

THE CERTAIN DECISION
I have a decided heart.

The Certain Decision for personal success is what fuels
your actions from the Active Decision. The clarity of vision
you maintain in your mind is directly proportional to the
effectiveness of your actions. A decided heart is unwavering
in the face of continual challenges and setbacks, and that
ensures victory and a lifetime of greater fulfillment.

From *The Traveler's Gift*

Truth is truth. If a thousand people believe something
foolish, it is still foolish! Truth is never dependent upon
consensus of opinion. I have found that it is better to be
alone and acting upon the truth in my heart than to follow
a gaggle of silly geese doomed to mediocrity.

—CHRISTOPHER COLUMBUS

The Certain Decision

In The Traveler's Gift, *Christopher Columbus presents David Ponder with the fourth Decision that determines personal success:*

I have a decided heart.

A wise man once said, "A journey of a thousand miles begins with a single step." Knowing this to be true, I am taking my first step today. For too long my feet have been tentative, shuffling left and right, more backward than forward as my heart gauged the direction of the wind. Criticism, condemnation, and complaint are creatures of the wind. They come and go on the wasted breath of lesser beings and have no power over me. The power to control direction belongs to me. Today I will begin to exercise that power.

My course has been charted. My destiny is assured.

I have a decided heart. I am passionate about my vision for the future.

I will awaken every morning with an excitement about the new day and its opportunity for growth and change. My thoughts and actions will work in a forward motion, never sliding into the dark forest of doubt or the muddy quicksand of self-pity. I will freely give my vision for the future to others, and as they see the belief in my eyes, they will follow me.

I will lay my head on my pillow at night happily exhausted, knowing that I have done everything within my power to move the mountains in my path. As I sleep, the same dream that dominates my waking hours will be with me in the dark. Yes, I have a dream. It is a great dream, and I will never apologize for it. Neither will I ever let it go, for if I did, my life would be finished. My hopes, my passions, my vision for the future is my very existence. A person without a dream never had a dream come true.

I have a decided heart. I will not wait.

I know that the purpose of analysis is to come to a conclusion. I have tested the angles. I have measured the probabilities. And now I have made a decision with my heart. I am not timid. I will move now and not look back. What I put off until tomorrow, I will put off until the next day as well. I do not procrastinate. All my problems become smaller when I confront them. If I touch a thistle with caution, it will prick me, but if I grasp it boldly, its spines crumble into dust.

I will not wait. I am passionate about my vision for the future. My course has been charted. My destiny is assured.

I have a decided heart.

The Purpose of Analysis

The fourth Decision states: *I have a decided heart.* More people fail at what they attempt because of an undecided heart than for any other reason. We all know people who make decisions with an undecided heart. They'll tell you about a decision they're trying to make, lament over the various options, ask for your opinion, and then talk to someone else about their decision, asking for more opinions! "What do you think? Left? Right? Up? Down? Orange? Green?" They even get opinions about the first opinion they got. "What do you think about what this guy said?"

Then, they take the decision back to their friends to discuss whether they should change their decision or stick with it. Life becomes an ongoing state of analysis.

But get this: *the purpose of analysis is to come to a conclusion!* It's not to continue to analyze. Get to it! To repeat what I've said before, successful people make their decisions quickly and change their minds slowly. Unsuccessful people make their decisions slowly and change their minds quickly. Many people spend so much time analyzing the decisions they have already made that they don't have any energy left to actually do what they decided!

The prospect of making a "right decision" scares people. I don't believe we can make right decisions all the time unless we were born with the ability to tell the future (which I won't believe until I see a newspaper headline, "Psychic Wins Lottery"). Unless you can tell the future, you couldn't possibly gather enough information to make right decisions all the time. We are, however, as we stated earlier, made with the ability to *make a decision and then go about the business of making it right.*

A Decided Heart

Dr. Billy Graham brilliantly noted, "I'm always amazed at how many people in trouble confuse God's will for their life with plain old bad decision making." The wisdom in that statement is profound, revealing how many people misunderstand the Certain Decision.

I have a decided heart. My destiny is assured.

So what is a decided heart? A decided heart has to do with how we make decisions and our conduct after that decision is made; it has nothing to do with action or persistence.

We all know people who get locked into endless analysis, never moving past the decision-making avalanche. The endless opinion-gathering process and uncertainty gathers momentum, like a snowball rolling downhill, getting bigger and bigger as the analysis gets more complex. When they finally make a decision, the analysis continues.

Although there are questions that cannot be answered, they can be decided. Remember, most of the time you won't have all the facts you need to give you a complete picture. You will, however, have all the facts you need to make a decision.

Do you remember the leadership discussion we had in the introduction?

"Where do you want to go eat?"

"I don't know. Where do you want to go eat?"

"Truly . . . wherever you want to go . . ."

Note that the people who make a decision and then make it right are the people we admire in our society. They have decided hearts, and their destiny is assured.

Do you know people who are absolutely sure that God has led them down a certain path until it gets tough, and then they're just as sure that God has led them in the opposite direction? If you know people who are determined to live their lives in that netherworld of wishy-washy decision making, tell them God said to leave Him out of it!

God doesn't change His mind. Did you know that even the Bible says wishy-washy people are dangerous? "A double minded man is unstable in all his ways" (James 1:8 KJV). An indecisive person allows instability into every part of his life. It touches everything—our families, our businesses, our hopes, and our dreams. And if we don't decide what's important in our lives, we're going to end up doing things that are important to other people.

When you exhibit a decided heart and commit yourself to the

fulfillment of the destiny you have chosen, your life will never be the same. People will follow you everywhere, seeking your wisdom and advice—all because you have a decided heart. Challenges that you previously thought were mountains in your life melt at your feet when you have a decided heart.

Identifying Your Drivers

At this point in our exploration of the Seven Decisions, you've identified numerous areas for growth and even committed to some actions. Now, based on what you've learned about yourself thus far, choose three specific decisions you have made in the course of working through this book.

For each decision, write all the reasons why it is important—why it is a MUST. What will following through on this decision give you? How will your life change? The drivers behind your decisions are what will give you the energy to see them through. The more powerful the driver, the more committed you'll become.

Finding Your Vision

One of the best ways to keep your heart decided is to make sure the destiny you're working toward is worth the hassle. Life can be a struggle. Success as a parent, a friend, a businessperson, a community-contributor, or success at any level and in any arena can be, and often is, a struggle. It's going to be a struggle to maintain a decided heart; otherwise what you're struggling for isn't worth the struggle in the first place!

Think big! If what you're working toward isn't big enough,

you're going to be ambushed by bigger things every day of your life. Remember: If you're hunting rabbits in tiger country, you gotta keep your eyes peeled for the tigers. But if you're hunting tigers, you can just ignore the rabbits!

A Mini–Goal-Setting Workshop

You never lack time or money—only an idea. Linus Pauling, the Nobel Laureate in chemistry, said, "The best way to get a good idea is to get a lot of ideas."

Now it's time to figure out some of the major goals you want to achieve. In your journal brainstorm a master list of goals you have for this lifetime—big and small. Do you want to write a book? Do you want to run your division? Start a company? Start a family? Travel to Australia? Read more poetry? Take a wine-tasting class? Learn a foreign language? Take a martial arts class? Master calligraphy?

Upon what new adventure do you wish to embark? What new skill must you master?

Your goals should help you move toward the Ultimate Vision of the life you want to create. Capture your goals for your professional and personal life.

Your Heart, Your Life

When I sat down to outline *The Traveler's Gift*, I listed people throughout history who best personified each of the Seven Decisions. When I got to the fourth Decision, "I have a decided heart; my destiny is assured," Christopher Columbus practically leaped out at me. Columbus, with all his failings, epitomized a person with a decided heart. One of the characteristics of a person with a decided heart is that he owns his Decision. "If you're with me, fine; if you're not with me, fine. I am going. I have a decided heart. You can come along for the ride or not. And if you're against me, I do not care what you think or say."

Columbus didn't care what anybody thought or said and, frankly, outside your personal board of directors, neither should you. As you embark upon your journey with a decided heart, I can promise you the clamor from your personal peanut gallery of doubters and not-so-well-wishers will roar. It will amaze you! The people you thought would be on your side—but aren't— might be a larger group than you imagined. If you worry about what other people think, you'll have more confidence in their opinion than you do in your own. Your future does not depend on the opinions or the permission of others.

If you are afraid of criticism, you'll have little impact on the world. Criticism runs rampant, and if you're inhibited by it, you'll drown in its deep waters. Anytime you do something unrealistic by other people's standards, they'll be braying like donkeys.

If you worry about what other people think of you, you will have more confidence in their opinion than your own.

Want to know why?

Sorry, I have no clue.

I've had this happen in my own life. I've seen it happen in the lives of friends and watched it as people worked to accomplish something great—and the critics come out of the woodwork. I don't know why people feel so threatened by their perception of your success that they manage to make you the focus of their lives. I do know, however, that you cannot let them become the focus of yours.

The Cortez Initiative

In 1519, an extraordinary man set sail on the final leg of a voyage from the shores of Cuba to the Yucatan Peninsula. On eleven ships, five hundred soldiers, one hundred sailors, and sixteen horses. The mission was clear: to take the world's richest treasure! It was a treasure of gold, silver, artifacts, and jewels. It had been held by the same army for six hundred years. This treasure was not a secret. The world knew about this treasure because army after army had tried to take it. Conqueror after conqueror had come with their forces to take this treasure, but nobody had been able to do it. Not for six hundred years!

Hernando Cortez was a conqueror. Today, this occupation would be politically incorrect, but back then, it was simply a job description. Doctors, bakers, conquerors . . . you get the idea.

Cortez was aware of the many conquerors who'd attempted to claim this treasure and failed. But his approach was different. He gathered an army committed beyond the level of the common man. Rather than signing up every recruit that applied, Cortez interviewed first. He talked to them about the treasure, what their lives would be like when they took the treasure, and what their families' and future generations' lives would be like when they took the treasure. He even fantasized about what it would be like the moment they put their hands on the treasure. He sold the people on the vision. They committed and set sail.

Most people fail at whatever they attempt because of an undecided heart. Success requires the emotional balance of a committed heart. When confronted with a challenge, the committed heart will search for a solution. The undecided heart searches for an escape.

Halfway through the voyage, Cortez had a problem. Many of the soldiers and sailors who were once "so certain" turned into whiners: "Mr. Cortez . . . we're not sure we should be on this ship at this time." Or "This isn't what we expected it to be . . ."

When they arrived at the Yucatan Peninsula, Cortez gathered everybody on the beach. They grew quiet, waiting for Cortez to say, "You go here, we'll go there. If the arrows start flying, meet me at this coconut stump . . . we're out of here."

Instead, he leaned in and said, "Burn the boats."

"Excuse me?!" they replied incredulously.

Cortez repeated, "Burn the boats. Torch the boats."

"If we go home," he added, "we're going home in *their* boats." And on their leader's orders, *they burned their own boats!*

And an amazing thing happened. They fought really well. For the first time in six hundred years—the treasure was taken!

Why? Because their choice was to take the treasure . . . or die!

Burning Our Boats

The question for you is simple: *What boats in your mind continue to float the excuses and limiting beliefs that are keeping you from getting what you say you want? What boats in your life do you need to burn?*

Most of us are scared to burn boats because we know we'll get criticized if we do. Have you ever been criticized for something you believed or for something you've done with good intentions or because you're different? Doesn't it hurt? It's a horrible feeling.

Do you want to find out right now how to overcome criticism and that awful feeling of being criticized?

There are some people in your life who are never going to like you. Some people won't like anything you do as you become more successful. Think about your favorite book or movie of all time. Now, go online and start reading peer reviews on Amazon.com or some other product review Web site. It doesn't matter if your favorite book has sold more than twenty million copies or if your favorite movie did over $500 million at the box office, you'll find plenty of critical reviews.

I was wondering the other day, *Does anybody in the world get a pass? Is there anybody in the world that everybody likes?*

That very evening, I heard someone on a talk show say, ". . . and that's just another example of the Oprah-fication of America!"

It was obvious the term was being used to imply, "I don't like her."

How can you not like Oprah? I thought. *This nice, wonderful woman who does good things around the world? She's generous, kind-hearted, smart, funny . . . How can you not like her?*

But somebody doesn't.

The Catholic Church has finished the beatification for Mother Teresa. They are declaring her a saint! As part of the process, they brought people into Rome to edify her. "Oh, she is wonderful," they declared. "She has performed many selfless acts," they would say. "If anyone should be a saint, it should be Mother Teresa."

As part of this process, they also have people argue against her sainthood. And what do they say? I have no clue. "We heard her cuss one time . . ." What could they say? But these critics do show up.

When we are bothered by criticism, what we most need is a good dose of perspective. So, here is ours. Folks . . . the critics are bad-mouthing Oprah and Mother Teresa! Who are we to be exempt? We must accept it for what it is . . . the babbling of rabble who ultimately cannot help you or do harm. Ignore them.

Unlocking Your Hidden Dream

If you had one "hidden dream," secretly nursed close to your heart, what would it be? In your journal describe it in great detail.

Thriving on Rejection

The fact is that criticism and rejection hurt, but you must shield yourself from them to protect your decided heart. Let me tell you what I do to protect my decided heart. When I was working on getting *The Traveler's Gift* published, the book kept getting turned down. I received a note from the top literary agent at William Morris. He wrote, "I found your story a bit melodramatic and lacking in concrete plot and characterization. Also, I didn't feel the characters you describe come to life."

Okay, so you don't like the story, I thought. *You don't like the plot or the characterization. And you don't like the characters. Other than that, what didn't you like?*

My little trick to keep my decided heart thriving, happy, and moving on the road toward my assured destiny during this trying time was to find other authors I admired who received this same kind of rejection.

Criticism, condemnation, and complaint are creatures of the wind. They come and go on the wasted breath of lesser beings and have no power over me.

I actually felt pretty good after I found a rejection letter of *The Diary of Anne Frank*. The publisher said, "This girl doesn't have any special perception or feeling that would lift that book above the curiosity level." More than twenty-five million copies of *The Diary of Anne Frank* have been sold worldwide.

When the manuscript for the classic *Lord of the Flies* was submitted, the publisher commented, "It does not seem to me that you've been wholly successful in working out this idea." More than 14.5 million copies have sold to date.

An unknown writer called Dr. Seuss presented a publisher with a manuscript titled *And to Think That I Saw It on Mulberry Street.* The manuscript was rejected by twenty-seven publishers, including one who said, "This is too different from the other books for juveniles on the market to warrant its selling. We pass."

Most of us read George Orwell's classic *Animal Farm* in school. The publisher said, "It is impossible to sell animal stories in the United States." *Animal Farm* has sold more than ten million copies.

I really felt I was in good company when I read the rejection letter sent to Rudyard Kipling for a manuscript he submitted entitled *The Jungle Book.* The publisher sent back this note: "I'm sorry, Mr. Kipling, but you just don't know how to use the English language." I thought, *Holy cow. I'm in good company.*

That's what I do to protect my decided heart.

Eliminating Debilitating Beliefs

Some of the greatest challenges to having a decided heart are our conscious and unconscious limiting beliefs. These limiting beliefs often translate into negative self-talk, such as, I can't do it, I'm not good enough, I'm not smart enough, or I can't make it work.

Many of these debilitating beliefs are hidden safely away from our conscious mind. They remain destructive to our growth until they are uncovered and understood, dismantled, and released. Often, simply becoming conscious of the limiting beliefs can help dissolve them.

What are five limiting beliefs you have about yourself? Think back to the fears you defined in the Overcoming Fear exercise on pages 289 and 290. Behind every fear is at least one debilitating belief about yourself. Uncover your destructive beliefs and write them down.

The Passion of Decisiveness

We're journeying toward a destiny that is assured because we have decided hearts. People such as Michael Jordan, Oprah Winfrey, Albert Einstein, Richard Branson, and Tiger Woods are so extra-ordinary because they have mastered life on their own terms, with decided hearts. With decided hearts, we learn to defy conventional standards with a childlike playfulness. We can actually develop a sense of excitement that triggers action in the face of criticism and rejection, breeding solutions and movement toward what we want instead of what we don't want. It awakens a burning desire and relentless determination when the odds are stacked against us.

Poor is the man whose future depends on the opinions and permission of others. Remember this: if you are afraid of criticism, you will die doing nothing!

Distilled into one word, the idea of a decided heart is *passion.* Passion comes from the heart. It has nothing to do with the mind. In fact, in times of decision, you might have heard somebody say, "The whole thing moved from my head to my heart." That's passion. Passion assists you when you have a great dream. It breeds conviction and turns mediocrity into excellence in everything you do.

Passion inspires other people to join you in your pursuit. You can set yourself on fire and people will come to watch you burn. Passion helps you overcome insurmountable obstacles. You become unstoppable! Your life becomes a statement—an example. Others will see their futures in your eyes.

Joan of Arc was only seventeen years old when she led the armies of France against the English. One afternoon as the armies of France were approaching the city, they saw in the distance tens of thousands of soldiers manning the barricades at every elevation. Joan of Arc told her leaders, "Immediately. Now. Now, we must take them. Now." The leaders were horrified at her boldness and passion for winning this battle against seasoned warriors! After all, she was a peasant girl leading a rabble of men from France.

"I intend to strike at the heart of the barricade," she said.

"If you go in, not a man will follow you," they told her.

Simply, she replied, "I won't be looking back."

This young girl's passion changed history. What can you do with the passion in your heart?

Architecting the Greatest Show on Earth

Phineas Taylor Barnum was born one day late, July 5, 1810. He would have preferred fireworks and a celebration coast to coast to commemorate the arrival of the Greatest Showman on Earth. But, as nature would have it, he missed the party by four hours. The name Phineas was well placed. Its biblical meaning is "brazen mouth." P. T.'s maternal grandfather had the most influence on the boy in his formative years. The bespectacled, mop-headed, boisterous old man dearly loved his grandson and spent much of his time pulling one over on him. In P. T.'s own words, "My grandfather would go farther, wail longer, work harder, and contrive deeper to carry out a practical joke than for anything else under heaven." This model served Phineas well in his later years.

His father died when he was fifteen years old, leaving the family bankrupt and Phineas as the sole supporter. Phineas worked as a clerk in a nearby general store (of which he owned half), where he discovered his ability for promotion and vision. And in July 1935, Barnum's destiny came calling. A man named Coley Bartram walked into the store and spoke of a woman called Joice Heth, who was allegedly 161 years old and the nursemaid of President George Washington during his infancy. The man currently in charge of the Joice Heth Show was eager to return to his home state of Tennessee and was looking for a buyer for the show.

Barnum was hungry for a bigger and better opportunity. They haggled over the three-thousand-dollar asking price, agreeing on one thousand dollars for the Joice Heth Show. To secure the purchase, Barnum talked the seller into a purchase-option arrangement for five hundred. Five hundred dollars was all the money Barnum had in the world, but he was certain he had made the right decision. Barnum sold his partner his half of the grocery store to get the money, and in a few short days, Barnum went from store clerk to showman.

Careful planning, staging, and promotion turned this 161-year-old woman of exceptional mind and wit into a small industry. Then the inevitable happened: Joice Heth went on to meet her Maker. True to his word, Barnum allowed a famous surgeon friend to perform a postmortem examination. Dr. David L. Rogers returned findings that shocked and frightened Barnum: Joice Heth was no more than eighty years of age at the time of her death. The scandal hit the paper with the headline: "HOAX!"

Barnum was devastated. He had done his research and was convinced that Heth's records were authentic. Barnum's decided heart began to waver. Although he knew his destiny, he feared this controversy marked the end of his career.

What actually happened was astounding. As the allegations flew and the story grew, a strange promotional phenomenon was born. The suspected hoax became a part of the promotional fabric of the Joice Heth story, actually increasing the value of the show. Once Barnum recognized what was happening, he moved the excitement and conflict of Joice's story into other shows that attracted huge paying crowds bent on figuring out their authenticity. Jumbo the Elephant, the mermaid from Fiji, the Cardiff Giant, the original Siamese Twins, and others—some real, some unreal, and all fun—were born out of the Joice Heth "hoax." P. T. Barnum became known as "The Greatest Showman on Earth" as he put together tour after tour featuring oddities from around the world.

In 1881, he joined with rival showman James Anthony Bailey to found the famous Barnum & Bailey Circus and change entertainment forever. World famous for removing social barriers against entertainment and using curiosity and sensation in promotion, Barnum was indeed The Greatest Showman on Earth. He was one of the first American entrepreneurs to realize the moneymaking potential of publicity.

Barnum learned from this Joice Heth experience to always move with a decided heart. He learned that even when things look hopeless, our belief doesn't have to align with the outward manifestation. Barnum most likely learned to manage his emotions carefully. Fear, dread, shame, and guilt can be piercing weapons against a decided heart. In Barnum's case, they nearly blinded him from the opportunity that led to the creation of the modern circus.

What if he had followed his initial shameful emotions out of town? What if he'd been frightened into another career? He might have died a store clerk in a small Midwestern town! That's nothing to be ashamed of, but it's certainly not the exciting life that was to be P. T. Barnum's!

Living a Life of Unlimited Possibility

With a decided heart, grab hold of your dream for your life, your family, and your future. Don't make choices based on facts or percentages—they'll always discourage you. I feel sad for the people who consider themselves "realistic." They live their lives according to *what is*. Please throw "what is" out the window. Forget "what is."

Let's start living life with *what if*. What if life could be exactly as you chose? What if your heart was so powerful it created the time you wanted with your children? What if you could be a full-time mom or dad? What if you could have all the kids' college education money saved up before they were freshmen? What if you could live without a house payment—with your mortgage paid in full?

If you could choose a perfect day, what would it look like? How early would you get up? How late would you sleep? Who would you choose to be around? And where on earth would you be?

All my problems become smaller when I confront them. If I touch a thistle with caution, it will prick me, but if I grasp it boldly, its spines crumble into dust.

The Certain Decision reminds us: you have the power to choose how you live your life because you have a decided heart and your destiny is assured. Choose wisely, and remember, most people fail because of an undecided heart. That is not you. Determine that you have a decided heart, and your success will require the emotional fortitude of that decided heart.

When confronted with a challenge, a decided heart searches for a solution—it is only the undecided heart that searches for an escape. You can't afford to wait for conditions to be exactly right. Why not? Because conditions are never exactly right!

You have vision for a reason. Your dream for your life and your family's is in your heart for a reason. That passion is a part of you. So, go! Proceed! Don't ask permission anymore. Take it! Go!

To wait, to wonder, to doubt, or to be indecisive is to deny the world of who you are and who you will become.

You have a decided heart, and your destiny is assured.

Architecting a New Self-Image

The five beliefs you highlighted earlier represent the major blocks to your decided heart. It's time to dismantle these negative beliefs and replace them with uplifting ones.

1. For each negative belief, determine its polar opposite. If you have a negative belief that says, "I'm too old to be creative and inventive," you might change it to, "My age gives me the wisdom and gift of creativity and invention."

2. Write down a new, positively stated belief for each negative one.

Recite these new statements as positive affirmations over the next thirty days. Through continual repetition of your affirmations, you'll reprogram your subconscious mind with your new belief (and erase the conflicting old one).

Real *Traveler* Profile:
General Norman Schwarzkopf

When someone mentions the word *leaders*, it's easy to think of General Norman Schwarzkopf. General Schwarzkopf was the commander of Allied Forces in Operation Desert Shield and Operation Desert Storm, and quite possibly the most popular American military figure of the past century. His strong and decisive leadership during the Gulf War helped bring an early end to that conflict.

History will long remember the skill with which Schwarzkopf coordinated a war effort in a country deeply suspicious of foreigners, all the while maintaining the secrecy so critical to the success of our troops—not an easy task during America's first internationally televised war.

It seemed appropriate for General Schwarzkopf to represent the Certain Decision. Here's a personal correspondence from the general:

Dear Andy,

When I received your invitation to share a time of discouragement in my life, my immediate concern was how to select only one. The years have presented me with a series of crossroads which have often taken me down a different path than I might have chosen.

It is, of course, understood that if this were a perfect world, I would not be writing this letter at all. My childhood would have been easy, my military career without detours, and there would simply be no story to tell. As you know, that is not the case.

In December 1972, the Army was considering officers in my year group for early promotion to full colonel. Routine promotions were in order two years down the road, but after having gotten feelers from various generals who wanted me for a colonel's job, I thought I had a pretty good chance. No one had a right to expect an early promotion; however, being promoted early boosted an officer's reputation, and I'd secretly let myself look forward to it.

As I walked into the War College on a Monday morning in January, I saw several of my peers patting themselves on the back. At that moment, I knew my name was not on the list. I realized that I would have another shot at early promotion the following winter, but this was the first time in my career when I was clearly no longer at the front of the pack. Friends offered condolences, which made me feel worse, as well as theories as to why I had been bypassed. I was disappointed, confused, and shaken.

The following November, I was nominated by the Army to serve as a military aide to Vice President Gerald Ford. I was honored and excited to be chosen out of all the lieutenant colonels in the Army. This was a prestigious job that would leave me with powerful connections in the event I decided to retire.

As the selection process went on, I got my hopes up. I was interviewed by the Vice President's assistant for national security affairs and even sat down with the Vice President himself. I thought we really hit it off.

In early January 1974, two events happened almost simultaneously. First, the Army released its list for early promotion to colonel and, to my shock, again I'd not been selected. Then, a few days later, I was called and told I had not been selected to work with Gerald Ford. In addition to the discouragement I felt, my frustration level was at an all time high.

At this point, I must tell you two of the most important lessons I learned from those and other challenges I have faced: (1) don't dwell on disappointment—determine to do your best anyway, and (2) we don't always know what's best.

Moving forward, I was soon commanding troops as a colonel in Alaska. This led to a troop command at Ft. Lewis, Washington, and promotion to brigadier general, followed by Pacific Command in Hawaii, and an assignment as assistant division commander of the 8th Mechanized Infantry—part of NATO's front-line defense in Germany.

After several other exciting assignments through the years, including command of the 24th Mechanized Infantry Division and participation in the Grenada student rescue operation, I took over Central Command headquartered in Tampa, Florida. My area of responsibility was the Middle East.

Looking back at my military career, I can see now that every struggle I endured pointed me toward my destiny in the Gulf War. The challenges we face in certain situations sometimes hold a purpose beyond our understanding at the time. We don't always know what's best. The tough times in my life often dealt with being put in positions not of my choosing, but the ultimate result is now a matter of history.

I am frequently asked if I miss the Army. I suppose the answer would have to be yes, but what I miss the most is the camaraderie of those who have suffered great adversity. This is the bond that links all old soldiers. Not surprisingly, it is also the bond that links successful people. Success without adversity is not only empty . . . it is not possible.

Sincerely,

—H. NORMAN SCHWARZKOPF, GENERAL,
U.S. ARMY

THE JOYFUL DECISION

Today I will choose to be happy.

*The Joyful Decision, when fully understood, becomes a
powerful catalyst for change in your life. Happiness is a
choice. This Decision can liberate your spirit with the
infinite joy available in each moment of every day.*

From *The Traveler's Gift*

*Our very lives are fashioned by choice. First we make
choices. Then our choices make us.*

— ANNE FRANK

The Joyful Decision

In The Traveler's Gift, *Anne Frank presents David Ponder with the fifth Decision that determines personal success:*

Today I will choose to be happy.

Beginning this very moment, I am a happy person, for I now truly understand the concept of happiness. Few others before me have been able to grasp the truth of the physical law that enables one to live happily every day. I know now that happiness is not an emotional phantom floating in and out of my life. Happiness is a choice. Happiness is the end result of certain thoughts and activities, which actually bring about a chemical reaction in my body. This reaction results in a euphoria, which, while elusive to some, is totally under my control.

Today I will choose to be happy. I will greet each day with laughter.

Within moments of awakening, I will laugh for seven seconds. After even such a small period of time, excitement has begun to flow through my bloodstream. I feel different. I am different! I am enthusiastic about the day. I am alert to its possibilities. I am happy!

Laughter is an outward expression of enthusiasm, and I know that enthusiasm is the fuel that moves the world. I laugh throughout the day. I laugh while I am alone, and I laugh in conversation with others. People are drawn to me because I have laughter in my heart. The world belongs to the enthusiastic, for people will follow them anywhere!

Today I will choose to be happy. I will smile at every person I meet.

My smile has become my calling card. It is, after all, the most potent weapon I possess. My smile has the strength to forge bonds, break ice, and calm storms. I will use my smile constantly. Because of my smile, the people with whom I come in contact on a daily basis will choose to further my causes and follow my leadership. I will always smile first. That particular display of a good attitude will tell others what I expect in return.

My smile is the key to my emotional makeup. A wise man once said, "I do not sing because I am happy; I am happy because I sing!" When I choose to smile, I become the master of my emotions.

Discouragement, despair, frustration, and fear will always wither when confronted by my smile. The power of who I am is displayed when I smile.

Today I will choose to be happy. I am the possessor of a grateful spirit.

In the past, I have found discouragement in particular situations, until I compared the condition of my life to others less fortunate. Just as a fresh breeze cleans smoke from the air, so does a grateful spirit remove the cloud of despair. It is impossible for the seeds of depression to take root in a thankful heart.

My God has bestowed upon me many gifts, and for these I will remember to be grateful. Too many times I have offered up the prayers of a beggar, always asking for more and forgetting my thanks. I do not wish to be seen as a greedy child, unappreciative, and disrespectful. I am grateful for sight and sound and breath. If ever in my life there is a pouring out of blessings beyond that, then I will be grateful for the miracle of abundance.

I will greet each day with laughter. I will smile at every person I meet. I am the possessor of a grateful spirit.

Today I will choose to be happy.

Beware of Conditioning

The U.S. Standard Railroad gauge—the distance between the two rails—is exactly four feet, eight and one-half inches. An odd number, but that's the way they built them in England, and it was the English expatriates who built the railroads in the United States.

So why did the English build their rails with such odd measurements? The same people who built the pre-railroad tramways built their rails with a gauge of four feet, eight and one-half inches.

And why did they build them like that? The tramways reused the same jig, tools, and measurements that had been used to build wagons, which used that same wheel spacing: four feet, eight and one-half inches.

And why did the wagons have that particularly odd wheel spacing? If the spacing had been different, the wagon wheels would've broken on some of the old, long-distance roads in England . . . which incidentally had wheel-ruts with the same spacing.

So who built the old rutted roads? The Imperial Roman Empire built the first roads in England thousands of years ago, and these roads can still be walked on today. The ruts are spaced exactly four feet, eight and one-half inches apart, because the Roman war chariots made the initial ruts. And every one of them had to match, for fear of destroying their wagon wheels and wagons. Since the chariots were made for and by the Imperial Realm, they were all alike in their wheel spacing.

So the U.S. Standard rail gauge of four feet, eight and one-half inches comes from the original specifications for an Imperial Roman war chariot.

This is a classic example of conditioning—people doing things because that's the way they've always been done. There are businesses in trouble today, headed for a cliff they don't see, because of how they've been conditioned—they were successful doing things a certain way in years past, and they don't see that the market has changed, or that the way they're doing things is no longer productive, or that they are out-of-date and out-of-style. They keep making decisions based on how things have always been done.

So next time you're handed some instructions or some idea and you wonder, *What horse's rear end came up with this?* you might be exactly right. You see, the Imperial Roman war chariots were made just wide enough, four feet, eight and one-half inches, to accommodate the back end of two warhorses!

Now here's an interesting twist to this story: When you see a space shuttle sitting on the launchpad at Cape Canaveral, you will notice two big booster rockets attached to the side of the main fuel tanks. These SRBs (solid rocket boosters) are manufactured by a company in Utah. The engineers who designed them may have preferred to make them a bit wider, but the SRBs had to be shipped by train from the factory site to the launch site. The railroad line from the factory had to run through a tunnel in the mountains, and the SRBs had to fit through that tunnel. The tunnel is slightly wider than the railroad tracks, and the railroad track at four feet, eight and one-half inches, is about as wide as two horses' rear ends. So, the major design feature of what is arguably the most advanced transportation system in the world was determined, literally, by the width of a horse's behind. Can you imagine?

A Happy Choice

When you consider the Joyful Decision, "Today I will choose to be happy," do you see why it's important to understand conditioning? The Joyful Decision has been conditioned *out* of most people. Most people don't realize happiness is a choice! They are doing the same things every day, just because that's the way they've always done it. They're waking up grumpy, going through the motions at work, sitting in traffic without a smile on their faces. Life is killing them.

The Joyful Decision is more controversial on its surface than any of the other Seven Decisions because people don't understand it. If you're looking for a key to increasing your financial portfolio, this is the Decision that will make you more money.

I was doing a radio interview about *The Traveler's Gift*, and I had a very cynical talk show host ask me about the Joyful Decision. He said, "I just have to tell you, I'm not into a lot of this personal growth stuff, but this one . . . this one really seems ridiculous to me."

I laughed and said, "Okay, tell me why."

Complaining is an activity just as listening to the radio is an activity. One may choose to turn on the radio, and one may choose not to turn on the radio. One may choose to complain, and one may choose not to complain. I choose not to complain.

He said, "Well, I understand why you would want to accept responsibility, and I understand why you would want to seek wisdom and be a person of action . . . I understand those decisions, but come on—in the economic climate that our country is in, with people out of work, how could choosing to be happy make a difference?"

I said, "You gotta be kidding me. Listen. Think about this: Consider yourself an employer. You have two prospective employees standing in front of you with the same educational background. They are basically the same age, have the same experience, and even look and dress the same. One of them gripes and complains, and the other one smiles and is happy.

"Who are you going to hire? Well, the happy one, of course, because that's the person you want to be around! Who wants to be around a complainer? And everyone else is just like you. They want to be around happy people too. And this is why, today, you must choose to be happy. It's the beginning of a new life!"

I urge you to choose to be happy. There are so many things about which we can choose to be happy! Happiness is not some emotional phantom floating in and out of your life. You can choose happiness every day. Laughter and enthusiasm are the fuels that move the world. The world belongs to the enthusiastic, and people will follow them anywhere.

Developing Your Happy Triggers

List five things you can do each day to make yourself laugh and smile. What can you think about? Is there a scene from a movie that always makes you laugh? Did your child do something so innocent and precious that it brought a smile to your face? Does your dog chase his tail?

The point is there are "happy triggers" all around us, but if we don't actively seek them out, we may only accidentally trigger them on rare occasions. By consciously identifying happy triggers, you can choose to be happy whenever you wish.

A Possessor of a Grateful Spirit

Now, if the last few paragraphs have irritated you . . . calm down. I don't *really* believe you can choose to be happy, snap your fingers, and have the feeling immediately. That is a bit ridiculous. I do, however, know for a fact that measures of happiness will result from simply choosing to be grateful.

Happiness—true happiness, that is—comes from deep within. Happiness comes from a grateful heart. It is impossible to be ungrateful and happy at the same time. Depression, anger, resentment, and other lower emotions may arise, but a grateful spirit keeps you from feeling sorry for yourself—the seeds of depression cannot take root in a grateful heart.

Occasionally, people come up to me in an airport and say, "I've heard you speak, and you know, I'm just not a happy person."

I might respond with, "Well, a great exercise for becoming a happy person is to sit down with a piece of paper and a pen and list the things for which you're grateful."

Occasionally they will reply, "Well, I just really don't have anything in my life to be grateful for."

I'll cross my arms, lean in confidently, smile, and ask, "Where are you flying to today?"

They'll tell me, and I'll respond, "You know, there's a lot of people driving to that city. There are even some people who want to get to that city and can't get there at all. Nice to be able to fly, isn't it?"

The realization hits them. "Oh, yeah, it really is nice to be able to fly."

"You know, you live in the United States of America. Isn't it great to live in a country that so many people complain about?"

They'll frown. And I'll say, "For all the complaining people do about our country, it's nice to live in a place that has freedom of speech. And as bad as some people think it is, where else would you want to live?"

Think about it: You can be grateful for the taxes you pay—that means you are earning money. You can be grateful for the mess you have to clean up after a party because it means you were surrounded by friends. You can be grateful for the nice clothes you're wearing. I would imagine there are some people in the world who don't have any clothes at all. And if they fit a little too tightly, it means you have enough to eat!

Just as a fresh breeze cleans smoke from the air, so does a grateful spirit remove the cloud of despair. It is impossible for the seeds of depression to take root in a thankful heart.

Sometimes I smile and say, "Have you eaten lunch yet? Where do you eat in this airport?"

And they'll tell me where, or they'll say, "Well, I haven't had lunch yet."

"Did you eat before you got here? Did you eat yesterday?"

"Well, yeah."

"Wow. You ate. A lot of people in the world don't have that luxury. Aren't you grateful you have something to eat?"

You can be grateful for mowing your lawn. You can be grateful for the windows that need cleaning, the gutters that are stopped up, that lock you haven't gotten around to fixing. In fact, you can be grateful for all the things that are wrong with your house! Why? You have a house!

You can be grateful for the parking spot at the far end of that parking lot, because that means you can walk. And if you're in a wheelchair, can't you be grateful that you have one?

You can be grateful for a huge electric bill. There are a lot of people who are not able to be warm or cool when they want to be. You can be grateful for aching muscles at the end of the day. You're able to work. And you can be so grateful for that loud alarm clock that goes off before daylight every morning. If you heard it, it means you're alive.

Several years ago, I went to Mexico City for World Vision International, and for a couple of days they walked me around a slum where a million people lived. I'd known there were poor people in the world, but I'd never seen a million of them in one place! I saw my own children in the eyes of the children who were playing there amid broken glass and dead animals. It was horrible to see what they had to do to get water and food.

You want something to be grateful for? Walk into your bathroom, turn on the faucet, and watch that clean water come out. Let it run over your hand. As long as you want that clean water, it's available in your own bathroom, from your own faucet. We're pouring this clean water on our lawns and washing our cars and dogs . . . yet there are a million people in Mexico City who don't have clean water to drink. The water is brought into the neighborhoods with trucks, and the people carry it home in pots, pans, and plastic bags.

I want to urge you to condition yourself, on a daily basis, to find things to be grateful for. *Become the possessor of a grateful spirit.*

From this moment on, you will ignore the conditioning that has pervaded your life to this point. You will ignore the conditioning that says you must wake up with a scowl on your face. You will ignore the conditioning that says children who laugh in a restaurant get on your nerves. You are creating new conditioning!

You are the possessor of a grateful spirit. You are grateful for the laughter of children, for situations that make you struggle and make you stronger. You are grateful for the ability to find your way out, because you will be able to lead others out. You are a leader. Your conditioning from this point on says, "Today I will choose to be happy."

Cultivating a Grateful Spirit

You can be grateful about anything: being alive, the ability to breathe, the trees, the air, the sun, the stars, indoor plumbing, abundant food, the country in which you were born, your family, your friends, your pet, music, love, romance, a great movie, your favorite book, the clouds, the mountains, a flower, a child's laugh, a puppy's curiosity, a new idea, the telephone, the Internet, paintings, sculptures, plays, heating and air conditioning. Get the idea?

Make a list of at least one hundred things for which you are grateful. Extra credit for extending your list to two hundred!

Who's Packing Your Parachute?

To condition yourself to be happy, you must possess a grateful spirit. Learn how to express gratitude. Expressing gratitude magnifies our happiness and brings us more happiness.

Most people don't get thanked. There are so many invisible people running in and out of our lives, providing services we take for granted, and they never get thanked. When you stop and say, "Hey! Just wanted to say thanks for what you're doing," the look on their faces will make you happy! It's easier to be happy when you are sharing happiness and gratitude.

I do not deny the reality of my situation. I deny the finality of it. This, too, shall pass.

Charles Plumb was a United States Navy jet pilot in Vietnam. On his seventy-sixth combat mission, his plane was hit by a surface-to-air missile. He ejected and floated down into enemy hands. Captured, he spent the next six years in a Vietnamese prison. He survived and now lectures on lessons he learned from that experience. One day, he and his wife were sitting in a restaurant, and a man at another table came up and said excitedly, "You're Plumb! You're Charles Plumb! You flew jet fighters into Vietnam from the aircraft carrier *Kitty Hawk*. You were shot down." He went on to reveal other details of the mission.

Plumb didn't recognize the man, so he asked, "How in the world did you know all that?"

The man replied, "I packed your parachute. I was in the navy too. I worked on the *Kitty Hawk*."

Charles Plumb couldn't believe it. He thanked the man for packing his parachute so many years ago. The man shook his hand and said, "Wow, I guess it worked."

Charles Plumb assured him, "It sure did. If your chute hadn't worked, I wouldn't be here today."

Plumb couldn't sleep that night—he kept thinking about that man. "I kept wondering what he had looked like in a navy uniform," he recalls. "White hat, a bib in the back, bell-bottom trousers. I wondered how many times I might have ignored him, not even acknowledged him with a 'Good morning, how are you?' You see, I was a fighter pilot. And he was just a sailor."

Charles Plumb thought about how many hours this sailor spent at that long wooden table in the bowels of the *Kitty Hawk*, carefully weaving the shrouds and folding the silks of each chute, each time holding in his hands the fate of someone he didn't know.

Today, Charles Plumb regularly asks people, "Who's packing your parachute?" Everyone relies on someone to make it through the day. There are so many people in our lives who are invisible to us, but they're packing our parachutes—mental, emotional, spiritual, and physical.

We need these parachutes; we need these people! Sometimes,

in the midst of our challenges, it's easy to forget to express our gratitude to these people, to say "Hello," or "Please," or "Thank you." Because we're so preoccupied, we don't congratulate each other or ask if anything difficult is happening in their lives. We don't compliment each other or commit random acts of kindness.

It's amazing how, when you condition yourself to have a grateful spirit, you will find yourself expressing gratitude and multiplying that feeling in your life. Stop your car beside the road when the garbage men are there, and just holler out the window, "Hey! I just want to tell you how much we appreciate you guys. I thought the other day, *What would our house look like after a few weeks if these men didn't show up?* We appreciate you!"

You'll stand out in a huge way because, I promise you, nobody else is thanking them. You can thank the person who reads your gas or electric meter and tell him how much you appreciate him walking through the heat or the cold to keep your home cool or warm. You can thank the UPS man or FedEx lady or the people who work behind the desk at the post office. Smile at the people behind the airline counters. Tell the kid collecting the shopping carts from your grocery store's parking lot how much you appreciate being able to pick up a cart inside instead of hunting one up from the lot.

The possessor of a grateful spirit who shares that gratitude with others is *conditioned* to be happy. He or she wakes up happy!

Capturing Your Moments to Remember

As technology advances, we seem to have more demands on our time. In an effort to "keep up," we often forget to remember the joyous, fun, even miraculous moments that unfolded before our very eyes.

What are some of the incredible moments to remember

you've had during the past week, month, or year? It could be a big event like a daughter's wedding, or a simple moment when you and your loved one shared a smile.

Capture ten of these moments right now to help cultivate a grateful spirit. (What if you did this exercise every week?)

The Magic of Smiling

I mentioned earlier that happy people make more money. How can choosing to be happy actually increase your financial portfolio? Why do happy people make more money? I'm amazed when I hear people say, "Oh, I'm having some hard times financially. We just never have good things happen to us. People never help us. Opportunities never come our way."

When someone mumbles, "People don't help me," I think to myself, *Of course they don't help you! They don't even want to be around you! Smile! Put some energy into your voice! Become somebody others want to be around.*

When I choose to smile, I become the master of my emotions. Discouragement, despair, frustration, and fear will always wither when confronted by my smile.

I believe opportunities come from our associations. Think about it— our opportunities, our encouragement, our information and knowledge are most likely to come from other people. If that's true (and it is . . .), then we *must* become people whom others want to be around.

People want to be around happy people—not whiners, moaners, and groaners. Happy people get more opportunities because opportunities come from people, and people are attracted by happy people. And obviously, opportunities often translate into financial success.

If you have to fake it initially, fake it! Nobody expects you to be happy every moment of every day. But you can choose to smile. Speak a little faster. Move. You will attract people and opportunities into your life when you become someone others want to be around.

Your smile is your calling card. It is the most potent weapon you have. With your smile, you can forge bonds, break ice, and calm storms. Use your smile constantly. The power of who you are is revealed when you smile.

The Smile Exercise

Smiles are contagious. Smiles affect your biochemistry. Smile for the next sixty seconds as you remember your favorite leisure activity. Why do you enjoy it? What benefits do you gain by pursuing that passion? Feel your smile through your entire body, including your breathing. And if you're having trouble remembering something that makes you smile, here are a few possibilities: your pet, your child, a sunset, a vacation, laughing with a close friend, your favorite show—whatever works for you!

How do you feel? Care to smile for more than sixty seconds? Go for it!

The Secret to Lasting Success

I'm about to reveal the biggest secret to the Joyful Decision. I don't talk or write about it much even though I've been asked the question many times. I've often considered what I would say if somebody ever brings me in to speak and says, "You've got one minute on stage. And this is the last minute you'll ever speak in your entire life. Tell them one thing that can change everything."

I've got the secret. Are you ready? It's going to blow your mind because it's so simple. You can learn it in a couple of days, and it will change everything.

Here's the secret: *Smile while you talk.* I'm not saying "smile a lot" or "smile at everyone you meet." I'm saying SMILE WHILE YOU TALK! Very few people do this. Watch . . . Even when people tell a joke, they don't usually smile until they get to the punch line. Most tell jokes with a serious expression furrowed in their brow, get to the punch line, and then laugh with everyone else. In everyday conversation, the vast majority of us speak to others with a serious or bland expression on our faces.

People are drawn to a person with laughter in his heart. The world belongs to the enthusiastic, for people will follow them anywhere!

Learn to smile while you talk, and your life will be forever transformed. And if you throw in a little chuckle while you're talking, even better. Why will everything change? People cannot help but smile at somebody who smiles at them!

I do this all the time when I speak. I'll walk around the room as I'm talking and look people in the eye, nod, and smile. Soon I'll have fifty or sixty people nodding with me in unison, because when you nod and smile at them, they will smile and nod back.

You want people to join the church softball team? You want them to buy the house from you? You want them to sign the deal? You want them to be clients forever? You want them to contribute to a cause? *Learn to smile while you talk!*

The same positive results will transpire with your family. Your spouse, your kids, your neighbors—everybody will react to you differently when you smile as you talk.

For many years, I toured as a comedian. I was not under any delusion that my material was the greatest in the world, yet I was very successful, due, in large part, to smiling while I talked. I was known for being able to connect with an audience immediately, and that was because I smiled when I talked. I would hear other comedians talking about dealing with hecklers. I never dealt with hecklers because I didn't have any—I was everybody's friend. People deal with and react to their friends in a totally different way. You can make friends instantly if you smile while you talk.

Smile-While-Talking Exercise

To do this exercise, you'll need to look into a mirror, so go into the bathroom, the bedroom, or any private place with a mirror.

For the next five days, for five to ten minutes each day, practice smiling while you talk. Incrementally add each of the following:

- A little chuckle, so a slight laughter comes through your voice
- An eyebrow lift and open eyes
- A little nod
- A faster cadence to your speech

Once you feel comfortable talking this way, begin practicing it causally with other people. Of course, you don't have to tell them you're practicing; just smile, nod, slightly chuckle, talk faster, and lift your eyebrows. It will change the way you interact with people and transform the opportunities that you will attract.

The Joy of Stupidity

As you begin fully living the Seven Decisions and becoming the person you want to be, you can choose to bring laughter into the lives of others. You can quickly become the funny person everyone wants to be around. When I was a comedian, it took me a while to understand where humor came from so that I could write it consistently.

Humor is discovered by considering a series of questions. Probably the biggest question comedians use to discover humor is, "What is stupid about this?" You can apply this question to everyday situations with your buddies, associates, and family. You'll find laughter that most people only dream about because there is no shortage of stupidity out there.

On the counter lay a frozen package of Mark and Spencer Bread Pudding. The instructions included directions on how to heat it up in the microwave, a conventional oven, or a convection oven. In large letters at the bottom, it read: *Warning. Product will be hot after heating.*

What is stupid about this?

On the packaging for Rowenta irons, there is a little notice on the bottom right: *Do not iron clothes on body.* Hmm . . . that would save a little time.

My smile has become my calling card. It is, after all, the most potent weapon I possess. My smile has the strength to forge bonds, break ice, and calm storms. I will use my smile constantly.

The label on the sleep-aid Nightol reads as follows, *Warning: May cause drowsiness.* And I'm taking this because . . .

A Sears hair dryer: *Do not use while sleeping.* Mm-hmm . . .

Swanson frozen dinners: *Number one serving suggestion: Defrost.* That's just a suggestion.

The directions on the box for Dial soap: *Use like regular soap*.

The box for Tesco's Tiramisu Dessert: *Do not turn dessert upside down*. And guess where that instruction is printed? That's right, on the bottom.

Most brands of Christmas lights: *For indoor or outdoor use only*. As opposed to what?

And, my favorite, on a Japanese food processor we got for Christmas, it reads, *Not to be used for the other use*. So, what is stupid about this?

You can come up with your own family comedy show. Just watch your kids; watch your parents. Remember what your parents used to say that you're saying now. I'm telling you, so many things will be funny.

We have two little boys at home, and we've learned that when you hear a flush and the words "Uh-oh," it's already too late. We now know to always look in the oven before we turn it on. (Tonka trucks don't do well at 375 degrees.) We also know now that a G.I. Joe's boot will pass through the digestive track of a four-year-old. There are so many things that, if you just look around, you can laugh at and be happy. As parents, as kids, and as kids with parents, there are so many things we all say that are crazy and funny! As we relate them to each other and laugh at ourselves, life is more fun.

Living a Dog's Life

We have a Dalmatian named Lucy. She was our "dog-daughter" for a long time until we had "real" children. Lucy is a part of the family and especially important to my wife. For years I have watched how Polly treated her, and occasionally, it irritated me. I told her one day, "You know, sometimes I think you treat that dog better than you treat me."

But I couldn't help noticing how Lucy acted . . .

When Polly came into the house after a morning out, I'd often be on the phone. I might say, "Hi," or if it was an important call, I might say, "Shh." Or if I was writing, we'd often say hello from across the room.

Lucy, on the other hand, reacts totally differently when Polly enters the room. When Polly enters, Lucy stands up and starts wagging her tail, as if to say, "Hey, it's my mom! I love you!" She walks over to Polly and licks her face. "Ooooh, ooh, kiss, kiss, kiss." (She does this even if Polly was just in the room five minutes before!)

It occurred to me that maybe if I treated my wife as well as the dog treated her, then maybe she would treat me as well as she treats the dog.

How do you treat people when they "enter the room"? Are they uplifted as they encounter you?

And while we're talking about it, how do *you* enter a room? Do you know people who brighten the room as soon as they walk through the door? Their presence alone puts a smile on people's faces. These rare souls focus their energy and attention on making others laugh and smile. They ask questions of people they meet and genuinely want to hear the answers. They take such an interest in others that others can't help but take an interest in them.

Most of us tend to lock ourselves in our own worlds. We're so focused on our own problems and challenges in life that we don't "see" the soul standing before us.

Next time you're in the checkout line at your local supermarket, notice that there's a real person on the other side of that counter, with his or her own problems, likes, dislikes, and beliefs. Look this person in the eye and connect with him or her. Wordlessly acknowledge him or her as another soul walking with us on the planet. What if you made it a point to try to make the cashier at the checkout or waiter in a restaurant smile? How might it positively affect your attitude and experience of life by focusing on sharing joy with someone you don't know? Transform your world by acting like a dog!

Real *Traveler* Profile:
Amy Grant

Music was always a part of this multiplatinum, multi-Grammy music star's life. Grant was "discovered" as an artist while working part-time sweeping floors and demagnetizing tapes at a Nashville studio. Her foray into the music business helped birth contemporary Christian music, a category that didn't exist at the time.

Twenty-five-plus years and many gold and platinum albums later, Amy has shared her music around the world. Amy is a great embodiment of the Joyful Decision.

Dear Andy,

Back in the spring of 1978, I released my first album. I was seventeen years old and full of dreams. That summer, after my class graduated from high school, I left on my first promotional tour. One stop on that tour was a book and record store in Southern California. I was to sign autographs and sing for ninety minutes. My mother was with me and we were very excited. The manager of the store had sent out 1,200 engraved invitations for the occasion. Obviously, everyone involved was expecting a large crowd.

Well, the crowd never made it. In fact, not one single person showed up! . . . Oh well—the store manager listened to me sing for an hour and a half. He listened to me sing by himself because even my mother left. (I'm not kidding!) This probably still ranks as the single most "distinguishing" event of my career.

I can't say, without a doubt, that quitting didn't enter my mind that day, but I'm glad that I didn't. That experience (and several like it) gave me a deep appreciation for the support of a kind of audience that I might never have gained otherwise. Besides, the memory of that afternoon still makes me laugh inside, just as it did the last time I looked out from the stage of the Pacific Amphitheater in Southern California to 20,000 smiling faces.

I know that there are no guarantees in life. I also know that good things rarely come about the first time around. And so my advice would be: Whatever your goals—don't give up! More important than talent, strength, or knowledge is the ability to laugh at yourself and enjoy the pursuit of your dreams.

Sincerely,

— AMY GRANT

THE COMPASSIONATE DECISION

I will greet this day with a forgiving spirit.

The Compassionate Decision changes the way most people view forgiveness. A forgiving spirit allows you to let go of the past and embrace a compelling new future. Harboring anger and resentment for others—regardless of whether or not "they deserve it"—poisons your soul and limits your growth. When you embrace forgiveness through the Compassionate Decision, your level of personal success becomes boundless.

From *The Traveler's Gift*

Forgiveness is a secret that is hidden in plain sight. It costs nothing and is worth millions. It is available to everyone and used by few. If you harness the power of forgiveness, you will be sought after and regarded highly. And not coincidentally, you will also be forgiven by others!

—ABRAHAM LINCOLN

The Compassionate Decision

In The Traveler's Gift, *Abraham Lincoln presents David Ponder with the sixth Decision that determines personal success:*

I will greet this day with a forgiving spirit.

For too long, every ounce of forgiveness I owned was locked away, hidden from view, waiting for me to bestow its precious presence upon some worthy person. Alas, I found most people to be singularly unworthy of my valuable forgiveness, and, since they never asked for any, I kept it all for myself. Now, the forgiveness that I hoarded has sprouted inside my heart like a crippled seed yielding bitter fruit.

No more! At this moment, my life has taken on new hope and assurance. Of all the world's population, I am one of the few possessors of the secret to dissipating anger and resentment. I now understand that forgiveness only has value when it is given away. By the simple act of granting forgiveness, I release the demons of the past about which I can do nothing and create in myself a new heart, a new beginning.

I will greet this day with a forgiving spirit. I will forgive even those who do not ask for forgiveness.

Many are the times when I have seethed in anger at a word or deed thrown into my life by an unthinking or uncaring person. Valuable hours have been wasted imagining revenge or confrontation. Now I see the truth revealed about this psychological rock inside my shoe. The rage I nurture is often one-sided, for my offender seldom gives thought to his offense!

I will now and forevermore silently offer my forgiveness even to those who do not see that they need it. By the act of forgiving, I am no longer consumed by unproductive thoughts. My bitterness is given up. I am contented in my soul and effective again with my fellow man.

I will greet this day with a forgiving spirit. I will forgive those who criticize me unjustly.

Knowing that slavery, in any form, is wrong, I also know that the person who lives a life according to the opinion of others is a slave. I am not a slave. I have chosen my own counsel. I know the difference between right and wrong. I know what is best for the future of my family, and neither misguided opinion nor unjust criticism will alter my course.

Those who are critical of my goals and dreams simply do not understand the higher purpose to which I have been called. Therefore, their scorn does not affect my attitude or action. I forgive their lack of vision and forge ahead. I now know that criticism is part of the price paid for leaping past mediocrity.

I will greet this day with a forgiving spirit. I will forgive myself.

For many years, my greatest enemy has been myself. Every mistake, every miscalculation, every stumble I made has been replayed over and over in my mind. Every broken promise, every day wasted, every goal not reached has compounded the disgust I feel for the lack of achievement in my life. My dismay has developed a paralyzing grip.

When I disappoint myself, I respond with inaction and become more disappointed.

I realize today that it is impossible to fight an enemy living in my head. By forgiving myself, I erase the doubt, fear, and frustration that have kept my past in the present. From this day forward, my history will cease to control my destiny. I have forgiven myself. My life has just begun.

I will forgive even those who do not ask for forgiveness. I will forgive those who criticize me unjustly. I will forgive myself.

I will greet this day with a forgiving spirit.

The Anger-Management Myth

Traditional wisdom tells us the most effective way of dealing with rage or resentment is a course in anger management. There are mental health professionals who deal exclusively in anger management. There are ads in the newspaper for anger management courses at your local college. It's part of our cultural consciousness—an athlete does something crazy, and the team sends him to anger management.

In 2006, football's Tennessee Titans defensive lineman Albert Haynesworth stomped on the helmetless head of a Dallas Cowboys lineman after the play was over in an act of sheer rage at a blown play. His outburst required dozens of stitches and reconstructive surgery to the lineman's face. Albert humiliated his team, and the NFL reprimanded Albert with a five-game suspension and encouraged him to take an anger management course.

We hear about celebrity court cases, with part of the sentence being an anger management course. Fortune 500 executives often enroll staff members in anger management courses. Jack Nicholson and Adam Sandler costarred in a movie entitled *Anger Management*.

This traditional wisdom is horribly flawed. Think about the term "anger management": Why would you want to *manage* something like anger? Forget about managing anger; let's get rid of it. Anger *resolution* can be accomplished by utilizing the Compassionate Decision: "I will greet this day with a forgiving spirit." And, yes, my friend, before you even ask the question, it really is just that simple!

The Ultimate Anger-Resolution Course

Forgiveness is the ultimate resolution of anger. For years, I thought forgiveness was something to hoard—something to be doled out on a case-by-case basis, determined by whether someone deserved it. It was like knighthood, bestowed upon the person who crawled into my presence, wailing and begging me for it. If I deemed him worthy, I would lay my sword upon his shoulder. "You are forgiven. Now depart from me."

Naturally, part of me thrived on that anger, and I held grudges for a long time. But as the grudges build, they can weigh us down. Eventually, we're so bogged down that we often can't remember who to forgive or the specifics of the original event. We become preoccupied by other people, and our lives become a catastrophic mess. By forgiving, we complete the ultimate course in anger resolution.

The bad news is that the past was in your hands, but the good news is that the future, my friend, is also in your hands.

I couldn't find a rule in any book I've ever read (including the Bible) that said in order for me to forgive somebody, the person who committed the offense had to ask for it or deserve it. And I couldn't find anything that said, "Well, you can forgive a person as long as he or she hasn't been doing the same stupid thing over and over again for twenty years."

Everything I read and everything I felt within my soul said, "Forgive. Let it go." I see now that by forgiving, I'm giving myself the ultimate gift, because forgiveness affects me much more than it affects another. It's not even mandatory that the person I'm forgiving be aware of it. Forgiveness often means more to the forgiver than it does to the person being forgiven.

Sometimes when I'm talking about this, people say, "So . . . they're just going to get away with it? I'm supposed to just forgive and forget?"

No, I'm not suggesting that at all. Forgiveness is about *you*. Trust is about *them*. Forgiveness is about the past; trust is about the future. Do we forgive somebody who steals from us? Yes. Do we continue to do business with him? No.

Forgiveness is a decision, not an emotion. If we approach it through our emotions, our emotions inevitably drag us the other way. But if you will notice, emotions follow decisions. When we decide to forgive, our emotions follow along.

The Gift of Forgiveness

How many times have you been trying to fall asleep at night, when suddenly your peaceful trance is interrupted and your eyes pop open? You remember what that guy at work said to you or what he did to you, and you can't believe it! You keep replaying what happened over and over, thinking about what you should have said differently or what you might say tomorrow if you have the chance. And you think about punching him out. (That's correct, ladies. Forty- and fifty-year-old men still think like boys in the sandbox.) You're consumed in the middle of the night, wide-awake, thinking about this person.

Or, perhaps you're driving along, and everything's fine. You're comfortable, having a great conversation with your family, when you remember something. Your spouse asks, "What's wrong?"

And you answer, "What do you mean, what's wrong?"

"Well, you just stopped talking. And you haven't said anything for five minutes."

You realize that you were thinking about that guy and what he said and what you wish you would have said.

Forgiveness is a secret that is hidden in plain sight. It is available to everyone and used by few. If you harness the power of forgiveness, you will be sought after and regarded highly.

Here's the crazy thing: 99 percent of the time, the people we're so irritated and bent out of shape about, these bozos who have offended us so deeply, are sleeping peacefully in their beds or living their lives, absolutely without a clue that we are even thinking about them! Often, they're unaware they've done anything to offend us in the first place.

So if they're not going to ask forgiveness, and if it doesn't matter if they ask or not, and if it doesn't matter if they deserve it or not, and if it doesn't matter how many times they've done it, and if they're not even thinking about it, but it's ruining your life . . . why should you forgive them?

Because it's ruining your life, not theirs! Trust me on this! You cannot become the parent, spouse, or friend you could otherwise be while consumed by an unforgiving attitude.

Forgiveness is a gift you give yourself. Receive it now!

The Resentment Discharge

Have you been harboring resentment toward anyone? Go back to when you were a kid and review your resentments:

who are the people who've imprisoned you through your resentment toward them?

Now, close your eyes and let go of your resentments for each person. Forgive them. Remember, your resentments only hurt yourself. Forgiving those toward whom you hold anger, resentment, or hatred liberates your spirit; life becomes infinitely more peaceful. To successfully complete this exercise, don't make any exceptions—forgive each person unconditionally (especially that one person you really don't want to forgive).

Commit from this day forward to embrace the Compassionate Decision of forgiveness unconditionally. We generally avoid unconditional forgiveness because of the secret payoff our egos get from harboring emotions like anger and resentment. Surrender the payoff of those "lesser" emotions, and embrace a new life filled with infinite freedom and joy!

The Miracle of Forgiveness

Do the names Jo Berry or Patrick Magee ring a bell for you? Probably not. Perhaps you remember the Brighton Bomb incident in 1984? The Irish Republican Army bombed the Grand Hotel in Brighton, England, in an attempt to kill Prime Minister Margaret Thatcher and her entire cabinet during a Tory Party conference.

Five people died in this enormous blast, including a gentleman by the name of Sir Anthony Berry, who left behind six children, including his daughter, Jo Berry. Patrick Magee was charged with planting and detonating the IRA device and was given eight life sentences by Judge Justice Boreham.

How does a daughter who lost her father under such devastating circumstances go about healing the painful anger that swelled within her? Jo came to realize that she must "seek to understand, not condemn." As she explains, "I'm beginning to realize that no matter what side of the conflict you're on, had we all lived each other's lives, we could all have done what the other did."

Through empathy, compassion arises; with compassion, we are less likely to judge others. But how can we learn to empathize in the face of swelling anger and grief?

As Jo explains, "An *inner shift* is required to hear the story of the enemy. For me, the question is always about whether I can let go of my need to blame and open my heart enough to hear Pat's story and understand his motivations. The truth is that sometimes I can and sometimes I can't. It's a journey and it's a choice, which means it's not all sorted and put away in a box."

It's difficult to imagine what this must have been like for Jo Berry. Her father was killed unnecessarily by this act of violence, but somehow, she held on to a hope that something positive would shine through this traumatic event. She went to Ireland and listened to the stories of courageous people who were entangled in the web of violence.

In 2000, Jo decided she wanted to have a face-to-face meeting with the person who took her father's life—she wanted to see Pat as a real human being rather than the enemy. Jo recalls, "At our first meeting, I was terrified, but I wanted to acknowledge the courage it had taken him to meet me. We talked with an extraordinary intensity. I shared a lot about my father, while Pat told me some of his story."

For more than two and a half years, Jo and Pat got to know each other. Each of them, it seems, is on a path toward recovering their humanity through forgiveness. Some might argue that a caring relationship between these two people under this difficult circumstance is nothing short of a miracle. Through the power of a forgiving spirit, the miraculous is possible.*

Hope-ful Forgiveness

Occasionally, you're on the flip side of the coin—someone is angry at you. Something you said or did offended someone. Now the other person has the opportunity to forgive you. Assuming that person is aware of the Compassionate Decision, as you are, you must give him the opportunity to work through his anger. It can be challenging to humbly ask someone for forgiveness. But it works.

Asking for forgiveness is an amazing experience, and one that only truly extraordinary people will do. It's much easier to simply let stuff slide, especially if the issue involves someone you're not going to run into again or someone who doesn't, on the surface, matter that much to you. But if he or she is a human being, a person on this planet with you, he or she matters. It takes courage to walk up to someone and say, "Hey, I need to talk to you. I owe you an apology, and I want to ask for your forgiveness." Oftentimes, your humility will create a bond or forge a new friendship that will benefit you in some way. This action almost always dissipates and resolves the anger.

When I was working with Bob Hope, he was very nice to me. This was a great man.

I was doing a television show one night, and the host said, "What's it like working with Bob Hope?"

And I replied, "Oh, he's great. He

Questions such as, "How do other people see me?" and "What don't they like?" can be quite revealing if answered honestly. When you become a person whom others want to be around, you will have become a person of influence.

---

* On www.AndyAndrews.com you can see a short video of Jo Berry and Patrick Magee discussing the situation.

is just so fun and, you know, as old as he is, it's amazing how sharp he continues to be. He's incredible. I really like him."

It was brought to my attention a couple of days later that Mr. Hope was not very happy about my comment on his age. Now, I could have just dismissed it and said, "Well, holy cow. You know, if he doesn't know he's old . . ." But here is a guy who had been very kind to me. I valued his friendship. I could not get it out of my mind that I had offended him. What I had done wasn't malicious or even harmful, but I said something that hurt his feelings. At that point, his feelings were much more important than my own. I kept thinking about it, and my wife said, "Well, if you're so concerned about it, you just need to call him."

I thought, *I'm not calling Bob Hope at his house*.

She said again, "You need to call."

So I did. I called Mr. Hope. The phone rang, and Mrs. Hope answered the phone. "Hi, Mrs. Hope. This is Andy Andrews. How are you doing?" We talked for a few minutes, and I asked, "Is your husband home?" He was.

Mr. Hope came to the phone. "Hi, Mr. Hope, this is Andy. Did I catch you at an okay time?"

"Yeah."

"Okay. Uh . . ." and I forged ahead. "You know, I was doing a television show the other night, and I don't know if this is accurate or not, but someone told me you were upset at something that I said on the show about your age."

And he said, "Yeah."

My heart sank. It was true.

"Mr. Hope," I began, "I deeply apologize. I am so sorry. I did not mean that maliciously, but I can understand how you would not have wanted me to say that, and I am so sorry that I did. I will watch myself in the future. I don't know what to do other than to ask you to forgive me. I truly value your friendship and our relationship. Would you please forgive me for doing that?"

The whole thing just melted. He said, "Of course, Andy. Don't worry about it. Man, if anybody understands saying something on television that you want to take back, it's me, so don't even worry about it. It's all forgotten."

He was absolutely terrific about it. It was one of the hardest things I've ever had to do. And now, since he's gone, I am so grateful that I didn't just apologize or say, "I'm sorry." Rather, I specifically asked for his forgiveness. And he gave it to me. I never have to feel badly about that again. Every time I think about Mr. Hope, I have good memories, and there's not even one little nagging, nit-picking thing in there. That's the power of forgiveness. It is resolution, not anger management. It erases the anger, gets rid of it completely.

A Powerful Act of Forgiveness

In *The Traveler's Gift*, Abraham Lincoln presents the sixth Decision: "I will greet this day with a forgiving spirit." In that chapter, Lincoln's conversation with David Ponder teaches him about forgiveness—its purpose, and its effects. As I researched Lincoln for the book, I discovered a thrilling connection between Lincoln and Joshua Chamberlain.

Chamberlain was a hero at Gettysburg, and here's David Ponder talking with Lincoln, months later

By the simple act of granting forgiveness, I release the demons of the past about which I can do nothing, and I create in myself a new heart, a new beginning.

in a tent, as Lincoln is about to give the Gettysburg Address. In the book, David Ponder asks Lincoln, "Sir, have you ever heard of a colonel from Maine, Joshua Chamberlain?"

Lincoln thinks for a moment and says, "No, I haven't. Should I have?"

David Ponder replies, "Well, maybe you should look him up when you get back."

Lincoln did go back to Washington, and he began to follow Joshua Chamberlain's career. Chamberlain led successful campaigns until the end of the war and was cited by the government four separate times for bravery in action. He was promoted to brigadier general for heroism at Petersburg, and a few months later he was cited for heroism at Five Forks and promoted to major general. At the end of the war, President Lincoln chose Joshua Chamberlain above all the Union officers to have the honor of accepting the Confederate surrender at Appomattox.

There, Chamberlain stunned the world with a show of forgiveness and respect: he ordered his troops to attention, saluting General Robert E. Lee and the defeated South. With that bold stroke, planned behind the scenes by Lincoln, of course, the president of the once-again *United* States of America began the healing of a nation and its people.

Healing a Wounded Heart

With a pen and journal in hand, answer the following questions and jot down any names that come to mind during this exercise. When you're finished, review each name. Ask yourself, "Is this a person I need to forgive, or is this a person from whom I need to ask forgiveness?"

Notice the quality of these questions. Too many people ask unconstructive questions like, "What's wrong? Why is this happening to me?" Remember, the quality of your answers is determined by the quality of your questions. Ask quality questions—questions that make you think—and you'll get quality answers.

Here is a list of questions you may ask yourself:

- What one decision would I make if I knew it would not fail?
- What one thing should I eliminate from my life because it holds me back from reaching my full potential?
- Am I on the path to something absolutely fantastic or something absolutely average?
- Am I running from something?
- How can I use my time better?
- What impossible thing am I believing and planning for?
- What is my most prevailing thought?
- What good thing have I committed myself to do that I've quit doing?
- Of the people I respect the most, what is it about them that earns my respect?
- What would a truly creative person do in my situation?
- What outside influences are causing me to be better? Worse?
- What gifts, talents, or strengths do I have?
- I know I don't have the answer right now, but if I knew the answer, what would I say?
- What is one thing I can do for someone else who has no opportunity to repay me?
- Who do I need to forgive?
- From whom do I need to ask forgiveness?

The Poison of Unforgiveness

In his classic book *An Enemy Called Average*, John Mason writes, "When faced with the decision to forgive, never make the excuse, 'But no one knows what that person did to me.' That may be true," he says, "but the question is, do you know what unforgiveness will do to you?"

What *does* unforgiveness do to us? Have you ever experienced the mental illusion that life has you cornered? Have you ever felt boxed in, discouraged, controlled by outside circumstances? When I have felt that way in my own life, I've determined over the years that there is generally someone I haven't forgiven or someone from whom I haven't asked forgiveness. The person's name sticks in the back of my mind, as if it's subconsciously tapping me on the shoulder, diverting my focus from where it should be.

There is a story an old Indian man tells his grandson about a fight going on inside between two wolves. One wolf was evil and full of anger, envy, sorrow, regret, greed, arrogance, self-pity, guilt, resentment, inferiority, lies, false pride, and ego. And the other wolf was a good wolf, full of forgiveness.

In order to be successful in all areas of my life, I must control my impulses—my thoughts. It is impossible to fight an enemy that has a fort in my head.

The grandson asked his grandfather, "Which wolf wins?"

The old man simply replied, "The one I feed."

Most likely, as you read these words, there is a fight going on inside you between those same two wolves. The fight is revealing itself to you as someone's name or a visual image of that face. You can kill the wolf that contains all that anger, sorrow, regret, and resentment by embracing the good wolf and choosing forgiveness.

There is one person you need to forgive that if you don't, your effectiveness as a husband, as a wife, as a mother or father, as a friend or a leader will suffer. The key to bringing your dreams into reality is forgiveness, and specifically, forgiveness of this one person. This one person, my friend, is you.

We have piled so much onto our own shoulders. There are many things we intended to do that we didn't do, so many promises we made but didn't keep, and so many goals we set that we didn't achieve. Over time, they've piled up on us, and the weight can be crushing. You have to forgive yourself!

I once broke my kneecap. It was the worst physical pain I had ever experienced . . . until I had an ear infection that landed me in the hospital. I wondered later why the ear was seemingly so much worse than the knee. The answer, of course, was that I could mentally "amputate" my knee. I was able to pull my mind away from the pain in my leg. But my ear? It was *in* my mind! I just couldn't get away from it.

The same is true of an unforgiving spirit. You cannot get away from it. It is impossible to fight an enemy that has a fort in your head. The only possible solution is to destroy the fort. Forgive yourself. Now.

Forgive Yourself

We tend to be our own worst critic, and judgment is a double-edged sword. In order to liberate yourself to begin to forgive others, you must first forgive yourself.

Using shorthand or personal "code words," list the things you need to forgive yourself for right now.

Beginning Anew

We now have the opportunity to begin anew, to drop the heavy weight of guilt resting upon our shoulders. Month after month, year after year, we've added to the load, and it's about to crush us. All the things we said we were going to do but didn't, the promises we made and didn't keep, the things we shouldn't have done but did anyway have piled up, and it's just too much for one person to bear. The guilt has turned into resentment, the resentment has turned into anger, and the anger, in its various forms, is taking over our lives.

For many of us, our greatest enemies have been ourselves. Every mistake, every miscalculation, every stumble we make is replayed in our minds. Every broken promise, every day wasted, and every goal not reached has energized the disgust we

From this day forward, my history will cease to control my destiny. I have forgiven myself. My life has just begun.

feel about our predicament. This dismay develops into a paralyzing grip. When we disappoint ourselves, it sets in motion a continual cycle of disappointment. It's true. It *is* impossible to fight an enemy living in our heads.

Forgive yourself. Begin anew. The simple act of forgiving yourself will change your life! You will be positioned to become the person you want to be when you finally ditch the weight of guilt and shame you've been piling on for years. Forgive yourself. Your family's not mad at you. Your friends aren't mad at you. I'm not mad at you. God's not mad at you. *You* don't need to be mad at you either. Let it go. Forgive yourself and begin again.

From this day forward, your history needs to stop controlling your destiny. Your life has just begun! Your forgiveness is valuable only when you give it away. By the simple act of forgiveness, you can release the demons of your past and create a new beginning for yourself.

Forgive the people who don't ask for it. Forgive yourself. From now on, your act of forgiveness will free you from unproductive thoughts. Your bitterness, resentment, and anger will be gone. It's time to begin again.

"I will greet each day with a forgiving spirit."

The Appreciation Letter

The purpose of this letter is to appreciate and free yourself from whatever you've been harboring against yourself. Commit to releasing something that you don't need to hold on to any longer. Example:

Dear (your name),

I've missed you. It has been too long since I've seen the fun, happy person I know you to be. So now I want to ask for your forgiveness about something. You will remember, it was five years ago . . . (describe the event)

[Ending] In closing, I want to acknowledge that you are one of the most special people in the world. These are the things that I appreciate about you . . . (list them)

Thank you for magical moments that you create for so many. The ripples that you create by the way you live reach many more than you could ever know . . .

Love,

(your name)

Now it's your turn. Draft an appreciation-forgiveness letter to yourself.

Real *Traveler* Profile:
Norman Vincent Peale

Dr. Norman Vincent Peale was a minister and an author of forty-six books, which have been translated into forty languages, including the perennial inspirational classic, *The Power of Positive Thinking*. Along with his wife, Ruth Stafford Peale, he started a magazine called *Guideposts*, which is enjoyed by more than fifteen million monthly readers. More than thirty-one million copies of his inspirational booklets have been distributed over the years, and he maintained a full speaking schedule until his death in 1993. Peale received twenty-two honorary doctoral degrees and was one of the few private citizens in history to be honored in a White House ceremony when President Reagan presented him with the Presidential Medal of Freedom.

Norman Vincent Peale said, "When God wants to send you a gift, he wraps it up in a problem, and the bigger the gift that God sends you, the bigger the problem." It's easy to assume that the man who wrote *The Power of Positive Thinking* didn't have to worry about positive thinking. We figure that the author of a book that has sold thirty million copies to date must have had it easy, right?

Here, then, is the great letter I received from a man whose very life embodied the Compassionate Decision. It is a story that will surprise you—and one I am certain very few have heard.

Dear Andy:

I suffered rejection when I wrote a book called *The Power of Positive Thinking*. Actually, I wanted to call it *The Power of Faith*, but my publisher insistently demanded that I change the title to a phrase . . . [from] the book, "The power of positive thinking."

It soon, to my surprise, hit the bestseller lists; in fact, it was on the *New York Times* bestseller list for 186 weeks, which at that time was a record. This projected me into the most vehement criticism I ever received. I considered the book a vitally Christian book, but some ministers castigated me as an archconservative, a tool of capitalistic interests, who was turning Christianity into a way to get rich. One bishop, a scholarly and gifted man, usually dispassionate and objective, became quite intemperate in his attacks on the book and upon me personally. Many ministers even preached against some terrible thing labeled "Pealism." And one distinguished pulpiteer called my work a perversion of the Christian religion. This hue and cry became so violent that I actually wrote my resignation from the ministry, though my church stood by me valiantly. I took a train upcountry to see my aged father who perceived that something was bothering me. And he, even in that remote area, knew of the scathing attack upon me.

So my father, sitting in his rocking chair, said, "Norman, you have always been true and loyal to Jesus Christ. You believe in and preach Bible truths. You have always been in the mainstream of Christianity, never following any temporary faddism. You have united the pastoral office with the best in the scientific and healing arts. You have blazed new pathways of positive thinking to counter the old destructive negatives. You are my son, and your old father who has known good men and not so good men for eighty years and more, both in and out of church, says you are a good and loyal minister of Jesus Christ." He was silent and thoughtful for a long minute. "Besides, and remember this, the Peales never quit. It would break my heart if one of my sons was a quitter, afraid to stand up and face any situation."

My father was a gentle-spirited man, and in all my life I had never heard him use any expression that included a swear word. Imagine my shock when he said, "And Norman, there's just one thing more."

"What is it, Dad?" I asked.

"Tell 'em to go to hell," he declared, to my astonishment.

Stepping into another room, I tore up my resignation and threw it into the wastebasket. Needless to say, I came away fortified in spirit. The book has sold upwards of twenty million copies worldwide and has become, in book statisticians' opinions, one of the few books in American history that has sold the most. The title has become part of the language and culture in not only America but the world.

A lady who was at one time president of the National Council of Churches, Cynthia Weddell, meeting a friend of mine, said, "How's Norman?" And the friend replied, "He is fine." And added, "He has outlived his critics." "No," said Mrs. Weddell, "he has out-loved them."

In every rejection you learn something, and I learned that if you just go about your business and love people and not hate anyone, you ultimately gain a victory. Now it so happens that very few people criticize me, wherefrom I deduce that perhaps I am slipping.

Cordially yours,

Norman Vincent Peale

NVP:SEL

377

THE PERSISTENT DECISION

I will persist without exception.

Your success with the other six Decisions rests on your ability and willingness to embrace and master the Persistent Decision. To persist without exception means to ultimately ensure success in your endeavors.

From *The Traveler's Gift*

Great leaders—great achievers—are rarely realistic by other people's standards. Somehow, these successful people, often considered strange, pick their way through life ignoring or not hearing negative expectations and emotions. Consequently, they accomplish one great thing after another, never having heard what cannot be done. That is precisely why one should never tell a young person that something cannot be done. God may have been waiting centuries for someone ignorant enough of the impossible to do that very thing!

—ARCHANGEL GABRIEL

The Persistent Decision

In The Traveler's Gift, *the archangel Gabriel presents David Ponder with the seventh Decision that determines personal success:*

I will persist without exception.

Knowing that I have already made changes in my life that will last forever, today I insert the final piece of the puzzle. I possess the greatest power ever bestowed upon mankind, the power of choice. Today, I choose to persist without exception. No longer will I live in a dimension of distraction, my focus blown hither and yon like a leaf on a blustery day. I know the outcome I desire. I hold fast to my dreams. I stay the course. I do not quit.

I will persist without exception. I will continue despite exhaustion.

I acknowledge the fact that most people quit when exhaustion sets in. I am not "most people." I am stronger than most people. Average people accept exhaustion as a matter of course. I do not. Average people compare themselves with other people. That is why they are average. I compare myself to my potential. I am not average. I see exhaustion as a precursor to victory.

How long must a child try to walk before he actually does so? Do I not have more strength than a child? More understanding? More desire? How long must I work to succeed before I actually do so? A child would never ask the question, for the answer does not matter. By persisting without exception, my outcome—my success—is assured.

I will persist without exception. I focus on results.

To achieve the results I desire, it is not even necessary that I enjoy the process. It is only important that I *continue* the process with my eyes on the outcome. An athlete does not enjoy the pain of training; an athlete enjoys the results of having trained. A young falcon is pushed from the nest, afraid and tumbling from the cliff. The pain of learning to fly cannot be an enjoyable experience, but the anguish of learning to fly is quickly forgotten as the falcon soars to the heavens.

A sailor who fearfully watches stormy seas lash his vessel will always steer an unproductive course. But a wise and experienced captain keeps his eye firmly fixed upon the lighthouse. He knows that by guiding his ship directly to a specific point, the time spent in discomfort is lessened. And by keeping his eye on the light, there never exists one second of discouragement. My light, my harbor, my future is within sight!

I will persist without exception. I am a person of great faith. In Jeremiah, my Creator declares, "For I know the plans I have for you . . . plans to prosper you and not to harm you, plans to give you hope and a future" (29:11 NIV). From this day forward, I will claim a faith in the certainty of my future. Too much of my life has been spent doubting my beliefs and believing my doubts. No more! I have faith in my future. I do not look left or right. I look forward. I can only persist.

For me, faith will always be a sounder guide than reason because reason can only go so far—faith has no limits. I will expect miracles in my life because faith produces them every day. I will believe in the future that I do not see. That is faith. And the reward of this faith is to see the future that I believed.

I will continue despite exhaustion. I focus on results. I am a person of great faith.

I will persist without exception.

The Habit of Quitting

The Persistent Decision is the key to the other six: "I will persist without exception." Without this particular Decision, the other six are meaningless. When you make and own this decision, the other six Decisions are certain to work.

Committing to the Persistent Decision means you accept responsibility. You constantly seek wisdom. You never stop being a person of action. You have a decided heart, without exception. You choose to be happy every single day. You greet each day with a forgiving spirit. Every single one of the other six Decisions hinges on your acceptance of the seventh: "I will persist without exception." It's the one that brings them all together.

I *really* love to watch football. I don't even care who's playing—I just love football. It amazes me that I love watching football so much. Football is a true passion, and yet, in the sixth grade, I hated playing. I wanted to quit so badly that I gave myself headaches. I hated the practices, the coach, and staying late after school until dark. But my dad would not let me quit. I couldn't believe it. "You started it and you're gonna finish it," he said.

Even my mother got on his case: "You know, he has headaches. This is not for him. He obviously wasn't built for this. He's a skinny kid, and look at those big kids out there."

My dad replied, "He doesn't have to play next year, but he will finish what he started this year." My dad took me aside. "Son, I want you to know that persistence is a habit. And so is quitting. One of the greatest favors I can do for you is to make sure you have the habit of persisting and never develop the habit of quitting."

I never did develop the habit of quitting. It was simply not accepted in my family. Once you started something, you finished it. If I signed up to sell seeds door to door, the other kids could turn their seeds back in, but I was selling every one of them. If I signed up to sell Christmas cards, every single card was going be sold. "You may be selling them in May, Andy, but you will sell every one of these cards," my dad would tell me. He wanted me to understand that every significant thing I would accomplish in my life would be hard and would require persistence.

This was just something expected in my house, and I'm so grateful for it today. Every single day, I watch people cave on stuff that I know if they had just stuck to it, they would see great things. Persistence opens doors in life you've always dreamed about.

. . . Without Exception

It's easy to shrug off the Persistent Decision: "Well, duh, who hasn't heard that before?" We've all heard we have to persist—we shouldn't give up. The unique twist is the last part: I will persist *without exception*. "Without exception" is what everyone tends to leave off.

When you persist without exception, miracles occur. You find a way where there is no way. Anytime you make a statement that you're going after something big—that you're going to do something unusual, something great—and the reward is also big, it's going to be hard. There is only a big reward for things that are tough to do. If it were easy, everyone would be doing it, and the reward would be small.

How long must a child try to walk before he actually does so? How long must I work to succeed before I actually do so? A child would never ask the question, for the answer does not matter. By persisting without exception, my outcome—my success— is assured.

Anytime you go after something big, a time will come when it seems obvious to everybody that it's "over"—it can't be done.

It may even seem obvious to you that it's over. If you get to that point and you have persisted, then others will tell you that it's okay to quit—because you've persisted. You hung in there, and you can quit with a clear conscience with encouragement from people around you because you gave it your best shot: "You tried. Lord knows you tried. We've watched you work. You're killing yourself! It's time to quit, honey. It's okay." People will encourage you to quit if you've persisted, because society no longer holds a penalty for quitting . . . as long as you persist a little bit.

However, if you persist *without exception*, you will have to find a way where there is no way. And that is when miracles occur. Anytime you hit the wall, anytime you come to the end of the road, what you're lacking isn't money, mentorship, or time; you're lacking an idea. That's all—an idea.

> "Let me tell you the secret that has led to my goal. My strength lies solely in my tenacity."
>
> —LOUIS PASTEUR

I can't tell you how many times I've worked with people who have come to that point. They'll say, "It's just over. I know it. I understand *persist without exception*, but I think this might be the case where . . ."

I'll reply, "Well, what have you done? What have you tried?"

"We've tried everything. We've exhausted every possibility. There is nothing that could be done that we haven't tried. We just . . ."

"I know that there's nothing else you could possibly do. You don't know where else to turn." (This is a great little game you can play with yourself.)

"That's right, that's right. We don't know where else to turn."

I'll reply, "I know you don't know, but if you *did* know the next move you would make, what would you do? If we were pretending, what would you say the next move might be?"

"Well, if I did know, I would probably do . . ."

And I'll say, "There you go. Do that!"

Remember . . . even when you are in the "deepest woods," you are only lacking an idea.

A Commitment to Persistence

I have a friend with whom I have lunch occasionally. He's a little older than I am, but he played football as a kid too. He was better than I was, and his dream was to play professional ball. He was a quarterback all the way through high school, and he even got a scholarship to play college ball.

But his dream of playing in the NFL, the National Football League, did not looking promising when he injured his back and didn't play in his senior year. By the last round of the NFL draft, the anxiety and disappointment were just crushing. Finally, the phone rang. One team had made him their choice in the final round . . . and at that time the NFL drafted *seventeen rounds!*

He was so happy; he would have signed for practically nothing. And, in fact, he did—$6,500. Of course, making the team was going to be the toughest challenge. He was competing against four other quarterbacks, but he wanted this more than anything in the world.

He spent the weeks before his first training camp getting into shape and refining his passing skills. He threw thousands of balls through an old tire hung from an A-frame at his in-laws'

You must know in the game of life, nothing is less important than the score at halftime. The tragedy of life is not that man loses, but that he almost wins.

house. And although his friends and family members were proud of him, they didn't really expect him to make the team.

In July, when he reported to camp, he was ready but scared to death. It was obvious the coaches didn't really expect him to make the team. When the jerseys were given out for the first photo session, they didn't even give him a quarterback's number. (In fact, if you get a rookie card of this guy, it shows him wearing number forty-two.)

Training camp was tough, and the competition was fierce, but his early preparation paid off. His confidence helped him perform well in scrimmages and preseason games until, with the final squad reduction, he was given a new jersey—number fifteen. He'd made the team!

Over the next three years, he sat on the bench and watched the team struggle through three of the most dismal years in the history of the franchise. They went through two coaching staffs; morale was horrible.

In his fourth year, in a bold move, the team hired a little-known assistant coach to be the head coach of the team. Nobody had ever heard of this guy. It turned out this new coach had traveled a similar path as my friend. He had come up through the ranks. He had never been a good player, but he loved the game so much he wanted to coach.

Some people thought this new leader was too volatile for the coaching profession. Many people said he couldn't relate to the players because he was wound too tight. He was given the opportunity to coach fairly late in his life, and then only because the team was so bad. My friend recalls, "If I thought it was tough to make the team, proving myself to this coach was even tougher."

My friend was a quiet guy, and the coach wasn't impressed with him. But he was impressed with his work habits, his stability, his confidence, and his ability to persist without exception. The coach saw a little of himself in my friend—not the greatest natural talent, but an innate inability to back down or quit.

In my friend's fourth year, the starting quarterback went down with an injury. My friend was ready. This was what he had worked so hard for! He went into the game and brought the team back from behind. After that game, Bart Starr became the starting quarterback for the Green Bay Packers.

Vince Lombardi, that little-known coach, and Bart Starr led the Packers to one of the greatest all-time records in the history of the NFL. At one point, they won five championships in seven years, including the first two Super Bowls, and Bart was named Most Valuable Player in each of those games. Bart was named the Player of the Decade in 1970, and has also been inducted, along with Vince Lombardi, into the Professional Football Hall of Fame.

Today, Bart lives in Birmingham with his wife, Cherry, and his children and his children's children. He's been just as successful in business and in his personal life as he ever was on the football field. Bart will tell you that a large degree of his success has come from developing the habit of persistence without exception.

Becoming a Force of Persistence

You've done an excellent job so far defining what you want your life to be like and identifying the obstacles you had unknowingly allowed in your path. We all know how new obstacles and challenges tend to show up (even after we've clarified what we want). For this reason, we must arm ourselves with the tools and understanding to overcome obstacles so they don't become excuses for quitting.

Right now, define a powerful set of beliefs for yourself that you can call upon in your moments of need. Identify three core internal obstacles that often stand in your way. Perhaps you identify yourself as a procrastinator and you put off taking action. Or maybe you tend to let fear guide your actions and decisions. List three of these personal limiting obstacles.

Next, in the form of affirmations, write down the attributes you are committed to that are aligned with your persistent spirit. For example, next to the procrastination obstacle you may write, "I am committed to achieving my objectives" or "I will see this through. I am guided toward my vision." For the fear obstacle you can say, "I am bound by nothing. With persistence, I can achieve anything" or "With faith and courage, I persist until I succeed."

Write them down in your journal and on a note card you can carry around with you. Remind yourself of your new affirmation every time you find your old obstacle presenting itself.

Faith or Fear

So what is the difference in people? When faced with struggles, why is it that one person quits and another keeps going?

In *The Traveler's Gift*, the archangel Gabriel delivers the seventh Decision to David Ponder in a warehouse. It's my favorite part of the book. If you haven't read the book, I won't tell you exactly what this warehouse is because it's the jaw dropper of the whole story, but I can see that place very clearly. It's frightening to me to believe a place like this might actually exist.

Reason can only be stretched so far, but faith has no limits. The only limit to your realization of tomorrow is the doubt you hold fast today.

In the warehouse, Gabriel asks David Ponder, "Does faith guide your everyday actions and emotions? Or does fear guide what you do?"

One or the other drives us, and both emotions are an expectation for an event that hasn't come to pass, or a belief in something that can't be seen or touched. To have faith is to believe in the hopeful potential of what one has not seen, and the reward of faith is to have the potential manifest. The emotional energy of faith is uplifting. Fear, in contrast, is also to believe in the dark potential of what one has not seen, and the only reward of fear . . . is more fear. The emotional energy of fear is life draining. Fear can be used as a catalyst for action or, by default, it imprisons a person to a life of mediocrity.

A man of faith reaps perpetual reward, and a man of fear lives on the edge of insanity. Fear is a vapor—a myth—and if you think that fear is some kind of warning from above to keep you out of trouble, you can forget that. There's no instance in the Bible that says fear is from God. Fear disrupts you and keeps you from your goals, dreams, and destiny. Fear and worry are interest paid in advance on something that may never come to pass.

Through the years, I've discovered that it's often the smartest people who are most susceptible to fear in the first place. I couldn't figure out why that is until I finally realized that fear is imagination run amok. What you fear doesn't even exist—it is the misuse of the creative imagination God has placed in you. And in the lives of these creative, intelligent people, somehow fear jumps into the mix and shuts down any possibility of moving toward their goals and dreams. It stops everything. The word *worry* is derived from an Anglo-Saxon term, meaning "to strangle" or "to choke off." Worry and fear choke off any creative flow or intelligent movement that people might have otherwise had.

Ignore fear. Cast it out of your life. There is no reward for fear. The reward is in faith and in seeing what you have believed come to pass.

"I will persist without exception. I am a person of great faith."

The Doorway Beyond Fear

Ralph Waldo Emerson said, "Always do what you're afraid to do."

What are the closed doors in your life? Many times, they stand as a limitation you've created in your mind. Your very limitations are segues to your dreams. If you will confront those limitations and deal with them rather than fear or avoid them, you will transcend them to experience unlimited possibilities for your life.

I have a friend named Erik Weihenmayer. Erik is one of the most amazing people I have ever known. He was born with a rare genetic disease, and by age thirteen, he was blind. At first he was aggravated, scared, and bitter. He could have decided the world was a terrible place to live and given up. He could have believed that God dealt him a horrible hand. Instead, Erik took his handicap and did what many said was impossible— he turned his blindness into a powerful tool that would allow him to live the life of his dreams.

All men are driven by faith or fear—one or the other—for both are the same. Faith or fear is the expectation of an event that hasn't come to pass or the belief in something that cannot be seen or touched. A man of fear lives always on the edge of insanity. A man of faith lives in perpetual reward.

Erik loved sports. But what sport can a blind guy play? He began with wrestling and became one of the high school team's star wrestlers. At sixteen, Erik discovered his passion for climbing. He was an active skier. He became a marathon runner, a skydiver, and a scuba diver. He loved adventure and chose to do the things that pushed him beyond what anybody else thought a blind man could do.

Early on, Erik decided he would use his handicap to live a life of growth, expansion, and risk. He chose to move beyond the retreat, fear, and limitations of his blindness. Instead, Erik challenged himself to grow enormously and to move beyond the black door of his handicap.

Was Erik always a world-class climber? Not at first. As a blind boy, he was angry. He fought the cane. He fought learning Braille. He fought anything that would label him. "I didn't want to be known as the blind kid," Erik recalls. "I wanted to be known for doing or being something cool."

For a while he floundered emotionally and academically; he flunked math his freshman year of high school because he had not learned Braille. But he bounced back.

Erik's passion for climbing was bigger than any disability or fear. Experiencing nature so tactically, feeling the different textures of the rocks, sensing the wind blowing off the side of the mountain, listening to the sounds—for a blind person, it was sensory overload, and Erik loved it!

Fear was always there for Erik. It will be there for you, too, but Erik chose to use his fears constructively.

Erik was on the cover of *Time* magazine as the first blind person— and one of the few of any kind of person—to climb Mount Everest.

Fear is a poor chisel with which to carve out tomorrow.

When Erik went after Mount Everest, he knew that 90 percent of the climbers who attempted to reach the summit do not succeed, and many don't come back alive.

Did you know that more than 10 percent of the people who have attempted to climb Mount Everest have died? Would you get in a car if you knew you had a one in ten chance of dying? Yet, here was a blind man who climbed the highest peak in the world at twenty-nine thousand feet, with temperatures of up to thirty degrees below zero and winds exceeding one hundred miles per hour—not to mention the challenges of navigating an extremely rugged terrain that was always blowing, changing, falling, and shifting, with sharp ice, deep chasms, and dangerous crevices that must be traversed in order to reach the top. Literally, one false step could mean death!

What if you saw fear as a door that must be walked through—as Erik Weihenmayer does? He has climbed the highest peak on each of the seven continents. Erik acknowledges that sometimes he is scared and has to push through his paralyzing fear. "Rock climbing helps me to understand that a lot of life is just reaching out into the darkness," Erik muses. "It can be scary because you don't know what's there."

Erik believes that the hold he's reaching for is out there, even though he doesn't have a lot of time and will fall if he doesn't find it. His fingers will give out if he holds on too long, but he's hoping, praying, and believing that he's going to find what he's looking for. Erik understands that there are no guarantees, but he refuses to be paralyzed by fear.

"A summit isn't a place on a mountain," Erik reveals. "A summit is a symbol to remind us that, with the power of our minds, our bodies, and our souls, and with the power of these two small hands, we can transform our lives into something miraculous. When we join our hands with those around us, we can do more than transform our own lives. We can transform the very face of the earth." *

Breaking Through Fear

What are some of the fears that keep you from achieving what you want, from participating in your passions? Write down the

---

* You can watch a fifteen-minute video conversation with Erik Weihenmayer on www.AndyAndrews.com.

top three fears you have about life. These fears can affect your relationships, finances, career, or family. They can also affect your spiritual, emotional, and physical well-being.

Underneath each fear, write down two or three ways it manifests in the various areas of your life.

What would happen if you didn't act out these fears? What would you do instead? Write down one thing you would do to replace each fear with a different emotion the next time it showed up.

Are most of your fears real or imagined? The degree of risk and uncertainty you are able to handle in your life will determine the level of fulfillment and reward you experience. Would anything be worthwhile if it wasn't tough, if it didn't carry risks, if it wasn't uncomfortable?

Reviewing each of your fears, what are two actions you can take in each area that would immediately diminish the fear holding you back? If Erik can scale Mount Everest, can't you work through some of your fears by taking focused, courageous, determined, deliberate actions?

What will it cost you if you don't take these actions? And when, specifically, will you take these actions within the next twenty-four hours?

True Rainmakers

In Australia, there is a story about a tribe of Aboriginal rainmakers. This particular tribe of rainmakers *always* made it rain. Now, Aboriginals are known for their rain dances, but some tribes were more successful than others, and word got around that this particular tribe was always able to make it rain. When the white communities were in trouble due to drought, they began to call this particular tribe to do their rain dance. On one such occasion, the leader of the white community went to the king of this renowned group and said, "Why is it that every single time you dance, it rains?"

The king replied, "It's very simple, actually. We dance till it rains."

An athlete does not enjoy the pain of training; an athlete enjoys the results of having trained.

Hanging in there, staying the course, and waiting for the success to happen is your best strategy! Do you know you cannot fail at whatever you've chosen to do? The only way you fail is if you quit. Failure and success are totally in your hands!

Some people might say, "You'll never make it; it'll never happen. Why are you wasting your time?"

You've got to remember that one day, somebody's going to be wrong, and somebody's going to be right, and it's going to be really obvious to everybody who's who. Let those words wash over you. You're totally in charge. You have not failed until you quit. "I will persist without exception."

Creating Your Private Chamber for Results

To employ the Persistent Decision, it is helpful to find ways to move toward your goals more effectively. For example, you may have a specific project you're trying to plan, such as a long-overdue vacation for you and your spouse. Even though you often think about doing this, something always comes up: The phone rings, an e-mail dings, your cell phone vibrates, your child screams for help with math homework, dinner is ready, and then you are tired and need to sleep.

Life is demanding, and it's easy to get swept away in a never-ending sea of tasks and ongoing actions. Sometimes it's necessary to close your doors (temporarily), shut off your e-mail program, and turn off your cell phone so you can work on a goal that's important to you.

Select a goal you've identified in an earlier Decision exercise and schedule time to work on it. The time should be viewed as sacred and nonnegotiable—just like an important business meeting.

The Unlucky *Traveler*

Henry Wadsworth Longfellow said, "Perseverance is the great element of success. If you only knock long enough and loud enough at the gate, you are sure to wake up somebody."

Probably the best story I could tell you about perseverance in my own life has to do with my book *The Traveler's Gift*. So many people assume because it was the *Good Morning America* Book Club selection and on the *New York Times* bestseller list, the book was a no-brainer for the publishing world and was accepted right away. That's not even close to the case!

When I completed the manuscript for *The Traveler's Gift*, I was convinced it was the best work I had ever done. I just couldn't convince anybody else. I couldn't get a publisher to publish this book. It took three years, three different literary agents, and fifty-one rejections from the biggest publishers in the world.

Now, that shook me a bit. People would be amazed to know how many times I've locked myself in my room and read my own manuscript. Because of the Persistent Decision—the seventh

Decision—I knew I could not fail. I knew this book would be published if I just stayed the course.

Friends would read the manuscript and say, "This book changed my life," and then publishers would read the manuscript and say, "We don't get it. Pass."

Month after month, and what turned into year after year, I could not get this book published. Of course, something was happening in the background that I could not see. I knew there were reasons things happened as they did. I can see some of the reasons now. But at the time, it was frustrating!

I kept working and kept waiting, tempted by detours, but knowing I had to stay the course. Finally, a company that had already turned *The Traveler's Gift* down published it. Part of persistence is trusting you will find a way where there is no way!

How did I do it? I found someone more powerful than a publisher—the publisher's wife. We were at a dinner party one night, and I made sure we were seated across from the publisher and his wife. I knew at some point in the evening, someone would ask, "So, what do you do?"

And someone did.

"Well, I'm working on a manuscript," I replied, and I laid out the story.

"Wow, I'd love to read that sometime," the publisher's wife responded.

"I have a manuscript in the car," I said. "This is just for you, now. Don't let him read it," I added, pointing to her husband, the publisher.

We laughed, and that was the beginning of finally publishing the book. I found out later that she and her husband stayed up all night reading the manuscript. She stayed up all night reading, and he stayed up all night because as she read, she often elbowed him, saying, "Hey, listen to this part."

A week later we had a deal on the book. Persisting without exception. Amazingly, when you persist without exception, miracles happen!

In spite of all the publishers turning it down, we succeeded, and this publisher was the place it needed to be. The timing was right. When I saw Diane Sawyer stand up on national television—on *Good Morning America*—and hold up *The Traveler's Gift* and say, "This is a book that America needs at this time," it occurred to me that when I wrote the book, our country wasn't in the turbulent, uncertain aftermath of 9/11 and did not have the same needs. What I perceived as rejection or delays was really divine orchestration for the right time.

One day I was talking to a group of people after a speaking engagement. A lady approached and told me she had written a book that she was having a tough time getting published. In fact, after a year, more than twenty publishers and agents had turned her down. I said, "Well, let me ask you something: does knowing that *The Traveler's Gift* was turned down for three years with fifty-one rejections help you feel more encouraged?"

She said, "Actually, yes. No offense, but yes. It does make me feel better knowing you were turned down a lot more than I have been."

I replied, "Well, there you go. There's another reason for me to have persisted through my rejections—to be able to encourage you. I would never have chosen it, not in a million years, but I was allowed to go through this process, to prove my persistence, and to hang in there to tell you my story to encourage you."

People of Persistence

Thomas Jefferson said, "Never fear the want of business. A man who qualifies himself well for his calling never fails of employment."

So what is success for you? A new house? A child? A certain job? A raise? Certainly you and I both agree that success doesn't happen by accident. You must know what you want and what you're willing to give in order to get it. Two things will be required: first, a decision, and second, consistent action and follow-through until you succeed.

What does follow-through mean? It means continuous, tenacious action toward your goal—intended, planned, effective action. You won't get anywhere by waiting for God to give it to you. Remember: He feeds the birds but does not throw the food into their nests! Following through—intending success—means relentless commitment to achieving your outcomes through drastic action. Many people fall into the trap of deciding on a destination or goal without the commitment to follow through. One or two actions typically won't give you the success to which you're committed. Massive, consistent action is what's needed to get you there.

Constant detours do not bring a man into the presence of greatness. Detours do not build muscle. Detours do not provide life's lessons. Between you and anything significant will be giants in your path.

There are a million stories of success, and they generally involve persistence. Unsuccessful people bail or quit. Successful people persist without exception. When you hear stories of triumph, if you're like me, you put yourself in them and you think, *What would I do in that situation?* Sometimes the stories are so traumatic you think, *Boy, I hope I could hang in there!*

Imagine a pre-pizza-delivery world. What if your dream was to open a new kind of pizza place in town that featured a guaranteed delivery service within thirty minutes of every order?

Your pizza place, because it was so different, struggled at first. Just as you begin to build momentum, your pizza place burned to the ground. Would you start again and stick with the dream that you had, knowing that you were on the verge of success? People had yet to accept the idea of having food delivered to their homes, but you were sure they would. Would you persist without exception?

Tom Monaghan did. He rebuilt his pizza place and then built another, and another, until Domino's Pizzas were literally all over the world.

What if you were a quarterback in high school and everybody said you could not play that position because you were left-handed and your throws were hard to catch because the ball came off your hands in a reverse spiral, spinning the wrong way? Would you persist in your dreams of playing quarterback on your high school football team? And deal with the critics again when you were going into college? And again before the NFL draft? Would you hang in there to become the NFL's Most Valuable Player, as the Oakland Raiders' Super Bowl champion and four-time All-Pro Ken Stabler did?

What if you were a singer and you were told that your voice was nasally and not particularly pleasing, and you were turned down by every major record label in the world—twice? Would you go around the block a third time and knock on doors again with another song and a smile on your face, the way Randy Travis did?

What if you had an idea for a new version of popcorn people had been eating for years? Would you spend forty years cross-breeding three thousand hybrid varieties of corn to perfect the exact moisture content in each kernel—13.5 percent—so that every single kernel would pop? Orville Redenbacher did.

All these people wrote to me detailing the rejection they endured and the persistence that finally won the day. I have their letters along with several hundred more. There are a myriad of exceptional stories that support persisting *without exception*, past the temptation to quit when circumstances aren't favorable or when the doubters' voices drown out your dreams.

Strategic Planning: Moving Toward Your Goals

Building momentum toward your goals helps you more effectively live the Persistent Decision. A solid strategy for results planning can expedite the realization of your goals:

1. What is a goal you really want to make happen? Choose something you have wanted for a while, though it has been out of reach. Really consider what you want and why you want it.

2. With your goal in mind, brainstorm ways to move toward it. Write down any actions—big or small—to help you achieve your goal.

Now, take at least one action in the next twelve hours to bring you closer to living your dreams! Schedule time each day or each week to move closer to achieving your goals.

Embracing a World of Crisis

We all enjoy hearing success stories, sweetened by the struggles people go through to achieve them. When it's your life, however, sometimes doubt creeps in and life seems harder than expected.

You might be going through the worst time in your life—or

you may know someone who is. Remember: you're not alone. We are all either in a crisis, coming out of a crisis, or headed for a crisis. It is just part of being on this planet.

If you're still breathing, your purpose on earth has not yet been fulfilled. There is a reason you're still with us. There's more fun to have, more success to enjoy, more people to encourage, more children to teach, more laughter to share. Your work is not done! You're only at halftime. It's time to take a breath, get up, and get ready to go again.

Times of calamity and distress have always been producers of the greatest men. The hardest steel is produced from the hottest fire; the brightest star shreds the darkest night.

Beware of the temptation to detour! Distractions are everywhere: movies and television, music, and another universe on the World Wide Web. Detours don't build muscle; they don't provide life's lessons. Detours will only distract you from greatness, and greatness is your destination!

Nelson Mandela said he was just an ordinary man who became a leader because of extraordinary circumstances. He ran away from his guardian to avoid an arranged marriage as a teenager and joined a law firm in Johannesburg as an apprentice.

Years of daily exposure to the inhumanities of apartheid, where being black reduced one to the status of a nonperson, kindled in him a kind of absurd courage to change the world. Instead of settling into the easy rural life he'd been brought up in, or even modest success as an attorney, he determined that his only future certainties would be sacrifice and suffering—he chose this to change others and their lives.

In the revolution to transform a country of racial division and oppression into an open democracy, Mandela demonstrated that he wasn't afraid. His real qualities of forgiveness, patience, and persistence, however, revealed themselves after he was released from prison. He served a twenty-seven-year sentence for leading a nonviolent strike and for his involvement in the African National Congress's resistance against the ruling National party's apartheid policy.

Times of calamity and distress have always produced the greatest people. The strongest steel is produced from the hottest fire.

Wherever you are in your life at the moment, you are only at halftime. Yes, they ran up the score on you in the first half. You made some mistakes, but you're about to run out on the field again with the lessons you learned; you will play a different game! Nothing is less important in life than the score at halftime. The tragedy would not be that you lost; the tragedy would be that you almost won and quit.

Think back to the people profiled throughout this book, like Buckminster Fuller, Bob Hope, George Washington, Joshua Chamberlain, Joan of Arc, Norman Vincent Peale, Amy Grant, and General Norman Schwarzkopf. They all had problems, just as you do, just as you *will*. Problems are the "black door" to your opportunities.

Our problems represent opportunities to enlarge our territory. In *The Prayer of Jabez*, Dr. Bruce Wilkinson reveals the power of a little prayer. He explains that we must ask and seek to have our personal territories enlarged and expanded. Will you allow your territory to be enlarged?

Persist without exception. From this day forward you will believe in the certainty of your future. Fear has no place in your life. It's time to have faith! Believe in the future, and watch your future manifest.

Transforming Problems into Opportunities

Problems are part of life. What are your three biggest problems right now? List them in your journal. Then answer the following:

- What makes them so big? Or why do you believe they are big?

- What could be great about each of these problems? List five reasons each of these three problems could be great. If one of your biggest problems is massive credit card debt, this can be positioned as a great opportunity for you. You can create a clear and measurable goal of eradicating all your credit card debt.

- List a few ideas for dealing with these problems right now.

- List three creative solutions to handling these problems.

Next, choose your biggest problem and the best solution you can implement immediately, and do it. Remember, during times of trouble, we're not lacking money, time, a mentor, or a leader. We're only lacking an idea.

An Idea Backed by Ceaseless Persistence

For my first book (it wasn't *The Traveler's Gift*), I came up with the idea to compile stories from "overnight successes" recalling their worst rejection in life. I asked, "What was the worst time or the worst rejection you experienced in your life before you became successful?"

I wanted the letters printed on their letterhead, in their own words, with their signatures at the bottom. It was a great idea! I just couldn't get anybody to do it. I had to get turned down by four hundred people before I finally had the fifty-two letters I wanted for the book. And that wasn't the difficult part.

I went to William Morris, the talent agency that was representing me at the time—one of the biggest agencies in the world, with literary departments in London, Berlin, New York, and Los Angeles—and presented them with my idea and the fifty-two letters, and they turned it down—as did numerous other agents and publishers.

Many people around me thought it was over, but I had an idea: I would publish the book. I didn't have any money, so I mortgaged my condo to print the books.

I had 10,000 copies—weighing tons—delivered to my condo. In my comedy routine, I started talking about the worst time in my life. Perhaps if you were encouraged by another person's worst time, your "worst times" wouldn't seem so bad. People started buying the books at my shows. We ended up selling more than 100,000.

Circumstances are rulers of the weak, but they are the weapons of the wise.

At that point I went back to the publishers and gave them the news, assuming they would now want to publish the book. I figured it would be a no-brainer. Instead they said, "Wow, obviously we were wrong. We certainly missed the boat on that. But you've sold all the books you're going to sell."

After I had sold 200,000 books on my own, I went back to all the publishers with the same offer. And they had the same response. "What are the odds on us being wrong twice?" they said. "Obviously, we missed the boat, but now it really is over."

I didn't even go back to the publishers at 300,000 or 400,000 or 500,000 copies sold. At 600,000 copies sold, my manager and I thought, *Ya know, maybe this is okay. We don't have a distributor or publisher or bookstore selling a single book and taking a cut. It's unfortunate that we didn't have any help, but we did get to keep all the money.* Thirteen dollars times 600,000 books—you do the math. I suppose things ended up okay.

Real *Traveler* Profile: Joan Rivers

Joan Rivers was one of the biggest headliners in Las Vegas. She toured the country, playing to sold-out theaters, and had a nationally syndicated television program, *The Joan Rivers Show.*

When people find out that I toured as Joan Rivers's opening act for two years during that time, they all ask the same question: "What is she *really* like?"

Joan Rivers is one of the nicest, most generous people with whom I have ever had the privilege of working. She never refused to sign an autograph, and even when she was in a hurry, she took time to really talk to the people who stopped her. And she always had time for me as well. She encouraged me, she bugged me to get married, and she was constantly watching out for my money. "Make a sandwich in my dressing room, Andy," she would say. "Did you see how much hamburgers were at the hotel? Ride in the limo with me. Don't you dare pay for a taxi!"

I'll always be grateful to Joan—she set a wonderful example of how to treat people. The following letter from her exemplifies the Persistent Decision.

Dear Andy,

You want an example of one rejection in my life? Only one rejection?!! I'd be lucky to keep this letter to one page! As far back as I can remember, I wanted a career in show business. And as far back as I can remember, people were telling me no. On December 7, 1958, I walked into The Showbar in Boston. I was to be paid $125 for the week, two shows a night. I had already checked into the hotel across the street. It was a dirty, horrible place, but I didn't care. This was my first job.

I had already been turned down by every agent in New York when I found Harry Brent. He was the man willing to work with me, mold my act, and ultimately book me into The Showbar as Pepper January . . . "Comedy with Spice!" Things were really looking up . . . or so I thought. After the first show, the manager called me over. "Hey, Pepper," he said, "you're fired."

I was devastated. *Fired!* Fired from my first job! I went back to my crummy hotel room and collapsed. I literally could not stop crying. I cried as I stood under the shower in that filthy tub, my feet protected with socks, the curtain open so that the killer from *Psycho* could not stab me! Standing in that dirt-blackened tub, I no longer knew whether the thing inside me struggling to get out was talent or only an obsession. But I didn't give in.

Soon, I was booked and fired from my second job. Harry Brent also left me, taking the "Pepper January" name with him. "Women comics I can find," he explained, "but a name like this is hard to come by!"

Meanwhile, I was back to square one. Let me condense this letter, Andy, by telling you that I tried everything and called on every one. Very little worked and everyone said no.

My own mother said, "You have no talent. You're throwing your life away."

One of the most powerful theatrical agents in the business told me, "You're too old. If you were going to make it, you would have made it by now." The talent coordinator for *The Tonight Show* said, "We just don't think you'd work on TV." The verdict certainly seemed to be in, but I just couldn't quit.

I had no money. My office was a phone booth in Grand Central Station. I lived out of one small suitcase and slept in my car while my father threatened to have me committed to Bellevue. All in all, not an easy time. It did, however, serve to shape the determination and an inner strength I have called on in my life many times since.

Even as I write this, it is far easier to recall my successes than the failures I've experienced. We all tend to forget the tough times. Children especially, I believe, sometimes see success as a "lucky lottery ticket" that one chances upon. And that is why I think it important to note that in my case, I was thirty-one years old. Thirty-one years of hearing no. Thirty-one long years before the acceptance began. Even in my darkest moments, I knew instinctively that my unyielding drive was my most valuable asset. Perseverance, my dear, will always be just as important as talent.

Never stop believing! Never give up! Never quit! Never.

—JOAN RIVERS

CONCLUSIONS
Final Thoughts on the Seven Decisions

Although these are some final words and reinforcement of what we've learned together, they merely represent the beginning for you. Each day that you commit to mastering the Seven Decisions, a deeper meaning will be presented. Each day you choose to live each Decision, a new world of higher levels of love, happiness, wealth, and laughter awaits you.

Do You Really Matter?

I was in a hotel room a couple of months ago ironing a shirt, somewhat listening to the television that was on at the other end of the room. I heard an anchor on one of the network news shows doing a "person of the week" feature. I heard him say, "And so, the person of the week is Norman Borlaug."

I put the iron down and ran to the television. I couldn't believe it: Norman Borlaug! The reporter continued, "Norman Borlaug, our person of the week, is credited with saving the lives of over two billion people on our planet."

I was blown away. I didn't know the guy was still alive—ninety-one-year-old Norman Borlaug. I knew who he was. Borlaug had hybridized corn and wheat for arid climates. He won the Nobel Prize because he discovered how to grow a specific type of corn and wheat that saved the lives of people in Africa, Europe, Siberia, and Central and South America.

Borlaug was being credited with saving, literally, two billion people on our planet. The reporter was misinformed, however; I knew it wasn't Norman Borlaug who saved the two billion people. It was Henry Wallace.

Henry Wallace was the vice president of the United States during Franklin Roosevelt's first term. However, the former secretary of agriculture was replaced for Roosevelt's second term in favor of Truman. While Wallace was vice president of the United States, he used the power of that office to create a station in Mexico whose sole purpose was to hybridize corn and wheat for arid climates. He hired a young man named Norman Borlaug to run it. So Borlaug got the Nobel Prize and person of the week, but wasn't it really Wallace who saved the two billion people?

Or was it George Washington Carver? Before Carver ever made his amazing discoveries about peanuts and sweet potatoes, he was a student at Iowa State University. There, he had a dairy sciences professor who allowed his six-year-old son to go with Carver on botanical expeditions on Saturday and Sunday afternoons. Carver instilled in him a love for plants and a vision for what they could do for humanity. George Washington Carver pointed Henry Wallace's life in that direction long before that little boy ever became vice president of the United States.

So, when you think about it, it is amazing how George Washington Carver "flapped his butterfly wings" with a six-year-old boy and just happened to save the lives of two billion people and counting. So perhaps Carver should be person of the week?

Or should it have been the farmer named Moses from Diamond, Missouri? Moses and his wife, Susan, lived in a slave state, but they didn't believe in slavery, which was a problem for a group of psychopaths called Quantrill's Raiders, who terrorized the area by destroying property, burning, and killing. One cold January night, Quantrill's Raiders rolled through Moses and Susan's farm, burned the barn, and shot and grabbed some people. One of these was a woman named Mary Washington, who refused to let go of her infant child, George. Mary Washington was Susan's best friend, and Susan was distraught. Quickly, Moses sent word out through neighbors and towns and managed to secure a meeting with Quantrill's Raiders a few days later.

Moses rode several hours north to a crossroads in Kansas to meet four of Quantrill's Raiders. They showed up on horseback, carrying torches, flour sacks tied over their heads, with holes cut out for their eyes. Moses traded the only horse he had left on his farm for what they threw him in a burlap bag.

As they thundered off on their horses, Moses knelt and pulled a little baby out of that bag, cold and almost dead. He put that child inside his coat next to his chest and walked him home through the freezing night. He talked to the child, promising him he would raise him as his own. He promised to educate him and honor his mother, whom Moses knew was already dead. And he told that baby that he would give him his name.

And that is how Moses and Susan Carver came to raise that little baby, George Washington Carver. So, when you think about it, it was really the farmer from Diamond, Missouri, who saved the two billion people—unless . . .

The point is that we could continue this journey back through to antiquity. Who really knows who saved those two billion people? Who knows whose actions at a particular time were responsible for changing the entire course of the planet—two billion people and counting!

And who knows whose future will be changed by your actions today and tomorrow and the next day and the next.

There are generations yet unborn whose very lives depend upon the choices you make, because everything you do matters—not just for you, not just for your family, not just for your hometown. Everything you do matters to all of us—forever.

Pioneering Your Own Life

By mastering the Seven Decisions, you are becoming a pioneer of new and unknown territories—both inwardly and in the world at large. A pioneer is somebody who goes into previously uncharted or unclaimed territory with the purpose of exploring it—and possibly colonizing, settling, or selling it. Pioneers take their destiny and the destiny of future generations into their own hands. This commitment opens the door to an exciting adventure with new allies, new treasures, and new discoveries to be made about humanity.

Will people follow you? What are you doing that is different from the throngs of humanity? What trails will you blaze for others to follow?

Pioneering leadership requires responsibility. In embracing the Seven Decisions, you become a leader and steward for others. As you lead others to success and a life of their dreams, the life you seek and deserve will be revealed to you.

How are you contributing to the lives of others? What will attract people to you? The first territory a pioneer must conquer is the internal terrain: *Who would I have to become for this to happen? Who do I want to come with me?*

Becoming a Pioneer

To chart your goals and dreams, answer these questions in your journal:

- Where am I going?

- Who must I become in order for these things to happen?

- What must happen in order for me to get there?

- Who do I want to come with me?

- What are the potential obstacles I must deal with right now and along the way?

The Obstacles on Your Path to Greatness

Overcoming obstacles, setbacks, and pitfalls is a requirement for navigating your path to greatness. You must be aware of the potential challenges that lie ahead—otherwise, you'll be sabotaged and blindsided throughout your journey.

Your first obstacles are within: fear and doubt. The secondary obstacles are the ones outside of you: other people and their criticism, doubts, weird looks, and rolling eyes.

Average people compare themselves with other people. That is why they are average.

I compare myself to my potential. I am not average. I see exhaustion as a precursor to victory.

What are some of the most oppressing questions that come to mind when you think about your goals? *What if I fail at this? What if people laugh at me? What if I don't have what it takes to succeed?*

413

We all have doubt or fear patterns that limit us in some way when confronting our dreams. Don't feel bad about having them. Be aware of them. Bring them to your conscious mind.

Wouldn't it be great if we could live our lives as if we'd already achieved everything we set out to do? Have you ever taped a football game? Maybe it was the biggest game of the year, and you were just dying to see this game. You were avoiding everyone because you didn't want to hear how it ended. Just as you were walking inside your house, your neighbor called out, "Hey, did you see how we won right at the last second? That was incredible!"

Man, how frustrating!

Because it was the biggest game of the year, you watched the entire thing anyway, but it wasn't the same. When your team fell behind in the first half, you didn't feel that sick feeling in your gut. As your team entered the third and fourth quarters, there was no reason to yell at the television screen, "A few more passes!" "Just hang on to the ball!" You weren't afraid because you knew you were going to win. You weren't sure how it was going to play out, but you *already knew* you were going to win.

Can you live your life as if you have already won? You know there will be pitfalls. You know there will be difficult times ahead, but you're not going to get scared or angry. Why? Because you are going to win!

Success Through Failure

If success in any endeavor is to be accomplished, then failure must be embraced as well. As you have already seen, failure is a constant in the lives of successful people and, in fact, is often a precursor to their success. Anytime we view failure as the "final word," we rob ourselves of an incredible future that might have been ours.

As an engineer for 3M Corporation, when Spenser Silver set out to create a hyperbonding glue, his reputation was at stake. He had been the lead researcher on many successful adhesives that 3M had branded and sold in the past. This time, however, the "king of stickiness," as his co-workers called him, produced an adhesive that was flabby, weak, and consistently dry. Despite the laughter of his col-

Failure is the only possibility of a life that accepts the status quo. We move forward, or we die!

leagues, Spenser noticed two distinct qualities of this particular failure: the adhesive could be used again and again, and it left no residue *on any surface* as it was removed.

Perhaps because of these two qualities, Spenser patiently (and with good humor) endured the workplace jokes and determined that he would share his discovery with everyone in the office. One of his co-workers, a man named Arthur Fry, sang in his church choir and was often aggravated by losing his place in the hymnal. Having heard about Spenser's failure, Arthur Fry saw an immediate use for an adhesive that could be removed easily, didn't leave a residue, and could be used repeatedly. Post-it Notes became a huge success! But first . . . they were a failure.

Failure is often the pathway to something greater than expected. In fact, you can reliably depend upon failure as a pathway to new perspectives and new ideas. So put the "agony of defeat" in its proper place . . . a place of honor! After all, the "thrill of victory" is just one more reward for the person who rightly sees failure as a learning experience, a mill for ideas, and an opportunity to prove to ourselves, and others, that we are adaptable, imaginative, and strong.

The Realm of Endless Possibilities

If we're driven by fear and doubt, we can't enjoy winning the game. Instead of asking, *What if I fail?* turn that fear-based question on its head: *What if I succeed?*

Who might I reach? What if I loved myself in spite of someone else's judgments? What if this marriage did work? Whom would I have to become, and what would I have to do?

Life's real rewards—love, happiness, and contentment—come through our internal growth. When you stretch yourself, you grow, and life's rewards are attained through this growth. A life of growth will bring you never-ending fulfillment, and mastering the Seven Decisions will help you have that life, paving the way to unlimited possibilities.

Through your efforts, you must prove you are worthy of obtaining the goal you set out to achieve. Ultimately, this journey is about uncovering the deeper level of greatness God has placed within you. Will it take effort? Sure! It'll take every last bit of effort and energy you have to realize your potential.

Sooner or later, every man of character will have that character questioned. Every man of honor and courage will be faced with unjust criticism, but never forget that unjust criticism has no impact whatsoever upon the truth. And the only sure way to avoid criticism is to do nothing and be nothing.

Zechariah 13:9 says, "I will bring you through the fire and make you pure. Just as gold and silver are refined and purified by fire" (author's paraphrase). The golden parts of you already exist. You just need to uncover them by bravely walking through the black doors of fear in your life. Walking through your fears will help you find your freedom. You may *believe* this, but you won't *know* it until you face your fear and remove its roadblocks so you can realize your natural greatness.

It seems so scary and foreboding to walk through our fears because they contain so much "unknown." What if there was a reliable method for breaking through fear? Would you follow this method if you knew doing so would turn your dreams and visions into reality? Lock these words into your mind and heart: *Do what you are afraid of.*

If you're afraid of death, go volunteer in a nursing home or an assisted living center for several hours a week. If you're afraid of rejection, ask the most important person in your neighborhood to lunch. If you're afraid of public speaking, take a course in public speaking or go speak at your local Toastmasters Club. If you're afraid of failing, do exactly the thing you are afraid to fail at doing. Fail miserably and discover all the opportunities that failure offers.

What will happen when you do what you're afraid of? You may feel uncomfortable at first. You may feel insecure or uncertain or even worthless, but doing what you fear is like peeling an onion: it will reveal layers of unnecessary baggage that you're carrying around with you. And as each layer presents itself, you can peel it off, expose the illusion for what it is (not real), and cast it away. On the other side of this experiment is freedom from fear, and the realization of your dreams!

An Endless Web of Decisions

What are the hidden forces at work in our lives, and how can we trace them? What effect do our decisions have on the rest of the world?

In 1980, Tim Berners-Lee was doing a six-month stint as a software engineer at Cern, a European laboratory for particle physics in Geneva. He was noodling around, trying to come up with a program for organizing his notes.

He had devised a piece of software that, as he put it, "could organize all the random associations one comes across in real life and that brains are supposed to be so good at remembering but sometimes aren't."

He called it Enquire, short for Enquire Within upon Everything, based on an encyclopedia from his childhood.

Our very lives are fashioned by choice. First we make choices. Then our choices make us.

Building on ideas in software design at the time, Tim fashioned a kind of hypertext notebook where words in a document could be linked to other files on his computer, which he could index with a number. (Remember, there was no mouse to click back then.) When he punched that number, the software would automatically pull up its related document. It worked splendidly and confidently—and nobody else could use this software. It would only work on Tim's computer.

Tim wondered, *What if I want to add stuff that's on someone else's computer?* After he obtained permission, he would have to do the dreary work of adding the new material to a central database. An even better solution, he thought, would be to allow others to open up his document on their computers and allow them to link their stuff to his. He could limit access to his colleagues at Cern, but why stop there? *Why don't we open it up to scientists everywhere?* In Tim's scheme, there would be no central manager. There wouldn't be a central database and absolutely no scaling problems. The thing could grow crazy like a jungle. It would be open-ended and infinite.

He later revealed, "One had to be able to jump from software documentation to a list of people, to a phone book, to an organizational chart, or whatever." He cobbled together a relatively easy-to-learn coding system he called Hyper Text Markup Language—HTML. Of course, HTML has come to be the language of the Web—it's how Web developers put up most Web pages that include formatted text, links, and images.

He designed an addressing scheme that gave each document a unique location, a Universal Resource Locator, or URL. He hacked a set of rules that permitted these documents to be linked together on computers connected by phone lines. He called that set of rules Hyper Text Transfer Protocol—HTTP.

And at the end of the week, Tim cobbled together the World Wide Web's first browser, which allowed users anywhere to view his document on their computer screens.

In 1991, the World Wide Web debuted with a coding system that brought order and clarity to information organization. From that moment on, the Web and the Internet grew as one—often at exponential rates. Within five years, the number of Internet users jumped from 600,000 to 40 million. At one point, it was doubling every fifty-three days.

Tim Berners-Lee, trying to organize his notes, literally changed the way we live. Tim Berners-Lee works in a cubby at MIT now, but he has changed the world. He didn't cash in on his "invention" like a lot of people would have. He's content to labor quietly in the background, ensuring that all of us can continue well into the next century able to *enquire within upon everything*.

24 Hours and Counting . . .

What you do today matters for all of us. What you don't do matters equally. Remember that our mistakes are in the past. We must forgive ourselves and move on. We choose what we want our lives to be about. What do you choose?

To unleash the greatest creative faculties that God has planted within us, live each day as if you only have twenty-four hours left on this earth. How would you act? How would you look? How would you get out of bed tomorrow morning? How would you have dealt with that crazy person who cut you off in traffic? How would you address your five-year-old differently? What would you say to yourself before you went to sleep tonight? What would you say to your spouse before you went to sleep tonight, or your parents?

24 Hours to Live

With your eyes closed, take fifteen minutes and quietly allow yourself to mentally peruse all the ideas, thoughts, and energy that you've gleaned from this book and your journal. Let your mind open to the possibility of a bright future.

Ask yourself, Who would I like to become, and what would I like to do with the next twenty-four hours of my life? If twenty-four hours of your life is all you have left, what are you going do? Take ninety seconds and, in your journal, write down every single idea that comes to mind.

Next, pick out your top three ideas and rank them in order of importance. Alongside or beneath these top three ideas, write why each is so important to you.

Finally, write down what you will do right now to move toward accomplishing these three things within the next twenty-four hours. Use your imagination, and remember, you have twenty-four hours to live!

A Different Choice

Your whole life is nothing more than a canvas of choices. What one choice could you make right now to change your life in a significant and lasting way?

Know this: You are different from everyone else. On planet Earth, there has never been anyone like you, and there never will be again. Your spirit, your thoughts and feelings, your ability to reason—all of these things exist collectively only in you. Your eyes are incomparable—they are windows to a soul that is also uniquely yours. A single strand of your hair contains DNA that can only be traced to you. Of the multitudes who have come before you and the multitudes who may follow, not one of them duplicates the formula by which you are made. You are different from everyone else! You are special! You are chosen. The qualities, many of them rare, that make you one of a kind are no accident.

Why have you been created different and unique from everyone else? You have been made different so that you might make a difference. In some way, you are changing the world! Every choice you make and action you take matters. Every choice you do not make, every action you do not take, matters just as much. Millions of lives are being altered, caught up in a chain of events initiated by you this very day. You choose what chain of events you will initiate, whether you realize it or not.

Understand that you have been given everything you need to act, and the choice is yours alone: *Beginning this very moment, you will choose wisely! Never feel inadequate again. Do not dwell in thoughts of insignificance or be content with wandering aimlessly. You are powerful. You matter. You have the choice and you ARE the choice. You have been chosen to make a difference.*

Living the Hero's Adventure

As the hero of your own adventure, you now stand at a cross-roads. The decisions you make from here on out will determine your destiny—so choose wisely. As David Ponder and hundreds of thousands of fellow Travelers have used the Seven Decisions to transform their lives, you have the power to do the same. Integrate these Seven Decisions into your way of being with the world, and the adventure will transform your life.

The Responsible Decision: The buck stops here.

The Guided Decision: I will seek wisdom.

The Active Decision: I am a person of action.

The Certain Decision: I have a decided heart.

The Joyful Decision: Today I will choose to be happy.

The Compassionate Decision: I will greet this day with a forgiving spirit.

The Persistent Decision: I will persist without exception.

With all that you've learned as you've read this book, what new shifts within yourself have you already begun to identify? What's changed? How are you different? How are you better prepared to play the hero's role and positively impact humanity? Write these distinctions in your journal.

A Destiny with Success Meditation

The following is a reminder you can read aloud daily after you've completed all the exercises in this book. This meditation is designed to help reinforce everything you've learned. Read it aloud every morning upon arising and each night before retiring to bed for the next twenty-one days. Please feel free to edit or change the wording where applicable.

I'm going to be the parent I've always wanted to be, the son or daughter I've always wanted to be, and I'll be the greatest friend in the world. I'll be a leader people look to in times of distress.

My destiny is assured. I've accepted responsibility for where I am, and I understand what I need to do to move forward in my life. *The buck stops with me.*

There is a thin thread that weaves only from you to hundreds of thousands of lives. Your example, your actions, and, yes, even one decision can literally change the world.

I'm on a constant search for wisdom, through my associations and the books I read. I understand that a year from now, through the people with whom I associate, the books I have read, and the choices I have made, I can actually be a different person. I am moving into my destiny with a servant's spirit.

I choose to act now. *I am a person of action. I am seizing this moment.*

I have a decided heart, and I will move; my destiny is assured!

And I will move toward that destiny with a smile on my face, because *I choose to be happy.*

I have a light heart because I've *forgiven* everyone who has offended me. And most important, I've forgiven myself. Life has truly begun again, because I understand the principles that will guide me through the second half.

The second half is where I win! The future begins right now. *I will persist without exception.*

BIBLIOGRAPHY

Chapter 1

The Quotations Page Web site. Thomas Edison quote, retrieved January 3, 2007, from http://www.quotationspage.com/quotes/Thomas_A._Edison/.

Chapter 2

Buckminster Fuller Institute Web site: http://www.Bfi.org/.

Chapter 3

Chamberlain, Joshua Lawrence, *Bayonet Forward*. Gettysburg, PA: Stan Clark Military Books, 1994.

———— *Through Blood and Fire at Gettysburg*. Gettysburg, PA: Stan Clark Military Books, February 1994.

Desjardin, Thomas A. *Stand Firm Ye Boys*. Oxford University Press, 2001.

"Kentucky Boy Scout to Meet President After Heroic Act." *Bowling Green Daily News* (February 7, 2003), retrieved January 17, 2005, from http://bgdailynews.com.

Monticello, The Home of Thomas Jefferson Web site, retrieved December 14, 2004, from http://www.Monticello.org.

Mulick, S. "Heroic Boy Helps Stop Blaze." *The News Tribune* (August 16, 2004), retrieved January 15, 2005, from http://www.thenewstribune.com.

Persico, Joseph E. *My Enemy, My Brother*. Da Capo Press, 1996.

Pullen, John. *The Twentieth Maine*. Alexandria, VA: American Society for Training and Development, 1980.

Shaara, Michael. *Killer Angels*. New York: Ballantine Books, 1987.

Chapter 4

Barnum, P. T. *Life of P. T. Barnum*. Whitefish, MT: Kessinger, 2003.

The Literature Network Web site, "James—The Holy Bible—King James Version," http://www.online-literature.com/bible/James/.

Pagden, Anthony, trans. *Letters from Mexico*. New Haven, CT: Yale University Press, 2001.

Chapter 5

Charlie Plumb Motivational Speaker and Author Web site. "Captain J. Charles Plumb Book Excerpts," http://www.charlieplumb.com/book-insights.htm.

Chapter 6

The Forgiveness Project Web site, retrieved February 21, 2005, from http://www.TheForgivenessProject.com.

Chapter 7

An interview with Erik Weihenmayer, Homiletics Online Web site, retrieved May 20, 2005, from http://www.homileticsonline.com.

Time Magazine Web site, "The Time 100," retrieved February 3, 2005, from http://www.time.com/time/time100/leaders/profile/mandela.html.

Weihenmayer, Erik. *Touch the Top of the World*. New York: Plume, Reissue edition March 26, 2002.

Conclusion

Andrews, Andy. *The Lost Choice*. Nashville, TN: Thomas Nelson Publishers, 2004.

My Prime Time Web site. "Special Feature: Celebrate Failure," by Ashley Ball, retrieved January 21, 2005, from http://www.myprimetime.com/play/culture/content/postyourfailure/index.shtml.

"*Time* Magazine's 100 Most Important People of the Century," retrieved February 13, 2005, from http://www.time.com/time/time100/scientist/profile/bernerslee03.html.

ACKNOWLEDGMENTS

I am blessed to be surrounded by friends and family who have become a team of which I am thrilled to be a part. If I can ever be perceived as a person who makes good and informed choices, it is only because of my reliance on these people's wise counsel. Thank you all for your presence in my life.

To Polly, my wife and best friend. You are beautiful, smart, and witty . . . after nineteen years it is still a great combination.

To Austin (7) and Adam (5), our boys. You bring me joy and perspective. I never knew I could love so much.

To Robert D. Smith, my personal manager and champion. After twenty-six years together, you still amaze me every day.

To David Dunham, who took this project under his wing.

To Duane Ward and the whole incredible gang at Premiere Speaker's Bureau: You are not just partners—you are friends.

To Gail and Mike Hyatt, who gave life to my career as an author.

To Reneé Chavez, my editor, whose careful eye and quick mind made this a much better book.

To Joel Miller, publisher; Kristen Parrish, senior editor; Dave Schroeder, marketing director; and Curt Harding, publicist, from Thomas Nelson.

To Todd Rainsberger, who helped shape the thoughts that became the words that led to this book.

To Sandi Dorff, Paula Tebbe, and Susie White, who direct the daily parts of my life. Without the effort, prayer, and attention to detail of these three ladies, my own efforts would not come to nearly so much.

To Jared McDaniel, for his sense of humor and artistic ability. (Except for the picture of me, Jared, I love the cover you designed for this book!)

To Nicholas Francis for his Web mastery.

To Ken Davis and José Catano, for making my office a place in which I want to write.

To Bailey Callaway and Ryan Saulter for their help here at home.

To Katrina and Jerry Anderson, Don Brindley, Sunny Brownlee, Foncie and Joe Bullard, Brent Burns, Myrth and Cliff Callaway, Gloria and Bill Gaither, Lillian and Edward Gilley, Gloria and Martin Gonzalez, Lynn and Mike Jakubik, Patsy Jones, Liz and Bob McEwen, Edna McLoyd, Mary and Jim Pace, Glenda and Kevin Perkins, Brenda and Todd Rainsberger, Kathy and Dick Rollins, Shannon and John D. Smith, Jean and Sandy Stimpson, Katherine and Christopher Surek, Maryann and Jerry Tyler, Mary Ann and Dave Winck, and Kathy and Mike Wooley. Your influence in my life is undeniable, and your example is very much appreciated.

To Scott Jeffrey, the Bear Bryant of "life coaches," who took the words from my speeches and helped form them into a coherent narrative. His superior skill at bridging the contextual gaps, polishing, and refining were indispensable, and, Scott, you are "inexpendable" (don't edit me!).
(www.scottjeffrey.com)

ABOUT THE AUTHOR

Andy Andrews

Hailed as a "modern-day Will Rogers who has quietly become one of the most influential people in America," Andy Andrews is a best-selling novelist and in-demand speaker for the world's largest organizations. *The Traveler's Gift*, a featured book selection of ABC's *Good Morning America*, has been translated into nearly twenty languages and was on the *New York Times* bestseller list for seventeen weeks. Andy has spoken at the request of four different United States presidents and toured military bases around the world at the request of the Department of Defense. Arguably, there is no single person on the planet better at weaving subtle yet life-changing lessons into riveting tales of adventure and intrigue—both on paper and on stage.

Learn more about Andy at AndyAndrews.com.

The
NOTICER

NEW
YORK TIMES
BESTSELLER

Sometimes, all a person needs is a little perspective.

YOUR CHANCE TO REGROUP, TAKE A BREATH,
AND BEGIN YOUR LIFE AGAIN AWAITS IN THE
SIMPLE WISDOM AND HEARTWARMING STORY OF
A MAN NAMED JONES.

"This is the best book I have ever read in my life."

—NANCY LOPEZ,
LPGA Hall of Fame Golfer

ISBN: 978-7852-2921-6

THE TRAVELER'S GIFT TREASURY

The Traveler's Gift: It's the book that moved millions. In the tradition of bestselling books by Og Mandino, Andy Andrews' blend of fiction and allegory will inspire you to find true and lasting success in your life.

The Traveler's Gift Journal: The perfect companion to *The Traveler's Gift*, this journal gives you the opportunity to record your own experiences as you personally take hold of each of the seven decisions.

The Young Traveler's Gift: Adapted from the *New York Times* bestseller *The Traveler's Gift*, this book will provide young people with the wisdom needed to make powerfully sound decisions in today's turbulent world.

Timeless Wisdom from the Traveler (9 CDs): Join Andy Andrews for an in-depth analysis of the lessons revealed in his modern classic, *The Traveler's Gift*.

Mastering the Seven Decisions LIVE (2 CD Set): Be moved to life-changing action with this groundbreaking two-hour special in which Andrews shares new insight into the powerful principles conveyed in his *New York Times* best-selling sensation *The Traveler's Gift*.

Mastering the Seven Decisions LIVE (DVD): In this riveting, thought-provoking and often very funny live performance, Andy Andrews proves that everything you do matters, not just for you and your family—but for generations to come.

Put what you've learned into life-changing actions with **The Seven Decisions Perpetual Calendar.** The calendar lays the foundation to your success of incorporating The Seven Decisions into your daily way of thinking and living. When you read The Seven Decisions as laid out in the *New York Times* best-seller *The Traveler's Gift*, and combine those principles with the tools offered through these calendar formats, you will be able to develop the habits that will turn your goals and dreams into daily realities!

**Andy Andrews' Seven Decisions Perpetual Calendar is offered as a
FREE DOWNLOAD online at <u>AndyAndrews.com/Calendar</u>**

For this, and other exciting, life-changing resources, visit